Managing School Library
Media Programs

School Library Media Management Series

Blanche Woolls, Series Editor

Managing School Library Media Programs. By Blanche Woolls.

A Model for Problem Solving and Decision Making: Managing School Library Media Programs. By Mary K. Biagini.

MANAGING SCHOOL LIBRARY MEDIA PROGRAMS

BLANCHE WOOLLS

1988
Libraries Unlimited, Inc.
Englewood, Colorado

LIBRARIES UNLIMITED, INC.
P.O. Box 3988
Englewood, CO 80155-3988

Library of Congress Cataloging-in-Publication Data

Woolls, Blanche.
  Managing school library media programs.

  (School library media management series)
  Includes bibliographies and index.
  1. School libraries--Administration.   2. Media
programs (Education)--Management.   I. Title.   II. Series.
Z675.S3W873   1988   027.8   88-2689
ISBN 0-87287-590-3 (alk. paper)

Libraries Unlimited books are bound with Type II nonwoven material that meets and exceeds National Association of State Textbook Administrators' Type II nonwoven material specifications Class A through E.

Contents

Illustrations

Preface

The school library began with a small collection of books on the teacher's desk and grew to become multistoried facilities with large print and nonprint collections. Information available in-house is supplemented by telecommunication links to databases. Interlibrary loan opportunities provide additional resources from throughout the world.

Providing administration and management information for school library media specialists who will be administering library media centers in the year 2000 and onward is beyond the scope of a single volume. For this reason, a series of manuals for school library media specialists has been planned, including a complete case study volume containing background information and examples for use by faculty and workshop leaders. Another volume will trace the history of school library media centers since the period covered by the Cecil and Heaps work, *School Library Service in the United States: An Interpretative Survey* (New York: H. W. Wilson, 1940) reprinted in Bowie, *Historic Documents of School Libraries* (Englewood, Colo.: Hi Willow Research, 1986). One volume will provide direction for planning and conducting inservice training programs. Two volumes for supervision of media programs, one for large school districts and a second for the smaller district, will be prepared as well. Manuals on the budgeting process and planning the media center facility are also planned.

The present volume represents the first in the series. It contains an overview of the tasks currently assigned to a person managing a library media program, the person in charge of the materials, equipment, facility, and staff. Chapter 1 offers a brief history of school library media programs. The second chapter describes preparation programs and job seeking behavior for the potential library media specialist. Chapter 3 discusses the first week on the new job. Information that is needed, and where it may be located, is stressed, and a brief introduction to the analysis of the facility, the collection, and personnel matters affecting administrators, teachers, and students is included.

Chapter 4 is a more detailed presentation of the tasks required in managing the school library media program and facility. Planning and scheduling the library media center and reviewing the ambiance of the facility itself are considered. The chapter that follows explains the interaction of personnel, including staff, students and volunteers. Steps in the management of the media center with administrators and teachers are described.

Collection management is the subject of chapter 6. The right to privacy of all media center users is presented; decisions for selection of automation, database systems, and collection development are discussed; and defending the contents of the collection and de-selecting materials for the media center are explained.

Chapter 7, on managing the budget, includes sample forms, records, and other examples to aid the library media specialist. The fiscal year is described and details are given for writing specifications and for preparing proposals for funding and program expansion.

Chapter 8 discusses the process to follow to decide which services should be offered. This sequence is set in the context of teaching methods, classroom assignments, the media specialist in the classroom, and the media center as classroom. The following chapter presents marketing activities and preparation of presentations for groups interested in media center activities.

The evaluation of the media center is the subject of chapter 10 and is divided between qualitative and quantitative measures; it also includes a discussion of staff or performance appraisal. The following chapter traces cooperation and networking and provides some guidelines for choosing which types of network to join.

Chapter 12 offers suggestions for the school library media specialist as a leader in the district and in professional associations. The final chapter makes some predictions for the future of the school library media center.

Each section presents exercises for use in the classroom and in a workshop setting. Those designed especially for the classroom assume that students will have ready access to one or more school library media specialists presently serving in an active media center with an integrated program. Beginning school library media specialists as well as veteran workers should be shown examples of teaching teams that are developing and using resource-based teaching units. In addition to exercises, case studies are given from Biagini's *A Model for Problem Solving and Decision Making: Managing School Library Media Programs* (Englewood, Colo.: Libraries Unlimited, 1988).

1 School Library Media Centers
Past and Present

American education has been, is, and always will be in a state of change. New theories are developed, refined, implemented (usually before they are tested adequately), and then discarded in a cycle which finds educators reinventing wheels. Administrators accept innovation, teachers follow administrative leadership, and students become recipients of each educational teaching theory, mode, and method currently in vogue.

One educational innovation of the twentieth century which has escaped complete recycling has been the school library. It was transformed, at midcentury, into the school library media center and was defined in the 1975 American Association of School Librarians (AASL) standards as a unit within the school to

support and further the purposes formulated by the school or district of which it is an integral part, and its quality is judged by its effectiveness in achieving program purposes. A media program represents a combination of resources that includes people, materials, machines, facilities, and environments, as well as purposes and processes. The combination of these program components and the emphasis given to each of them derive from the needs of the specific educational program.[1]

The choice of emphasis to be given to each program component is made by the school library media specialist, who must see that this combination of people, materials, machines, facilities, and environments is smoothly integrated. School library media specialists and their staffs understand the potential effectiveness of different actions and use those tasks which provide the most efficient services to clientele. The materials must be selected from a myriad of sources to meet the needs of individuals, organized for easy access, and circulated with procedures that ensure accountability. Equipment must be maintained in good working order, sent to and from locations for use (often with a student or technical operator), and returned promptly to meet the request of the next teacher or student. Attractive and efficient arrangement of facilities expands the potential uses of materials, aids in monitoring the behavior of students, and allows for a wide variety of activities by more than one group of students.

The last program component in the 1975 AASL standards document is the environment, a factor which greatly affects the attitudes of human beings. Commercial agencies spend large sums of money to create an environment which will attract the public to visit, relax, and buy goods and services. A pleasant environment is important to learning, and learning is the reason for having a library media program in every school.

All of the above are vital to the school library media program. However, the most important aspect of this learning environment is the person who chooses which components to emphasize. School library media specialists provide leadership for their individual programs, and these programs must be well managed if they are to meet the needs of students, teachers, and curriculum as defined by the school community. To be an effective manager, the library media specialist should build both from the perspective of the past and from a vision of the future.

1

History of School Libraries and
Library Media Centers

The history of the development of libraries and library media centers in schools is relatively short when compared with the much longer history of librarianship in other types of libraries. This program is indeed an educational innovation of the twentieth century. The first school librarian, Mary Kingsbury, was appointed in 1900.

Prior to 1900 schools had built collections of books into "libraries" to the point that, in 1876, *Public Libraries in the United States* reported 826 schools of secondary rank with libraries containing nearly 1,000,000 volumes, or, a little over 1,000 volumes per library.[2] Between 1876 and 1900 statistics reported the number of volumes but not the number of high school libraries, so further comparisons are not possible.

Growth in the number of libraries was slow, and the growth of the size of collections was even slower. In 1913 Edward D. Greenman wrote: "Of the 10,000 public high schools in the country at the present time, not more than 250 possess collections containing 3,000 volumes or over."[3] He continued:

> The libraries are well managed, and are frequently under the supervision of a trained librarian. The students are given practical training in the use of the library, in cataloging, classification and in the value of reference books.[4]

The condition of school libraries was further described by Mary E. Hall in 1915. She had been the second person to be appointed a school librarian in the nation when she was named to the Girl's High School in Brooklyn in 1903. She wrote that

> to realize what we mean by a "modern" high school library one must actually see it in action.... To have as your visitors each day, from 500 to 700 boys and girls of all nationalities and all stations in life, to see them come eagerly crowding in, 100 or more every 40 minutes, and to realize that for four of the most important years of their lives it is the opportunity of the library to have a real and lasting influence upon each individual boy and girl, gives the librarian a feeling that her calling is one of high privilege and great responsibility.[5]

The activities were rapidly outgrowing a single reading room and new facilities were being built that included a librarian's office or workroom. At Mary Hall's own school, a library classroom was proposed.

> The library classroom adjoins the library reading room and should be fitted up to have as little of the regular classroom atmosphere as possible. It should be made quite as attractive as the reading room and have its interesting pictures on the walls, its growing plants and its library furniture. Chairs with tablet arms on which pupils can take notes, one or more tables around which a small class can gather with their teacher and look over beautiful illustrated editions or pass mounted pictures and postcards from one to another, should surely form a feature of this classroom.... There should be cases for large mounted lithographs ... for maps and charts, lantern slides, mounted pictures, and clippings. A radiopticon or lantern with the projecto-scope in which a teacher can use not only lantern slides but postcards, pictures in books and magazines, etc.... For the English work and, indeed for German and French, a Victrola with records which make it possible for students to hear the English and other songs by famous singers, will help them to realize what a lyric poem is.... This room will be used by the librarian for all her classes in the use of reference books and library tools, it will constantly serve teachers of history, Latin, German, French, and be a boon to the departments of physical and commercial geography. After school it will be a center for club work. Reading clubs can be made more interesting.... Classes will be scheduled for a regular class recitation there when a teacher wishes the aid of the room in awakening interest.[6]

She goes on to state that this library had come a long way from "the dreary room with its glass cases and locked doors, its forbidding rows of unbroken sets of standard authors, its rules and regulations calculated to discourage any voluntary reading."[7]

In spite of the enthusiasm of Mary Hall and others, school libraries continued to develop very slowly. The impetus to expand secondary school libraries accelerated in the mid-1920s when regional accrediting agencies specified a high school library with a trained librarian as a requirement for all schools seeking to be accredited by their associations.

Although elementary school library standards were published in 1925, not many elementary schools had libraries or librarians. If monies were allocated for the purchase of library books, these books were kept in individual classroom collections. Size and quality of such collections were a direct result of four criteria. The first two were the budget allocated and the skill of the teacher in selecting suitable books. The third was the relative stability of the teacher's grade assignment. Many books ordered by a teacher for students in an above-average fourth grade arrived at the end of the school year. In the fall the teacher's assignment might change to a below-average third grade for whom past selections were no longer appropriate. The last criterion for the possible quality collection was the longevity of the teacher in a particular classroom. When teachers left a school, their classroom collections, if not redistributed by the teachers before their departure, were "raided" by other teachers before replacements arrived. The demise of the classroom collection was a slow and painful process for many teachers who did not wish to lose control over their old favorites. It seemingly took a rocket to blast books out of the classroom and into a library.

The upheaval in education in the 1950s with the launching of Sputnik caused members of Congress to provide funds for workshops, special programs, and institutes for training and retraining teachers. Funds also became available for materials and equipment to supplement classroom textbooks, especially in math, science, and foreign language. The National Defense Education Act (NDEA) reimbursed school districts fifty-one cents on each dollar spent, but these materials and equipment were rarely housed in the school library. High school libraries were inadequate in size and staff to add these materials, and elementary schools had no libraries at all.

Several events in the early 1960s had great impact on the expansion of school libraries and the initiation of the concept of elementary school libraries in the United States. The first was the completion of *Standards for School Library Programs*[8] in 1960 which updated *School Libraries for Today and Tomorrow*[9] published in 1945.

Immediately following the publication of the 1960 *Standards*, the AASL was awarded a grant by the Knapp Foundation, Inc. to assist in the development of school libraries. A motion picture, *And Something More,* was produced to show to parents and members of the community and to encourage the support of the concept of an elementary school library program. In December 1962 the Knapp Foundation awarded the AASL a grant of $1,130,000 for a five-year demonstration project to be conducted in three phases. First, pilot programs began in five elementary and three secondary schools at locations throughout the United States. Cooperation with a teacher education program was required, and library science degree students were placed in the Knapp Schools to complete their practicum or field experience requirements. When the sites were in full operation, administrators in school districts were invited to apply for grants to visit the model libraries. Originally it was planned for six teams of six persons each to visit during two visiting periods per year at each site. Many more than this number did, in fact, view these centers.[10]

Another event which had an impact on the development of school libraries was a report prepared by Mary Helen Mahar and Doris C. Holladay for the U.S. Office of Education. In this document it was shown that fewer than 50 percent of the elementary schools in the United States had school libraries.[11] The report attracted the interest of private industry and additional materials were prepared to bring the plight of school libraries to the attention of the public.

The International Paper Company launched a national campaign in newspapers and periodicals with full-page ads encouraging the development of school libraries. Free packets of information were also available from Remington Rand, a library furniture manufacturer, to help prepare a public relations campaign to build and expand library services in all schools.

These efforts in the early 1960s brought the plight of children with no school libraries to the attention of Congress. Cora Paul Bowmar, in her discussions with Congressional representatives, put on the "saddest face one could ever imagine" because she had "a vision of 10 million children going to 40,000 schools with no library."[12]

These factors led Congress to consider school libraries during the passage of the Elementary and Secondary Education Act (ESEA) in 1965, and funds were placed in Title II specifically to purchase library materials. These funds were then combined with local initiatives and volunteer efforts to build school libraries in elementary buildings and to expand libraries in the secondary schools.

ESEA Title II was designated as categorical aid. This title provided funds to school districts for the purchase of *print* and *audiovisual* materials for use in *school libraries,* but few professional librarians were available to choose these materials or to organize them for use in the elementary schools. When the amount to be spent was distributed to school districts, many administrators were unsure of how to spend it wisely and certainly had little idea how to organize the collection for use. Huge quantities of materials flowed into school districts, and the high school librarian, often the only professional librarian in small school districts, did not have the time to process the high school materials, much less those materials for other schools. To overcome this problem, a librarian was appointed coordinator or supervisor of the processing center, the new district media center, and the school library program. In the beginning the school secretary became part-time manager of the elementary school library. Later, personnel were selected to work in elementary schools and to organize the tasks of parent volunteers.

Twenty years after ESEA Title II many changes have occurred in school library media centers. While the number of students in private schools has risen slightly, the number of students in public elementary and secondary schools has decreased steadily from 1970 through 1985 (see table 1.1). With the reduction in school enrollment, school library media specialists were asked to share buildings. As buildings were closed in districts, library media specialists often returned to the classroom.

At the same time, federal funding guidelines were rewritten and categorical restrictions were lessened. Library media specialists now competed with other programs, not only for declining federal dollars, but also for declining state and local funding. The monies spent for microcomputers further decreased funding for other types of materials and equipment found in school libraries, and, in the early 1980s, the school library media picture seemed bleak.

Table 1.1. Numbers of Children in Elementary and Secondary Schools in the United States

Total	1970	1975	1980	1985 estimated
Elem-Secondary	51,272,000	49,791,000	46,318,000	45,050,000
Public Elem/Sec	45,909,000	44,791,000	40,987,000	39,350,000
Public K-8	32,577,000	30,487,000	27,674,000	26,920,000
Public 9-12	13,332,000	14,304,000	13,313,000	12,430,000
Private Elem/Sec	5,363,000	5,000,000 est.	5,331,000	5,700,000
Private K-8	4,052,000	3,700,000	3,992,000	4,300,000
Private 9-12	1,311,000	1,300,000	1,339,000	1,400,000

Source: W. Vance Grant and Thomas D. Snyder, *Digest of Education Statistics 1985-86* (Washington, D.C.: Office of Educational Research and Improvement, U.S. Department of Education, Center for Statistics, 1986).

School Library Media Centers and the Reading Program

Cecil and Heaps, in their 1940 *School Library Service in the United States,* credit Governor De Witt Clinton and William L. March, both from New York, and Horace Mann of Massachusetts with traveling to Europe to bring back the best ideas for educating children to put into practice here.

> These educational leaders and others of the day realized that the development of intelligent citizens depended not only upon teaching reading but also on providing reading opportunities. It was for the purpose of providing such opportunities that the school district libraries came into being.[13]

Unfortunately, the educational thinkers of the late nineteenth century did not specify the development of libraries in schools as the ultimate method to teach reading. Certainly library services in elementary schools did not begin or progress with the enthusiasm that these leaders might have envisioned. There seem to be two reasons for this. The first reason is the activity of the public library. The expansion of the public library services to children through the creation of children's rooms and the beginnings of training for children's librarians in the Carnegie Library of Pittsburgh in the early 1900s seemed to meet the need for reading opportunities. Children's librarians provided schools with collections of books and some programming for children. Public librarians were assigned to schools and entire library collections were provided to create school libraries. Room collections of thirty or more books were sent regularly to individual teachers. Providing library books for elementary classrooms and entire library collections to high school released school officials from responsibility for these services within schools.

The second reason for the slow beginnings of school library services in schools related to the method of teaching. Reading was taught from reading textbooks which were written by reading "experts." These textbooks did not always appeal to children, particularly children with varied cultural and family backgrounds. The occupation of parent(s), life-style, the family composition, even the family color, excluded large numbers of children attending public schools in this country from any relationship to their reading texts.

Individualized reading proponents in the 1960s tried to move children from textbooks into school library books, but few school libraries existed. The movement to provide school libraries was more directly related to the need to increase understanding and competency in students, particularly in science and foreign language, not necessarily to help children learn to read better or faster.

The emphasis on creating and expanding school library programs in the mid-1960s provided the resources for library media specialists to begin extensive reading motivation in the media center. The Right to Read Program and Head Start programs focused attention of the need for children to learn to read, and media specialists began to offer "reading guidance" to children. However, this did not seem to progress beyond suggesting books that children might enjoy or giving book talks. The concept of "The Librarian as Reading Teacher" proposed by Lea-Ruth Wilkens in her presentation at the AASL Houston Conference, October 21, 1982, has yet to be realized.[14]

This missed opportunity is confirmed by the lack of mention of school library media programs in the major 1984 paper, *Becoming a Nation of Readers: The Report of the Commission on Reading.*[15] Several statements in this book describe activities for the school library media specialist. These include the following:

> The single most important activity for building the knowledge required for eventual success is reading aloud to children.[16]

> There is no substitute for a teacher who reads children good stories. It whets the appetite of children for reading, and provides a model of skillful oral reading. It is a practice that should continue throughout the grades.[17]

Children of every age and ability ought to be doing more extended silent reading.[18]

The amount of time children spend reading in the average classroom is small. An estimate of silent reading time in the typical primary school class is 7 or 8 minutes per day, or less than 10% of the total time devoted to reading.[19]

The reference to libraries is:

Analyses of schools that have been successful in promoting independent reading suggest that one of the keys is ready access to books. However, fully 15% of the nation's schools do not have libraries. In most of the remaining schools, the collections are small, averaging just over 13 volumes per student.[20]

At the end of the twentieth century, attention is being turned to the plight of the illiterate adult. The year 1987 was proclaimed "The Year of the Reader," and one state, California, proposed to halt the use of reading textbooks and turn to children's books to teach reading. School library media specialists are being made aware that the plight of the illiterate adult might be lessened if there were fewer illiterate children. It seems a good time to return to an emphasis on reading that can best be met through an excellent collection of materials to encourage reading in the school library media center. This is only beginning in the school library media center today.

School Library Media Centers Today

The school library media center in the late 1980s began to move into a new era, an era characterized by the changes in the teaching role of the library media specialist. Progress in school library media services has also been affected by the development of new technologies. Use of computing power, which had previously been limited to large academic and public libraries, became available in the smallest school library media center. School library media specialists were asked not only to learn how to use the microcomputer but also to teach its use to teachers and students. Attention was drawn to the media center as circulation and the card catalog were automated.

If school library media centers today were to have a motto, it might be, "Integrate with the Curriculum." Library lessons and library services no longer stand alone but are an integral part of the curriculum. While school library media specialists were trained teachers, the program they offered in the past *supported* the curriculum by providing, among other services, the teaching of research skills. Now the media center program is being *integrated* into the curriculum rather than merely offering a warehouse of materials for the shopper who may or may not choose to visit that store. Levels of curriculum integration were identified by David V. Loertscher who, in the February 1982 issue of *Wilson Library Bulletin*, presented a taxonomy similar to Bloom's. This taxonomy classified the activities of the school library media specialist and the media center as shown in figure 1.1.

Level One—NO INVOLVEMENT: The library media center is bypassed entirely. In this level of the taxonomy, the student as potential "shopper" has not chosen the school library media center as the "store" to visit.

Level Two—SELF-HELP WAREHOUSE: Facilities and materials are available for the self-starter. The library media center collection is well organized, the facility is inviting, the equipment is in working order and accessible, and the students and teachers who enter will find materials available. Services do not extend beyond acquiring, organizing, offering, and maintaining the information and equipment needed.

Level Three—INDIVIDUAL REFERENCE ASSISTANCE: Students or teachers get requested information or materials for specific needs, which places the school librarian in a position of visible assistance. Loertscher describes this as the "magician role—the ability to know where to locate important and trivial information and materials from a vast array of sources." This is similar to Gaver's "reader's guidance" service.[21]

Level Four—SPONTANEOUS INTERACTION AND GATHERING: Spur-of-the-moment activities and gathering of materials occur with no advance notice. The school library media specialist at this level responds to the instant need for information which occurs when a teacher or student wishes to expand the subject or unit under discussion. At this time, pictures of birds, maps of Civil War America, recordings of an opera, production of a transparency, or other activities or materials are provided at a moment's notice. While such service is needed and desirable, Loertscher warns that it should not serve as an "excuse for lack of planning by teachers or turn into a babysitting service."

Level Five—CURSORY PLANNING: Informal and brief planning is held with teachers and students for library media center involvement. A usual spot to begin Level Five is the teacher's lunchroom where the presence of the school library media specialist will remind the teacher of the need for library materials within the hour, day, or week. It may result from a teacher's need to generate enthusiasm for an assignment which may not be perceived by teacher or student as interesting. At this point the library media specialist should respond with new ideas, sources for help, and other activities which will increase interest in the task.

Level Six—PLANNED GATHERING: Gathering of materials is done in advance of class project upon teacher request. Planned gathering of information permits the school library media specialist to notify the public library of the probable demand as well as to gather materials for reserve or placement in the classroom. For many school library media specialists, the gathering of materials, placement on a book truck, and delivery to the classroom has been the highest level of involvement of the library with the classroom. School library media specialists in the 1980s often go beyond this to Level Seven.

Level Seven—EVANGELISTIC OUTREACH: A concerted effort is made to promote the multimedia individualized instruction philosophy and the library media center program. School library media specialists plan inservice training sessions for teachers to show those materials and equipment available to respond to classroom needs. Teachers are given sample lessons that use books and media from the library. Supplementary teaching aids are demonstrated or placed in the library for preview by teachers. Outreach for students includes the sharing of resources available to help them with their assignments. Library lessons describe the information available as well as the methods to find references in the card catalog or reference books. Teaching students to use online database searching serves as an excellent outreach activity destined to convert students into researchers.

(Fig. 1.1 continues on page 8.)

Fig. 1.1—*Continued*

Level Eight—SCHEDULED PLANNING IN THE SUPPORT ROLE: Formal planning is done with a teacher or group of students to supply materials or activities in response to a previously planned resource-based teaching unit or project. School library media specialists begin to meet with teachers and students before the library experience. Materials are provided for students; library media specialists may help transform information into a multimedia presentation. Goals and objectives for the lesson are interpreted, when requested, for the teacher as well. The library media center is included in the teaching plan, and students are given assignments that make use of materials both in and outside the media center. This level of the taxonomy is the team-teaching mode in which the library media specialist participates and contributes as a member of the teaching team, and students take as much responsibility for their own learning as possible.

Level Nine—INSTRUCTIONAL DESIGN, LEVEL I: The library media specialist participates in every step of the development, execution, and evaluation of a resource-based teaching unit. At this level, the library media specialist's involvement is still detached and considered merely enrichment or supplementary. Formal planning for units of instruction occur far in advance of the actual assignment of the unit to students. Teacher and library media specialist work together to plan the unit; they evaluate and modify the unit as instruction continues, and they work jointly to evaluate the unit at the close. The library media specialist is heavily involved in the planning and assumes a leadership role if the unit is multidisciplinary. Additional cooperation occurs in joint development of the goals and objectives for the unit and in the participation of the media specialist in the actual instruction given throughout the unit.

Level Ten—INSTRUCTIONAL DESIGN, LEVEL II: The library media center staff participates in resource-based teaching units where the entire unit content depends on the resources and activities of the library media center program. At this point library media specialists assume the teaching role so essential to the learning of students in any school. No longer a mere provider of materials, the media specialist has become an evaluator of student progress. Students recognize that the role of the school library media specialist is one which will impact on the final grade assigned for work in the unit.

Level Eleven—CURRICULUM DEVELOPMENT: Along with other educators, the library media specialist contributes to the planning and structure of what will actually be taught in the school or district. To achieve this level, the library media specialist must be recognized as a coequal teacher, a colleague, a contributor to learning within the school. Knowledge of the collection, not only in the school but in other libraries in the area or in the state or nation, bring together resources. To this knowledge is added knowledge of teaching strategies and learning styles. These two sets of knowledge are vital to curriculum planning and adoption within a school.

Fig. 1.1. The Loertscher taxonomy. From David V. Loertscher, *Taxonomies for School Library Media Programs* (Englewood, Colo.: Libraries Unlimited, 1988).

Library Lessons Integrated into the Curriculum

As the teaching role of library media specialists is recognized, method of presentation as well as content of library lessons has been modified. Rather than isolated instruction in the use of the card catalog or how to open a book, library instruction is presented with units taught as a part of regular classroom instruction, to meet an instruction need, and at a time when a related assignment has been made. For example, students are taught how to develop search strategies, locate citations, and request materials from other libraries only when a research assignment has been given by the teacher. When the instruction is totally integrated into the curriculum, the library media specialist helps assess the quality of student research papers based upon joint planning and teaching of the research process with expectations for student outcomes mutually determined.

While these sequences may be planned and taught in a single school, a planned curriculum may be in place for the entire school district. That is, the introduction to the use of the index in a book may be a skill to be taught initially in grade three in each elementary school library media center in the school district.

Districtwide coordinated media skills programs are in place from kindergarten through twelfth grade. Planned and developed by committees of library media specialists and teachers, research and reference units are directly related to specific areas of the curriculum. In the Lancaster, Pennsylvania schools, instruction in the use of *Readers' Guide* is placed in one or more units of social studies in the middle grades. Students are taught to use this reference tool as a part of a social studies research assignment. In the Lancaster schools integration of instruction into curriculum units is required rather than "voluntary" on the part of the teachers. Teachers and library media specialists present the research skill as a part of planned curriculum units.

Library instruction is mandated from the state departments of education in Pennsylvania and New York. In Pennsylvania students at three levels must be given thirty hours of library instruction during the school year. A curriculum guide has been published by the Pennsylvania Department of Education to help library media specialists plan for these integrated library media experiences. In some locations curriculum has been designed and distributed at the district level. In others school library media specialists have gone directly to teachers to choose which areas of the curriculum and which classes will be used to offer this instruction. A committee made up of teachers and the library media specialist designs the actual presentations and decides who will teach which lessons.

In New York forty-five minutes per week of library instruction is mandated for each junior high student. A syllabus was developed to help teachers and school librarians work together to meet this regulation. If successful, expansion into elementary and high schools is likely.

Many library media specialists have welcomed these opportunities because as one high school media specialist explained to the author, it has presented her an opportunity to leave the media center to go plan with teachers. In her building she chose teachers who had not been regular media center users and was very pleased when these teachers became eager users of media center services.

Library Media Specialist as Computer Teacher

As microcomputers became available for use in public schools, it was no surprise that library media specialists took the leadership role in promoting this technology. Many saw microcomputers as a natural companion to other technologies already managed by the library media specialist. They justified centralization of microcomputers in the media center based upon the following:

1. The microcomputer has instructional applications across disciplines; library media specialists are accustomed to facilitating interdisciplinary activities from their unique vantage point in the school.

2. The microcomputer is yet another tool for teaching; library media specialists are routinely viewed as providers of instructional tools and materials.

3. Selection of microcomputer software is a critical aspect of the use of the technology in instruction. The library media specialist is the educational professional with the most training in selection of reference and research materials to expand the curriculum beyond the textbook.

4. Providing teacher inservice training on the use of technology in instruction has been a typical expectation for library media specialists.[22]

When library media specialists are responsible for computer teaching, it is in three forms: teaching teachers, teaching students "computer literacy," and teaching students through the use of computers.

The first, teaching teachers, should follow the pattern established for all inservice training, discussed in depth in chapter 5 in the section on managing with teachers. Training should start at the level of experience of individual teachers. Even though microcomputers have been available for some time, not all teachers have accepted the challenges or the possibilities that have been offered by this technology. Students who appear to be very knowledgeable threaten insecure or techniphobic teachers. It has also been difficult to get teachers to acknowledge their need for microcomputer expertise. Through the use of a fun, foolproof, and user-friendly program such as *Print Shop*, with its output of posters, banners, cards, and stationery, many teachers can overcome their reluctance to use the equipment and may even generate enough enthusiasm to try other software programs.

More advanced microcomputer experiences for teachers should include media specialists acquainting them with software that will help them with their teaching. Selecting user-friendly programs to generate spelling lists or unit tests and sharing possible software programs providing specific content within the curriculum will encourage the use of the microcomputer. With assistance, teachers may begin to develop computer assisted instructional (CAI) uses of microcomputer programs.

Computer literacy training for students will depend upon the school district's definition of "computer literacy." Originally this meant students should learn BASIC programming. More recently applications such as word processing and database management programs are taught as a part of the library media instruction sequence. Many school library media specialists have been very active in the design and implementation of the school's microcomputer program, including helping select software and hardware and promoting curriculum integration.

If LOGO is taught as a part of the computer curriculum, the library media specialist may be the primary teacher and the computers may be located in or near the media center. While this may appear to be unrelated to the information role traditionally assigned, it is essential that beginning computer experiences be under the direction of the library media specialist. Students and teachers will thus recognize the leadership of the media specialist in use of computers and be more willing to accept suggestions for the use of the microcomputer for computer assisted instruction.

Use of the microcomputer for classroom instruction can be encouraged if the library media specialist discovers appropriate programs, helps teachers integrate CAI into the classroom, and sees that students use the programs available with a formal, sequenced plan. Media specialists should provide current information about new programs as they come onto the market, choose the best from those available, and see that teachers are aware of the potential uses of any programs purchased.

Online Database Searching

The library media specialist with a microcomputer, a modem, a telecommunications link, and a database can offer a new world of information to students. The speed and ease of access to information found in commercial databases offer quick answers to reference searches and greatly help in locating additional materials in other libraries beyond the school library media collection. This opening to the world's information for students and teachers allows research for projects beyond what a local school or public library could normally provide.

Two types of databases available to school library media specialists include information and bibliographic databases. Information databases provide citations and some offer full text. They may be prohibitively expensive for schools with smaller media center budgets. When bibliographic citations are the output, articles must be located in the media center or through interlibrary loan.

A bibliographic database provides access to cataloging data. It may also provide location information to resources that can be secured through interlibrary loan and may even offer the opportunity to order the resource through the database communication network.

Online Card Catalogs and Circulation Systems

A number of library media specialists have attracted positive administrative attention by demonstrating the value of automated circulation systems. Others have adopted systems which may be used as online catalogs. Still others have promoted systems which would link schools within a district together or link school libraries to other types of libraries in the region. Initially careful consideration must be given to choice of functions and levels of automation. A decision must be made whether to remain self-contained or to choose automation systems which will interact with other locations.

The first level of automation is the system for a single building. School library media specialists may place their holdings on a hard disk drive and, with multiple terminals, support both a card catalog and a circulation system. With this plan there may be no communication beyond the media center. Choosing an in-house system limits use of the collection to students in the media center. It cannot provide online access to students in their classrooms who wish to locate library media center holdings from that location. Yet, in-house systems are being chosen by many media specialists at this time.

Such a system requires input of the media center records, a task termed "retrospective conversion of records," a process of converting a paper record, usually the shelflist, into machine-readable format. This means that the record chosen to describe the media center holding, usually the shelflist, is keyed into machine-readable format and, if input "in-house," becomes a very time-consuming clerical task. For media specialists who run the media center with no help at all, volunteers must be recruited. These persons turn shelflist cards (which may have inadequate or incorrect information) into less adequate or less accurate machine-readable records when a record is miskeyed. If the primary objective of media specialists is to facilitate writing overdue notices, purchase of a simple overdue writing software program may be more cost accountable and useful until an alternate method of retrospective conversion can be chosen.

Others are choosing a system which will permit access beyond the school to librarians in other types of libraries as well as to other library media specialists in the district, city, state, or nation. North Pole High School in North Pole, Alaska is on the CLSI system of the Fairbanks Public Library, and the Carmel, Indiana schools use CLSI with the Carmel Public Library. In this way, students can not only confirm the existence of a book or other item, but can determine if the item is on the library shelves or checked out by a patron.

Another option is to choose a system already in place in the local area or state. Some states have funded projects to place school library collections on state databases which may be accessed through microfilm or laser disk technology. Wisconsin's Mitinet project on microfilm and the Access Pennsylvania optical disk project are examples of this. Transfer of materials from one location to another may be easier if a state delivery system is in place as it is in Pennsylvania or if regional centers provide interschool delivery units such as is provided in Iowa, Michigan, New York, Pennsylvania, and Texas.

A final choice may be to join a national network for bibliographic access to university, public, and special libraries as well as to member school library media centers. A number of private schools and school districts are members of their state or regional networks and use the services of the Online Catalog Library Center (OCLC). Suggestions for joining networks are discussed in depth in chapter 11.

Automating the media center is no longer innovative. School library media specialists can seek suggestions from others who have systems in their media centers. These persons can explain the positive features and the problems of their systems.

No media specialist will want to change systems very often. Great care must be taken in choosing which system and what record—MARC or the present shelflist record. Using a MARC record, a standard format developed by the Library of Congress, can ensure compatibility. On the other hand, many shelflist records found in library media centers today lack many components of the MARC record. More information to assist in making this decision can be found in chapter 6.

Finally, media specialists must use care in determining which materials to input into this database. Automating the circulation system or placing the card catalog online are excellent opportunities to weed the collection. With most systems it is as time-consuming to withdraw a record as to put it into the system originally. Unused, outdated, irrelevant materials should be discarded so that students and teachers will not be deceived when the item appears as the result of their search only to find out that it is unusable.

A Day in the Life of a High School Media Specialist

With so many new roles and technologies to handle, what is it really like to be a library media specialist in the late 1980s? A look at a typical day might help.

The school library media specialist opens the door and glances at the bulletin boards to see if they have been finished for the week. Three announcements of contests are in the media center mailbox, the first from the state school library media association announcing this year's online searching contest for students, the second from the state Friends of Libraries announcing their First Amendment essay contest. The third notice is for a contest to honor the best written program for a microcomputer for students and teachers. The last item in the mailbox is the reminder for the evening's parent-teacher open house.

Before the school day begins, a small group of students create visuals to help them present their report. A second group uses the reference collection made up of both hard copy and electronic sources, including CD-ROM as well as the online database. A teacher comes in to pick up the films sent from the local intermediate unit and is disappointed to find a videotape was sent instead. This means a change in the equipment requested for the afternoon class.

The media specialist stops briefly at the administrative microcomputer to create brief documents such as notes to the Student Council to thank them for providing funds for students to make free copies on the photocopy machine and to remind the officers that continuation of funding for this project would be appreciated for the next year.

Since the media specialist is responsible for a microcomputer laboratory in the media center, used for teaching keyboarding and for computer assisted instruction modules, word processing, and database searching, a quick survey confirms that all microcomputers are on and working. Just before opening the plan book for the day, the media specialist picks up a questionnaire for a research study being conducted by a student at the local college. The requested statistics are available on a spreadsheet and the media specialist moves back to the administrative microcomputer to generate the requested information.

Looking at the plan book, the media specialist notes that the first group of students will be in soon to locate materials for their research reports. This group must be reminded to develop a sound search strategy before going to the CD-ROM players. A twenty-minute segment of time must be scheduled for teacher and media specialist to evaluate the team-taught unit which had just been completed. They will review their scoring of the research papers and the final grades which have been output from the computer used for the final test. Results of short student surveys show that materials were heavily used at one point because a second teacher had made a similar research assignment.

A brief block of time is left free to discuss the probable change in the English Literature curriculum with the principal and the chair of the English Department. The bibliography generated on the proposed topic may not be adequate, and additional funds will be requested.

When the warning bell rings to indicate five minutes before the first class, students who chose to take materials from the media center check them out at the circulation desk. The clerk behind the desk checks the status of materials already in each student's possession by running a bar code wand over the student's identification card.

Students entering for the first period go to the "card catalog," a terminal which connects to a CD-ROM disk containing the holdings of all libraries in the immediate area of the school. Students have access to materials in the school and items available in the local public library, the community college, and a nearby university. In addition, an online modem connects them to a wider bibliographic database listing the holdings throughout the U.S. Since one of their first "library lessons" in their elementary school was "how to complete an interlibrary loan form," this is an automatic process.

Students use both online and CD-ROM databases to select information sources and an electronic bulletin board to locate additional facts or holdings of libraries in other locations. The bulletin board is used to request locations or telefacsimile transfer of actual documents. Other students refer to the microform collection for some of their citations while still others use the online database for full text retrieval.

As each period in the day is checked off the plan book, notes are made of both successes and failures. At the end of the day a brief analysis will result in placing order suggestions on the acquisitions database, drafting memos to teachers, or outlining activities for library staff for the remainder of the week or semester.

The final note in the plan book is a reminder to call the local supplier of trophies to confirm the delivery of the Debate Club plaques. The media specialist cosponsors the Debate Club this year.

It will have been a busy day, and the media specialist thinks briefly of university courses where the activities of the media center were described in lectures given over fifteen weeks rather than accomplished in seven hours, activities which are repeated and rearranged daily, weekly, and monthly. It has been a particularly tiring day, and the media specialist begins to review the reasons for choosing this career. Turning the page on the plan book to see what is on the agenda for the next day, a letter from one of last year's students is clipped so that it can be answered. The letter reads:

My new school seems o.k. The media center isn't as big, doesn't have any good books at all, and there are very few computers. I'm back to signing out a book with my pencil, but I'm still thinking about being a media specialist when I go to college next year.

Exercises

1. Visit a library media center observing the media specialist for one or more days. Note especially the number of students given individual assistance, the interaction with teachers, and the content of any classes taught in the media center.

2. Create a timeline showing the development of school library media centers in such a way that it would be of interest to middle school students in an introduction to their library media center.

3. Related Case Studies: See

Case Study 4, "Technology Can Be Useful: Microcomputers for Library Media Management and User Studies"

Case Study 12, "What Is Appropriate Trent Student Behavior? Planning Library Media Orientation"

Case Study 13, "What Should Trent Students Know and When Should They Know It? Planning Integrated Library/Media/Research Skills, K-12"

Case Study 18, "Updating Trent Collections for Currency"

Case Study 26, "Are Trent Library Media Specialists Teachers, or ... Something More? Performance Appraisal."

All of these studies are in Mary K. Biagini's *A Model for Problem Solving and Decision Making* (Englewood, Colo.: Libraries Unlimited, 1988).

Notes

[1]*Media Programs District and School* (Chicago: American Library Association, 1975), 4.

[2]U.S. Office of Education, *Public Libraries in the United States of America; Their History, Condition, and Management, Special Report, Department of the Interior, Bureau of Education, Part I* (Washington, D.C.: Government Printing Office, 1876), 58. Reprinted in Melvin M. Bowie, *Historic Documents of School Libraries* (Englewood, Colo.: Hi Willow Research and Publishing, 1986).

[3]Edward D. Greenman, "The Development of Secondary School Libraries," *Library Journal* 38 (April 1913): 184.

[4]Ibid., 184, 186.

[5]Mary E. Hall, "The Development of the Modern High School Library," *Library Journal* 40 (September 1915): 627.

[6]Ibid., 629.

[7]Ibid.

[8]American Association of School Librarians, *Standards for School Library Programs* (Chicago: American Library Association, 1960).

[9]Committees on Post-War Planning of the American Library Association, *School Libraries for Today and Tomorrow, Functions and Standards* (Chicago: American Library Association, 1945).

[10]Peggy Sullivan, *Realization: The Final Report of the Knapp School Libraries Project* (Chicago: American Library Association, 1968), 5, 22.

[11]Mary Helen Mahar and Doris C. Holladay, *Statistics of Public School Libraries, 1960-61, pt. 1, Basic Tables* (Washington, D.C.: U.S. Office of Education, 1964).

[12]Cora Paul Bowmar, quoted in Bertha M. Cheatham, "AASL: Momentous in Minneapolis," *School Library Journal* 33 (November 1986): 38.

[13]Henry L. Cecil, and Willard A. Heaps, *School Library Service in the United States: An Interpretative Survey* (New York: H. W. Wilson, 1940), 41. Reprinted in Melvin M. Bowie, *Historic Documents of School Libraries* (Englewood, Colo.: Hi Willow Research and Publishing, 1986).

[14]Lea-Ruth Wilkens, "The Librarian as Reading Teacher: A New Emphasis," *School Library Media Quarterly* 11 (Winter 1983): 122-26.

[15]Richard C. Anderson, et al. *Becoming a Nation of Readers: The Report of the Commission on Reading* (Washington, D.C.: The National Academy of Education, The National Institute of Education, The Center for the Study of Reading, 1984).

[16]Ibid., 23.

[17]Ibid., 51.

[18]Ibid., 54.

[19]Ibid., 76.

[20]Ibid., 78.

[21]Mary Virginia Gaver, *Services of Secondary School Media Centers: Evaluation and Development* (Chicago: American Library Association, 1971).

[22]E. Blanche Woolls and David V. Loertscher, eds. *The Microcomputer Facility and the School Library Media Specialist* (Chicago: American Library Association, 1986), vii-viii.

2 Becoming a School Library Media Specialist

The choice of becoming a school library media specialist is made by a variety of persons and for a variety of reasons, examples of which are listed below. Some reasons might, of course, be perceived as more likely to provide a dedicated library media specialist than others.

1. Dedicated educators choose an opportunity to serve all the children in a school rather than a single classroom; they not only "love books" but appreciate the opportunity to share in the teaching and learning process of all students in one building.

2. Other types of librarians prefer the opportunity to work nine or ten months rather than twelve.

3. English teachers manage the high school library one or two hours each day rather than teaching another section of composition.

4. Teachers are "drafted" in times of media specialist shortages.

5. Furloughed teachers seek a permanent position when a school library media specialist position becomes vacant.

The opportunity to become a truly excellent school library media specialist is based on several criteria. Among these are outstanding teaching skills and enthusiasm for learning and for the continued accomplishment of students. A service orientation is necessary so that information flows steadily from the media center to the teachers and students, and a helpful attitude must be maintained at all times. Creativity is essential so that the most effective methods can be implemented and the program can be exciting, ever changing, and ever challenging to students.

Before choosing the school library media center as the preferred "classroom" assignment, interested persons should decide if they are willing to make the commitment to work to effect positive change in ALL students and to be flexible in methods to help them achieve success. The media center has grown far beyond the book collection to include information in a wide variety of formats, and the role is constantly changing. An interest in trying new things is essential because the skills, too, are ever changing.

Changes in the role of the school library media specialist coupled with new trends in technology in school media centers have radically changed the skills needed for persons managing and working in these information centers today. Programs to prepare new library media specialists and update the more veteran ones are available through institutions offering college credit. Other experiences with new materials, curriculum innovation, or other changes may be available through continuing education activities.

Preparing School Library Media Specialists

Programs to prepare school library media specialists exist in universities and colleges in Schools of Education and Schools of Library and Information Science at both undergraduate and graduate levels. Courses are selected by or assigned to students to help them meet the certification requirements for the state in which they plan to teach. State and local certification requirements are developed for and approved by each state's Board of Education. State board members usually delegate the responsibility for confirmation of appropriate certification to specific teacher education units within a state's Department of Education.

State departments of education may grant certificates to persons with bachelor's degrees. The number of semester hours required at the undergraduate level varies greatly. In Kentucky eight semester hours are sufficient to begin work in a school.[1] However, a total of twenty-four semester hours are required, and persons must continue their coursework until this number has been completed. Some states will permit a school library media specialist to work in an elementary school with fewer course hours than would be required in a junior high or high school. Twenty-two states require a practicum or internship, but the length of this experience also varies. Computer courses are electives in five states.

Two types of certificates may be awarded, temporary or permanent. Graduates of undergraduate programs may receive only a temporary certificate. Persons who begin their careers with a temporary certificate must replace it with permanent certification within a specified amount of time. The methods to achieve permanent certification also vary. Some states require teaching experience, but no further education beyond the bachelor's, while others demand a master's degree. Alabama requires not only a master's degree but also one year's teaching experience as prerequisites for certification as a library media specialist. This author is most familiar with certification requirements in Pennsylvania, a state requiring education beyond the bachelor's but not a master's degree.

Students graduating from a program approved by the Pennsylvania State Department of Education will be issued an Instructor I certificate. This is a temporary certificate that is valid for teaching for three years. At the end of that time, applicants must show evidence of three years of successful teaching experience and the completion of twenty-four credits of education beyond the bachelor's degree. Applicants are then given an Instructor II certificate, which is the permanent certificate valid for ninety-nine years. No further education is presently required by the Pennsylvania Department of Education.

Because persons attending institutions of higher education expect to be eligible for certification in a state upon graduation, university and college education programs respond to the certification requirements within their state and, whenever possible, meet requirements for adjoining states. State requirements therefore dictate the components of programs offered to certify school library media specialists. One trend has been to plan competency-based programs. Franklin reports that fourteen states presently have competency-based programs.[2]

More than one method exists for confirming the meeting of certification requirements. Granting certification is accomplished by one of the following means:

1. Department of Education staff review the transcript of an applicant to determine if the applicant's record meets state requirements.

2. Program approval is awarded to the school or department within the college or university based upon a visit to the location by a team of selected educators reporting to the Department of Education.

3. An independent group or agency confirms eligibility of the school or department.

In Pennsylvania certification follows the program approval process. Staff in colleges and universities write their response to a competency-based program meeting state standards established by the Pennsylvania State Board of Education. Pennsylvania Standards for Program Approval and Teacher Certification in Library Science are as follows:

Standard I
    The program shall require studies and training to enable the library science teacher to function as an integral member of the educational community.

Standard II
    The program shall require studies and training to enable the library science teacher to function as a disseminator of information.

Standard III
    The program shall require studies and training in the administration, supervision and management of a school library.

Standard IV
    The program shall provide studies and training to develop competencies to enable the library science teacher to develop professionalism.[3]

The Pennsylvania Standards further list the expected competencies and the academic and professional preparation areas (see appendix A). Faculties in school library certification programs plan a program which meets the academic and professional preparation areas. The method of ensuring that students in this program meet the competencies as listed in the Standards is outlined. Finally, this proposed program is sent to the Pennsylvania Department of Education for review.

The approval process in Pennsylvania continues with Department of Education personnel and other educators. After programs are presented to the Pennsylvania Department of Education, a team of reviewers is assigned the responsibility of visiting the college or university to determine if the standards are being met by the program as stated. Visits are made to faculty, present students, graduates of the program, and employers of graduates and other school administrators. If the program is approved by the team of reviewers, students who meet the program requirements, confirm their competencies, and graduate will be eligible for school library certificates when they have passed the Pennsylvania Teacher Certification Testing Program (PTCTP).

The PTCTP was approved by the Pennsylvania State Board of Education in September 1984 as an amendment to the Pennsylvania Code. All teacher candidates seeking their Instructional I certification after May 31, 1987 demonstrate that they have successfully completed examinations in their program specialization, basic skills (three separate tests in writing, reading, and mathematics), professional knowledge, and general knowledge (one test in social studies, literature/fine arts, or science).

When all requirements have been met, a certificate is issued. A facsimile copy of a Pennsylvania certificate is shown in figure 2.1.

Commonwealth of Pennsylvania

Professional Certificate

This certificate entitles

to practice the "art of teaching" and render professional service in the endorsement areas hereon in the schools of the Commonwealth of Pennsylvania

Type Code	Years Valid	Date Issued	Area of Certification	Type Code	Years Valid	Date Issued	Area of Certification

T C	01 Emergency	23 Vocational III	31 Educational Specialist I	40 Standard	60 Provisional	70 Permanent Standard	82 Supervisory II
Y O	05 Limited Special	25 Elem. Temp. Standard	32 Educational Specialist II	45 Normal Certificate	61 Instructional I	71 Perm. St. Stand. Lmtd.	83 Administrative I
P D	10 Partial	26 Coordinator I	33 Educational Specialist III	50 Interim	62 Instructional II	75 Permanent Equivalent	84 Administrative II
E E	21 Vocational I	27 Coordinator II	35 Interim Standard	51 Interim	63 Instructional III	80 Permanent	85 Master's Equivalent
	22 Vocational II	30 State Standard Limited	36 Vocational Interim	55 Provisional Equivalent	65 Normal Diploma	81 Supervisory I	86 Program Specialist
							90 Eligibility

00 COMPETENCY AREA REGISTRATION IN CONJUNCTION WITH VOCATIONAL INSTRUCTION
02 WAIVER OF CERTIFICATION GRANTED FOR ONE CALENDAR YEAR ONLY

Authorized by the Secretary of Education

DEHE-67 4/82

Fig. 2.1. Pennsylvania sample certificate.

The certification process may be handled differently in other states. Ohio lists certification requirements in "Quality Library Services K-12," one component in their Minimum Standards Leadership Series 1985. The following is a description of requirements for the Educational Media Certificate.

Requirements combine educational foundations, library science and audiovisual education competencies for the educational media certificate. There are two different educational media certificates and an educational media endorsement.

1. High school certificate (7-12)

2. Special certificate (K-12)

3. Endorsement

The high school certificate requires a bachelor's degree with 30 semester hours of specialized coursework in both print and nonprint materials. The special certificate has the same requirements as a high school certificate with the addition of six hours of work in professional education that encompasses the K-12 spectrum. An endorsement to a standard certificate to teach library/media requires twenty hours of work in both print and nonprint materials.[4]

The revision of the certification process in Ohio is yet underway. Methods to confirm program approval are being developed.

Programs at Kent State University and the University of Pittsburgh as they respond with course offerings to meet their state standards may be found in appendix B.

Education for the school library media specialist should not be over when permanent certification has been received. In some states and in many local school districts, continuing education is required of all teachers who wish to renew their teaching contracts. Such requirements as number of credits, college or workshop credit, and time allowed to complete the courses are all specified by the governing body. School library media specialists who wish to be employed in any school district must learn not only state certification requirements as they relate to permanent certification, but also continuing education requirements in effect for their school district.

Whether or not additional education is required, school library media specialists must remain on the cutting edge of education, and this can happen only through reading the literature and taking part in additional learning experiences. Programs carrying continuing education credits may be offered by the school district or by an intermediate or regional service unit. Often professional associations plan workshops and are able to offer these experiences for either college credit or continuing education credit. Many colleges and universities offer short courses or summer sessions designed to attract school library media specialists who wish to upgrade their skills.

Toward the end of the preparation period or when a job change is sought, the school library media specialist begins to look for an appropriate location. This job-seeking task requires some preparation.

How to Find a Job

In the mid-1970s finding a job was a matter of luck, being in the right spot at the right time. Reduction of numbers of students attending schools brought about a reduction in numbers of schools. Few teachers were being hired at any level, and school library media specialists were furloughed or returned to classrooms as the library media center was turned back to volunteers. This situation has been reversed in the mid-1980s, and it is anticipated that the need for certified school library media specialists will continue to grow.

The creation of media centers beginning in 1965 provided opportunities for graduates to choose the job of school library media specialist as a career. Positions were made full-time, increased from part-time classroom teaching with part-time responsibility for management of the media center. Now, more than twenty years later, teachers who transferred from their classrooms to the media center are retiring, often taking early retirements as states make such options attractive. Vacancies caused by these retirements cannot be filled unless large numbers of teachers and education students choose to earn their school library certification.

Jobs will be available, but matching preferences to position will require attention to the process. A résumé must be prepared citing all library experiences, for example, library page or aide during high school, summer work at the public library, experience in the college library. The practicum or field experience supervisor should write a very detailed letter about the experiences of the student while in the school so that potential employers have some idea of the capability of the applicant. Care must be taken to include reference letters from those professors who can attest to the competencies of their students to manage a school library media center, especially if their education prepares them for all levels from kindergarten through high school. It is usually preferable to ask for letters of reference before graduating. Seeking such a letter ten years after graduation may be difficult for any professor who has taught many students in the intervening years.

Next, the student should prepare a résumé and covering letter. These both must be kept up-to-date for they contain the date the resume was prepared, name, address, telephone number, educational background, schools attended after high school, and courses taken relevant to the job under consideration. Degrees received and specialization are followed by work experience, both full- and part-time, with emphasis on those positions that are related to school library media services. A brief description of related jobs and responsibilities should be included.

Finally, most educators are interested in the applicant's interests and hobbies. It is possible that one applicant would be chosen over another because of the ability to sponsor a student activity, such as the tennis or debate team, not directly curriculum-related.

Résumés should be well formatted on a word processor to allow for easy update. They must be eye catching in case they are one of many submitted for the job.

The covering letter is addressed to the prospective employer, states the information understood about the position, and cites the reasons why the applicant is interested in the job and well suited for it. This letter must be carefully proofread to assure the reader that the applicant is articulate, accurate, and acceptable.

After the résumé is prepared and the placement file is complete, the students begins the job search. Professors in the school library media training program often have information about openings because school officials check with the training programs when they have jobs they cannot fill. If the college or university provides a placement service, they will post job openings sent to the placement office.

Many state associations provide job hotlines within their states. However, while these may list more job openings for other types of libraries than for school libraries, they are a good first place to seek information. The professional literature will also provide information about openings in school districts.

Another method used by some students is to request that their field experience or practicum experience be assigned to a school district where they might like to find a position. This is positive from both sides. The prospective school library media specialist can assess the school district at the same time school district personnel are reviewing the competencies of the student.

The network of school library media professionals is another source of information. These persons will have immediate knowledge of resignations, transfers, and retirements in their district and may have information about neighboring districts.

State department of education personnel usually are aware of the openings within the school districts in their state and can be called for help. At the national level it is also possible to talk with persons in the offices of the federal government responsible for library programs. These persons talk regularly with state departments of education personnel, library school educators, and supervisors in large school districts. They may well be aware of openings that exist.

Professional association conferences are also a source of information about job openings. Many students plan to attend a state or national conference before they have graduated in order to meet and talk with media professionals about situations in school districts in a variety of locations. These experiences may aid in the decision process by helping match skills with preferences.

The Interview

Preparing for an interview will help the applicant remain calm during the process. A list of intelligent questions to ask about the school district can be formulated after a review of the situation there. It is wise to "check out" the district in much the same way the administrators will be checking the applicant—to see if this person will fit the district. Applicants will want to know if the situation will suit them. Some of the managerial questions are discussed at the beginning of chapter 3.

Applicants should always be on time for any interview. This means making sure of the location of the building and the amount of time it takes to arrive. An attempt to be calm and relaxed will fail if unexpected traffic rerouting or missed turns delay arrival.

The interview process is to find out as much about the applicant as possible. It is a time when one or more persons will be asking questions. The applicant should listen carefully to the questions posed and reply to the person who directs the question, not make a presentation to the entire review panel. Questions should be answered in as positive a manner as possible with mention of personal skills that are appropriate. While an applicant should appear to be interested and enthusiastic about the position, it is important to act naturally. Acknowledge when unsure about a response rather than attempting a clever guess.

Many books have been written about clothes making the person. This may not be true all of the time, but it certainly is true in a first meeting in the interview situation. If an applicant really wants the job, it is not time to try out the latest extreme fashion. It is a time to look professional.

The interviewers will learn a great deal about applicants—what kind of persons they are, their skills, their thoughts on significant education issues, and perhaps, a little of their philosophy of education. Practicing how to interview before an actual interview may help prospective media specialists formulate careful answers quickly.

The interview provides an opportunity for the interviewee to ask questions concerning the position. It is a time to find out about the school district and the organization of both the educational and the media center programs for the district.

After an interview, it is appropriate to send the interviewer a letter of thanks. At this time interest in the position can be restated.

Exercises

1. Request an application for a certification form from your state department of education. Carefully read the instructions and confirm the requirements for certification. See what information is necessary to be included, e.g., is a physical examination required? What fees are assessed and what method of payment is suggested? Are college transcripts necessary? To whom is the form to be submitted? What is the probable length of time between submission and return of the certificate?

2. Generate a list of questions you might ask about a school district during an interview.

Notes

[1]Ann Y. Franklin, "School Library Media Certification Requirements: 1984 Update," *School Library Journal* 31 (January 1984): 21-34.

[2]Ibid.

[3]Pennsylvania State Board of Education.

[4]Ohio State Board of Education.

3 Choosing and Beginning the Job

Graduation diploma and certification in hand, the new school library media specialist has located several positions that seem interesting, has submitted job applications and résumés, and has visited for a preliminary interview. If qualifications match needs within the school district and an applicant has interviewed well, a job offer should be forthcoming. Some questions must be answered before accepting a library media position and signing the contract. While it may be tempting to launch into the daily routine of the media center, a wiser approach would be to learn about the organizational and political structure of the school district.

Determining District Administrative Practice

A first group to research are the managers of the school district, the members of the board of education. Members of school boards are either appointed or elected. If appointed, the members are often selected by some public official such as the mayor, and these members maintain their positions as long as the appointing politician wishes them to do so. When elected, members appear on the ballot for the voters to choose. They may be in bipartisan elections, or they may be elected on a special ballot. Elected school board members serve at the pleasure of the voters of their community, and their decisions may be greatly influenced by community reactions. Individuals sometimes run for office to correct what they perceive as a problem, such as the actions of the superintendent currently in office, the addition of a new program to the curriculum, or the withdrawal of a program considered unnecessary or less necessary. The latter category may be assigned to programs begun with outside funds that are not continued when these funds are withdrawn.

School boards are legally responsible for setting policy for the school district. Since state sunshine laws mandate open meetings of public officials, school board meetings are open to the public. The school library media specialist should plan to attend meetings to observe the actions taken, the sides chosen by individual members, and the general attitudes toward certain issues. School board members are powerful individuals in the education of children in the community.

School board members review graduation requirements for high school students. While state boards of education establish criteria for curriculum within the state, a local school board may increase the requirements. That is, the state may require two semesters of physical education while the local school board may include in the requirement the ability to swim a prescribed distance.

School boards are responsible for the budget. They approve all budget allocations and confirm that monies are being sent as requested and approved. School boards are also responsible for purchasing and selling property owned by the school district. They must agree to the purchase of additional property and the construction of new buildings. These persons must hire architects, approve plans, award jobs to contractors, and see that the building is built as specified. They must also agree to the closing of school buildings when school populations decline or other circumstances require relocation of students. In Western Pennsylvania, a region heavily mined for coal, mine subsidence (the caving in of old mine shafts) can cause a school building to crack. Other schools may be plagued by the discovery of asbestos in the walls or ceilings. In these cases school boards must find alternative locations until buildings can be repaired or new buildings constructed.

Finally, the school board is responsible for interviewing and selecting the school superintendent and approving the hiring of all administrators, teachers, and staff. School board members must ensure that the regulations of the state are carried out with regard to certification of all employees. This may include ensuring that proper health tests are conducted, that police checks are made (some states now require confirmation that a prospective teacher has no arrest record), and that all teachers have the appropriate degrees and teaching certificates.

As stated earlier, the superintendent of schools is chosen by the school board. Length of appointment of the superintendent may be governed by state law. In Pennsylvania a superintendent must be given a four-year contract. Such mandatory contracts provide the superintendent some protection from the whims of the community. Superintendents are then responsible for the day-to-day management of the district program, for the selection of administrators and teaching staff, the development and implementation of curriculum, and the continuation of the school's program including the maintenance and upkeep of the buildings in the school district. Management of the school program requires, among other things, creating, refining, and presenting the school budget for the approval of the school board.

Superintendents choose administrators to work with them. These administrators are assigned to the central office staff and to the building-level programs. Central office staff are responsible for special areas of the school program and assume districtwide responsibility in a particular function (e.g., art coordinator, elementary supervisor, athletic director). Teachers in those functions are first responsible to their building principals and secondly to the coordinator of the more specialized program.

Building administrators include the principal, assistant principal, department heads, and lead teachers. Process for selection of any of these positions may be solely the responsibility of the superintendent, or, in the case of a department head, may be appointed by the building principal or elected by the department teachers. The administrators at all levels manage their programs. Who reports to whom is a system worked out in the central office by the superintendent and staff, and the school library media specialist should be aware of this in order to understand the process to be followed to be successful in effecting change.

A line and staff chart of the school district will show the relationships of the assistant superintendents to the superintendent and the reporting sequence of coordinators and their relationship to the principals. A chart of one school district is shown in figure 3.1.

As shown on the organization chart, the board of education is ultimately responsible for the school district. The superintendent serves as the liaison between this board and the administrators and teachers in the district. The Superintendent has several associate superintendents, one for Curriculum and Program Management, another for Contract Compliance, and a third for School Management. Among the division directors, the Division of Library and Media Services reports directly to the associate superintendent for Curriculum and Program Management. In this school district, principals report to the associate superintendent in charge of the Office of School Management. This would mean that the director of the Division for Library and Media Services would bring a building-level problem and its solution to the attention of the associate superintendent for Curriculum and Program Management who would transmit the request to the Office of School Management and that associate superintendent would bring the matter to the attention of the principal. This is a very large school district, and smaller districts will have more tasks assigned to fewer individuals.

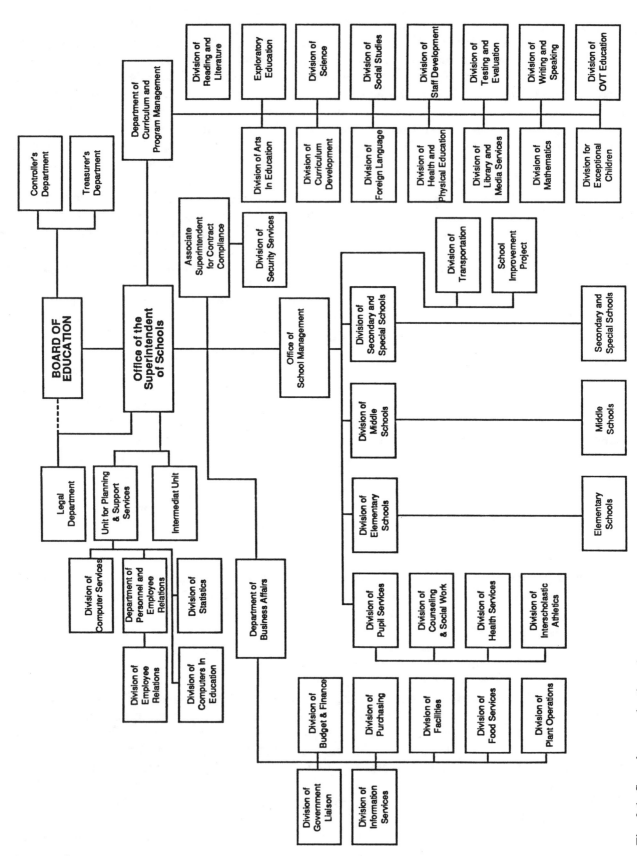

Fig. 3.1. Sample organization chart.

In school districts teachers may be selected by a district personnel office, by the building principal, or by the superintendent. Teaching areas are determined by certification, and curriculum is specified by the state with local modifications. Choices from a list of textbooks may also be dictated by a state or local approval process, but methods of teaching, choice of primary use of one textbook from the prescribed list, or alternate materials is determined by the classroom teacher. Nevertheless, superintendents are ultimately responsible for the total curriculum.

Superintendents must assure the school board that state requirements are met. They must respond to teacher and administrator suggestions for improvements or requirements going beyond state requirements. That is, teachers may consider it important for students to have additional writing experiences or insist that students pass a basic swimming test. These activities will then be required by the school district with the approval of the school board. The superintendent must keep aware of the trends affecting the education of students so that the school district can offer the best possible education to all students attending the schools.

Another responsibility of the superintendent is to see that facilities are maintained. Daily tasks in individual school buildings are the responsibility of the principal, but any major changes will need the approval of the superintendent who will make recommendations to the school board. If a media center is too small to provide services for the students and teachers, renovation or new construction must be brought to the attention of the superintendent through the principal.

The school budget is developed in a manner chosen by the superintendent and in such a way that it will be accepted by the school board. Some superintendents divide the budget into a per-pupil allocation with additional money given to special areas. That is, instructional funds may allocate a certain number of dollars for each student for textbooks (if they are provided by the district) and supplemental instructional materials, while art departments or school library media programs receive an amount based upon the number of pupils, or a lump sum is given to the district for distribution to these programs within the individual school buildings.

Once the positive and negative points have been weighed, the candidate accepts a position. At this time a formal contract is signed and the media specialist is ready to begin the job.

Beginning the Job

School library media specialists bring to any new position all their background experiences, their observations of other school library media specialists, their reading and learning in their educational program, and their perception of what makes a good media program. Sometimes many of the elements are in place in the selected position. At other times a position may be accepted that is less than desirable because of other circumstances, such as location of family or preferred location. In any case the school library media specialist's own goals and objectives should be initiated the first week. These goals and objectives may be refined in the first months on the job, but the initial projects to be planned will be evident from the first visit to the school, and objectives must be set if any plans are to be successful.

School library media specialists just beginning in a new job in a new location should try to learn as much about the system as possible in order to choose the most likely approach to a successful outcome for any plan. It is also important to find out as much as possible about what has gone before. This is not to propose that all that has gone before has been done in the most efficient, effective, or successful manner, but accepting a new position may provide a media specialist with a unique opportunity to decide exactly what changes to make and in what priority order. Ignorance of past procedures might innocently create problems which would be detrimental to the progress of other program changes. An understanding of past procedures can help in analyzing present problems. In fact, some procedures may not be problems at all. A proverb spoken by many is, "If it isn't broken, don't try to fix it." The review is useful to determine if something is, in fact, broken, or more broken than another procedure.

Beginning the job requires as much knowledge as possible about the human factors, collection factors, and the facility itself. Each of these will be discussed in turn in the context of what a media specialist who is new to a building should try to accomplish in the first few days on the job.

Facility Factors

While human factors are more important than factors which involve the facility itself, it is more likely that library media specialists beginning the job will be shown the facility before meeting any of the humans who work there or who come to the library media center for materials. A review of the facility will include attempting to find out just how the traffic flows through the library media center and locating the essentials such as the circulation desk, the reference collection, other materials in the library, and the division of spaces.

First, the new media specialist should locate the school library media center within the school. Is it near the classrooms or in another wing of a huge building? One school library media center with which the author is familiar is in the center of a campus of school buildings. Its very location means that the library media center must accommodate not just students but their outer garments in cold weather, raincoats and umbrellas on rainy days, and their lunches when they come to the media center the period before lunch.

Second, a count should be taken of the number of tables and chairs in the library media center. This figure points out the limits to the number of students and teachers who can use the center at one time. Then comes a review of the placement of tables and chairs. Tables and chairs all grouped together increase opportunities for social interaction among students. Noise can be disseminated if natural dividers can be erected. If no separate classroom exists in the library media center, can a "classroom" setting be created and still leave room for other students to come in as independent users?

Next, an analysis must be made of the traffic pattern within the media center. The circulation desk should be placed near the entrance so that students see it immediately when they enter and are reminded to check out materials before they leave. The circulation desk in one library visited by the author was located in a far corner of the library media center. When the bell ending the period rang, students would gather their materials and leave. Many times their exit with materials that were not appropriately checked out was an oversight because they were anxious to get to their next class.

While many new school library media specialists are fearful of making any changes in the facility, relocating furniture and shelving can generate a new perception of the facility to the users. Changing the layout of the library media center to improve the arrangement of activities may reverse negative attitudes of students and teachers or change their perceptions of the behavior's that are acceptable in this room. The person most likely to resist the change will be the building custodians, sometimes titled building engineers, who are responsible for the wax buildup on the tile floors or the fading colors in carpeted libraries. Few book shelves are bolted to floors and moving requires only the removal of books and rearrangement of shelves. It is usually well worth the effort to make the move.

Before actually moving the furnishings, areas should be analyzed to see that spaces will be adequate for the furniture and shelving to be moved into them. It is not always necessary to use a tape measure to do this; stepping off space one foot at a time can help give a fairly accurate measure. Counting the tiles on a tile floor or tile ceiling can also help make a quick measure. Once the appropriate traffic flow is determined, a move can be made.

To assist in a simple review of the layout, a graph sheet and corresponding scale drawing of tables and chairs is found in chapter 4, figure 4.3. This may be used to draw a rough layout of the present library media center so that it may be viewed from above and judgments can be made of the floor plan before actually moving any furnishings. Should the furniture be moved immediately? The decision is based on how tolerable any problem might be versus how a bad situation might influence the first weeks on the job. Time is a factor. If a single day is available before students arrive, there might not be sufficient time to rearrange the media center. On the other hand, changing a media center can help modify attitudes of those persons who had used the facility in the past. If it can be determined that an attitude adjustment is needed, then by all means a rearrangement should be carried out to see if it will help solve some of the problems.

Additional items the new media specialist should locate as soon as possible include the equipment. Since equipment may be stored in locations away from the media center, an inventory of equipment and its probable location throughout the school should be available in the school office, if not found in the school library media specialist's desk or file. Teachers will be using equipment as soon as classes begin. Some may even need to preview materials before school officially opens. Locating the equipment and making some analysis of the state of repair are essential.

A quick review of the media available is also of interest. Many library media specialists save media when it should be discarded. They may have the perception that the original purchase price was such that it deserves saving, or the small size of such media as filmstrips, make them so much easier to store. Weeding to make room for new items seems less necessary.

A quick check of the periodicals collection is also necessary. If no serials holdings list is available, one should be generated as soon as possible. Students will need to know what is available when they begin their research papers. Microforms should be checked. While most persons prefer hard copy to microforms, the only copy may be in microfilm or microfiche. Is a union list of serials available for the holdings of nearby libraries? What are their borrowing policies, and what about the delivery system for exchange of materials?

In reviewing the reference collection, a quick analysis should be made of the age and coverage and warning given if encyclopedias are more than three years old. The vertical file is another reference tool which should be reviewed. Often very dated materials remain in file drawers. This is one of the less likely reference sources to receive the attention it deserves.

Whatever the past excuse for leaving dated, irrelevant material in the library media center, it is not valid today. Useless materials and equipment should be removed as soon as possible. If doubt about any item exists, it should be removed from the shelves and held until the appropriate teacher has an opportunity to review and recommend or held for one year to see if any requests are made to use it. It is inappropriate to promise information on a subject when it is inaccurate. Students learn little except frustration when they must sift through the information for relevancy only to find that it has little value except as historical record.

Human Factors

Reviewing human factors requires a first look at staff in the media center, then administrators, teachers, and students. During the job interview, the numbers of professional and clerical staff should be discussed. When job descriptions for these persons are not available during the initial interview, an attempt to locate them should be made as soon as possible. If no descriptions are available, these must be developed in a way that covers the services and tasks, maximizes staff activities, and permits each person to feel self worth. This can be accomplished only when library media specialists can match tasks to human competencies.

Finding Out about Staff

Many school library media centers are one-person operations. In others, a newly hired media specialist may find that there are two professionals. Ideally, one is designated director, and they are not expected to share media center management responsibility. An argument has been made that two persons can share equally the administration of the media center, but this is seldom efficient. Someone must be responsible for policy decisions, final selection of materials, division of the budget, discipline of students, assignment of tasks within the library, and other routine functions. It takes two very cooperative persons to share such responsibility equally and consistently.

When the tasks of the library media center are divided, the division may be made in one of several ways. Perhaps the most common is to divide the readers' advisory and technical services functions as is often done in academic and public libraries. With this division of duties, one person works more closely with teachers and students while the other is responsible for ordering and processing materials. A second possibility for dividing duties is to separate print materials from nonprint materials. A third possible division is by grade level; that is, one person works with primary and another with intermediate grades or one with ninth and tenth grade, the other with grades eleven and twelve. A last division is by subject area. Again, similar to subject bibliographers in an academic library, one person works with English and literature teachers, another with science and math teachers, and the third with social studies and history teachers.

Division of clerical and professional tasks is accomplished following an analysis of program needs in relation to professional staff. Clerical staff may be assigned to work with individual library media specialists, or they may be given more independent roles such as maintaining the circulation desk and reserve books, reporting only to the director of the media center.

When a media staff exists, the new library media specialist should meet with the other professionals at the first opportunity to discuss the tasks and procedures in place in the library media center. If no other professionals are assigned, the clerical staff should be queried about procedures in place. In all cases, the strengths of each person should be noted so that an understanding can be reached of the assignment of the best person to accomplish any task. Initial meetings can help determine the perceptions of duties of professionals and staff so that plans for any changes can be made and reassignments occur smoothly.

Finding Out about Administrators

Certainly the school library media specialist needs to be aware of the building principal's perception of media programs in general and of the program currently offered in the building. An easy way to discover some things about administrators is to listen in the teachers' lounge. Knowing a principal's interests can be useful when it is necessary to get this administrator's attention. Finding out a principal's perceptions of media programs can also be accomplished by asking him or her to complete a checklist published in the National Association of Secondary School Principals (NASSP) *Bulletin* (see appendix C). This simple checklist can be completed by other school personnel, and reviewing the responses will be helpful in learning the perceptions which must be modified, changed, or overcome.

Finding Out about Teachers

The NASSP *Bulletin* checklist can also be used to determine the attitudes of teachers. Perceptions of principals may be compared with those of teachers to check similarities and differences.

A second method is to discover ways you can participate in the curriculum of the school. A check of textbooks is a beginning. Many school library media centers house single copies of textbooks and curriculum guides. If this is not true, collecting copies for future use is imperative. While not all teachers follow these guides or use the textbooks, certainly a large number will. A review of the curriculum guides will provide an outline of the topics to be covered in each semester. Teachers can be asked how long they spend on each unit, the research assignments they give as a part of the unit, and the information they feel should be provided by the library media center. At this point files should be searched to see if bibliographies are available. If they are not, bibliographies on each major area of instruction should be developed using a word processor for easy update.

Finding out teaching methods as well as curriculum followed is essential if the library media center is to respond to teacher needs. Some teachers may use media frequently, and some may use it incorrectly. If this is known, changes can be tactfully suggested. If teachers never use media, suggestions can be made of appropriate media that could be used with a unit. Library media specialists must learn about teachers, but they must help teachers learn about the media center and the services offered.

Teachers often have an incorrect perception of the role of the library media specialist. If the media center has been seen as an extension of the study hall rather than as an extension of the classroom, a sales program to develop a completely new image must be planned. An in-depth presentation of marketing strategies is provided in chapter 9. However, the school library media specialist should begin developing a sales program the first week. One method of doing this is to determine just what services the faculty may perceive they need and wish to have available to them. A checklist of services can be prepared, and teachers can be asked to rank or prioritize or "buy" those services of most use to them. A sample checklist is shown below:

Teachers: Using no more than 100 points, please "buy" the following services which you expect from your library media center. We will discuss your rankings at the next teacher's meeting.

Extended hours of service should be available to students
_____ after school classes end and until 4:30 (or later)
_____ on week nights

An interlibrary loan service is provided
_____ for teachers
_____ for students
etc. etc.

_____
100 Total[1]

In devising such a checklist, school library media specialists should take care to suggest those services which can be offered, unless they are trying to build support for a new service. That is, allowing teachers to choose "database searches" from a list of services would be pointless unless some plans were being made to add the equipment, the telecommunications link, and other necessary and costly items to the library media center budget. This process of analyzing services will be covered more fully in chapter 8.

Finally, the novice school library media manager must try to locate the "gatekeepers." A gatekeeper, in this sense, is that person, teacher, administrator, school secretary, or custodian, who holds information and shares it with an "inside" group. Gatekeepers often are able to analyze situations and, based upon their experiences, solve problems. The gatekeeper in a school may be able to suggest alternative plans of action to satisfy teachers when one course of action does not appear to achieve what is desired.

Finding Out about Students

The first step in finding out about students is determining the methods used to admit students to the library media center. In some situations admission to the center is by library pass signed by one or more teachers and countersigned by the library media specialist. As few obstacles as possible must be placed in the way of student use of the media center or most students simply won't bother. School library media specialists may argue that a relaxed pass system will fill the media center with loafers or escapees from the study hall, but this premise should be tested. An analysis of students using the center during one week may point out the type of use, e.g., study or recreational reading; the origination of the request for use of the media center, e.g., classroom or study hall; and the behavior of students from various sources, e.g., study hall students tend to misbehave.

The second step in finding out about students is checking when they are allowed to come to the media center. Rigid scheduling of the library media center may mean that access is severely limited and students can only attend once a week for forty-five minutes. Suggestions for moving from a totally scheduled program to partial scheduling to free access will be given in chapter 4.

The number of students may be regulated by rules and regulations for the library media center, and these should be printed. Regulations may state that only ten students may come from each study hall, no more than six students can be sent for small group study, and other requirements. These rules may also state the disciplinary action that will be taken in the case of misuse of the library media center or the materials housed there. School library media specialists should remember that all rules require an action for any infringement of the rule. Oftentimes the monitoring of the penalty is more troublesome than the action that prompted it.

After determining method of access for students, scheduling, and rules and regulations, inquiries should be made to see if students are assigned to the library media center as aides or work study helpers or in any other function that might secure student support of the media program. This author is opposed to assigning students dull tasks such as shelving books, reading shelves, or replacing magazines. On the other hand, many students enjoy planning bulletin boards, helping at the charge-out desk, moving media equipment to and from classrooms, monitoring the microcomputer lab, or preparing new books and other media for the shelf. Assisting in the library media center can be a learning experience if students can expand their reference skills, conduct online database searches, participate in selection of materials by reading reviews and matching materials available to topics needed, and helping other students learn word processing.

Collection Factors

School library media specialists who are entering a new position need to find out as much as possible about the collection of materials and the need for these materials in the various curriculum units being taught. During the process of finding out about the teachers, information about their teaching methods and their curriculum units was sought. Matching teachers' needs to the materials available in the curriculum is a collection factor.

Locating Bibliographies

A school library media specialist has usually developed a collection of bibliographies to match both curricular needs (e.g., community helpers or Civil War) and recreational reading (e.g., sports stories, mystery novels). The first week in the media center it will be helpful to locate any existing bibliographies. Each bibliography should be reviewed for when it was created as well as for the recency of materials listed and for the numbers of materials still available, that is, not lost, misshelved, or discarded. If no bibliographies can be found, teacher units should be determined for the first six weeks and bibliographies produced. This will help the media specialist quickly become familiar with the collection and be more helpful when students and teachers inquire about available resources. Also, when a teacher requests assistance in locating materials, a bibliography should be created for media center holdings under that topic.

When the collection is accessed by computer, determining the holdings in particular areas is greatly eased. Depending upon the program used in the original input of the library media center's holdings, materials on various subjects can be located and a bibliography can be prepared with a minimum of searching on the part of the media specialist. If a card catalog is the record of the media center's holdings, a more tedious search may be needed if materials are to be listed.

Once concerns about the materials have been analyzed, some decisions must be made concerning their distribution to the media center users. It may be that a written policy exists. If so, the circulation procedures should be reviewed. When no policy exists, the media specialist develops the rules for circulation.

Rules for Circulation

Two major areas of circulation are of primary interest: the circulation period and the policy for overdue books and fines. The two-week circulation period has long been a standard time period. However, just because it has always been done that way does not mean that the policy should be continued. A great deal of time is usually spent in reminding students that a book is overdue after two weeks. Some of this might be lessened if the period of loan was lengthened to three or four weeks or even a semester. A newly arrived media specialist may be able to make the transition to a longer loan period. Placing books to be used by entire classes on reserve to limit circulation is more appropriate than using the two-week loan period.

Fines are always a debate. It is the opinion of this author that fines are one of the worst possible public relations devices for any school library media specialist. The image of the library media center becomes punitive. Rather than teaching "responsibility," a prime excuse for collecting fines, it promotes clipping of pages or sneaking of items through the detection system. In some instances the library media specialist cannot even use the funds collected; rather, they go into the district's general fund and are used for other purposes. Even if the money collected from overdues is used to buy posters or other items for the library media center, the cost in the destruction of a positive school library media center image is far greater than any amount collected from students. A much better approach is to sell the library media center and its contents as the property of the students. To keep materials over a deadline when they are needed by other students is to be a poor citizen, and this behavior is not absolved by the payment of a fine. Again, a school library media specialist new to the building may be able to reassess the process and begin the school year with a new, less restrictive and punitive policy.

When the Students Arrive

First impressions are critical. The novice media specialist must dress as a professional. For a time it was difficult to distinguish between teachers and students. One of the author's favorite educators, a principal in Minnesota, insisted that teachers adhere to a dress code. The teachers in that building were to be role models for the students, not peers, and they were there to teach rather than be pals. A professional appearance on the part of the media specialist provides an air of competence and importance to the activities that take place within the media center. The following additional suggestions should be helpful to the new media specialist as students arrive.

Be visible when students first enter the media center. They will not know the new media specialist unless this person has transferred from one school to another with students also attending the new school. Learn students' names as quickly as possible. This shows interest in and respect for the student's presence in the media center.

Avoid at all costs being intimidated by students. A positive posture, use of guidelines of expected behavior, and a genuine regard for students as sincere researchers will bring a positive reaction.

Students must understand the expected behavior in the media center. It may be that these expectations are written on a handout or on bookmarks to be distributed, or are prominently displayed at the chargeout desk or elsewhere. Explaining behavior is as important as explaining location of books, magazines, and equipment.

Whenever possible avoid voice commands. A strident voice in the media center will disturb everyone there. Students quickly learn to read messages in body language and eye contact. These silent signals are far preferable to other means of attracting attention.

Address any discipline problems immediately. Ignoring a problem will encourage other students to create similar problems. Quickly respond to students when they misbehave so they understand that the consequences for bad behavior will be immediate, fair, and positive. Sarcasm or ridicule is as harmful to the giver as it is to the recipient. Unkind behavior is often returned in later situations and the media specialist will be the recipient.

Establish a reputation for being positive, fair, impartial, and flexible. Students should be the focus of attention. It is not fair to them if a media specialist's personal problems become a part of the classroom attitude. It is difficult to hide personal stress and strain, but students may not understand that the curt response was made because of something that happened elsewhere.

Beware of physical contact with students. Most states have laws against physical punishment of students. The media specialist should take care to intervene physically only in a situation where physical harm might come to another pupil. Again, eye contact and a soft voice are far more effective than more aggressive behaviors.

Take care not to punish the whole group for the behavior of some of the members. A private reprimand or a more public but personal acknowledgment of the misbehavior will be as effective. Depriving a group will only make the group angry and may, in fact, draw the group into support of the poor behavior of the few than to rally the group into support of the media specialist.

Do not return a student to the teacher for misbehavior. Teachers should not be allowed to send students to the media center when they have misbehaved. If the media center is not to be looked upon as a jail, the media specialist should show the same courtesy to the concept of the classroom. The author took a class in educational psychology in which the instructor pointed out that students misbehaved because they wanted to leave the classroom. To send them out of the classroom to the principal or back to the teacher is, in a sense, rewarding them just as the Fox rewarded Brer Rabbit by throwing him into the Briar Patch.

Finally, be prepared for the students when they enter. "Flying by the seat of your pants" may work occasionally for the veteran media specialist, but it is not very likely to work for the beginner. Well-developed plans with more activities than could possibly be carried out is preferable to running out of things to do, often an embarrassing situation. As the media specialist becomes more aware of the pace of activities, it will be possible to conduct activities with less detailed plans, but in the beginning the plan book should be carefully developed.

Having survived the first week in the new building, the school library media specialist must begin to plan for the immediate future, for the remainder of the school year, and for the long-term future of the school library media program. The following chapters expand the responsibilities.

Exercises

1. If unfamiliar with school district organization charts, visit the administration offices of a nearby school district and ask to see the district's organization chart.

2. If possible, interview a "new" school library media specialist after the first week on the job. Obtain impressions about this initial experience. Compare this with someone who is returning to a familiar situation.

3. Related Case Studies: See

   Case Study 1, "What Is the Value of the Trent Library Media Program? Planning a Needs Assessment"

   Case Study 5, "Is the Library Media Program Central to the Mission of the Trent Schools? Creating a Rationale"

   Case Study 7, "Providing Information for Decision Makers: Preparing a Presentation for the Trent Board of Education"

   Case Study 12, "What Is Appropriate Trent Student Behavior? Planning Library Media Orientation."

All of these studies are in Mary K. Biagini's *A Model for Problem Solving and Decision Making* (Englewood, Colo.: Libraries Unlimited, 1988).

Notes

[1]Model adapted from Mary Virginia Gaver, *Services of Secondary School Library Media Centers: Evaluation and Development* (Chicago: American Library Association, 1971), 123.

4 On the Job
Managing Program and Facility

The management of the media center is an assignment based more in the realm of business than it is in the teaching or education modes. While school library media specialists are educators, responsible for all parts of the school's curriculum and for the learning of all students in their building, they must also manage a many-faceted operation which involves staff, materials, equipment, facility, and furnishings. This is a great deal more complex than managing a single classroom and its students.

Classroom teachers are given uniform goals and objectives to reach during the year for their grade level or subject. These general goals and objectives are adapted by individual teachers as they plan their year's activities. Few school library media specialists are given the same basic outline to follow, and they must develop their own goals and objectives for their year. This planning process can easily follow a business model, with the first objective at the beginning of the year to establish an advisory committee.

Because the media center impacts on the entire school, few media specialists would feel comfortable with or capable of planning the entire program without input from the users, teachers, students, administrators, and parents. An efficient way to get appropriate comments from users is to form an advisory group that will meet regularly, as frequently as time allocates, but seldom less than one time per semester. This group will act not only as advocates of the media program, but will also be directly involved in setting goals and objectives and planning or revising programs in the media center.

The Advisory Committee

Teachers sometimes forget that the media center serves the entire school, not just the media staff. Requests for funding for the media program may be interpreted as support for the media specialist only. Advocates of the library media program can be very helpful because their efforts can in no way be construed as vested interest. The easiest way to promote advocacy is to see that an advisory committee is appointed. Choosing the members of this committee should be done jointly with the principal, who is in a position to help decide those who will be politically helpful. The committee includes administrators, teachers, students, and parents, all users of the media center.

Advisory committees should be given a charge so that they will understand their role. Members will want to have an active assignment if they are to consider the activity worthwhile. Again, development of the charge to the advisory committee should be a joint effort with the principal.

Many areas of the media program might be of interest to this committee. Members could assist in the planning for budgetary expenditures and take some of the pressure off the media specialist when requests far exceed resources. They can participate in developing policies such as access to the media center and help explain problems with media center scheduling. As an advocacy group, they could speak for additional resources for they would be very aware of needs. The media specialist uses the advisory committee to test new ideas and to help with needs assessment.

Managing the Program: A Business Model

The management of the school library media program is based upon the business concepts of planning, organizing, directing (actuating), and controlling. The first of these, planning, is the process of deciding what work must be done and then who should do it. During the planning process school library media specialists work directly with those persons who will carry out the plans. This group will include all members of the media center staff who should be involved in goals and objectives for the activities within the media center.

Planning

Planning is based upon a sound media center policy statement. At the theoretical level planning begins with a policy statement to describe library media services. Such a statement may be created at the district level. If not, the library media specialist should develop such a statement with the advisory committee. The Joint Policy Statement of the World Confederation of the Teaching Profession (WCOTP) Assemblies and the International Association of School Librarianship is shown in appendix D. This might be used as a model for the development of a policy statement.

Planning is the process of identifying problems. In this phase objectives, policies, procedures, and methods are developed based on the needs of students and teachers. A needs assessment is conducted and courses of action are adopted to meet these needs. Alternate strategies are determined in case the first course of action is not possible and the results of each alternative are discussed. A final step is to evaluate the program.

As mentioned previously, the advisory committee can be extremely helpful in establishing needs. For example, it is learned that a new world history textbook is being adopted. During the needs assessment process, an analysis of the textbook will be made to find topics appropriate for supplementary material. These topics will be matched to the present collection of material to see what is available, what must be ordered, and what is in print. A bibliography of available materials in the present collection is generated. Teachers will be queried about suggestions for additions to the present collection and asked to review the bibliography for an analysis of the relevancy of the materials found in the collection. Additions selected for purchase will be given a budgetary priority and, if funds are available, materials will be ordered immediately.

An alternate strategy might be to send a list of items to the local public library to see if they would be available for short-term loan. The public library collection is considered an alternate strategy because users anticipate locating needed materials in their own collection. The result of implementing the above strategy would be the temporary alleviation of a crisis situation which should be corrected in future plans and priority setting. One result might be the loss of public library materials from the school with the consequent loss of future cooperation with the public library. Whether or not materials are requested from the public library, public library staff should be notified of such curricular changes in order to prepare for student research papers at the appropriate time.

At each step of solving a problem alternatives may be reviewed in terms of cost accountability. This will be discussed in more depth in chapter 7. In the context of planning, one advocate of cost accountability is Stufflebeam. In his accountability model, Context, Input, Process, Product Evaluation (CIPP), he states that a good manager must answer both the *ends* and the *means* of a program.[1] His definition of *ends* include what objectives were chosen and why, how adequately the program personnel pursued the chosen objective, and how well the objectives were achieved. In the case of the new World History curriculum, the media specialist may or may not be involved in the setting of objectives for the classroom activities but will be involved and will involve teachers in those activities that take place in the media center.

Means includes the program design. Stufflebeam suggests that designs should be chosen for good and sufficient reasons. Designs should be evaluated to see to what extent they were properly implemented, and to assess the value of their primary, secondary, and tertiary effects. To complete this process, Stufflebeam states that four records should be maintained. They are (1) objectives and the bases for their choice, (2) the chosen strategy and the reason for the choices, (3) a record of the actual process, and (4) a record of attainments and recycling decisions.

Writing objectives after a needs assessment should be clear, and reasons (bases for their choice) for specific objectives are recorded. The participation of the library media specialist in curriculum planning is critical at this point. Many of the strategies chosen will be dependent upon the media center's collection and the services offered students and teachers. Strategies are determined and the reasons for these strategies will help decide adjustments if strategies appear to fail. Recording the actual process, perhaps in a log, can be helpful in reminding the library media specialist of successful activities as well as in learning the outcome of revisions. If successes are recorded, these attainments can be used in reporting back to teachers or to administrators for monthly or yearly status reports. Changes or "recycling decisions" are recorded to help other teachers who wish to implement a similar plan. These records will also help others understand the modifications that were accomplished.

Certainly the objective of our previous planning would be to provide each student with at least six in-house sources for research papers they would be assigned in this World History unit. One of the bases for the choice would be to add to the media center collection the materials needed to supplement the curriculum unit. Purchase for in-house use would be preferable because students would have immediate access when classes came to the media center.

A record of the actual process would involve choice and ordering of the new materials. Teachers might be asked to preview materials and make selections from several choices. Finally, the record of attainments and recycling decisions would be put into place at the close of the unit to see if the materials had been adequate, relevant, and recent enough for research.

Organizing

At the organizing stage, decisions are made as to who should do what work, what activities are involved in the work, and what facilities are available to accomplish the task. What is the nature of the media center involvement in component activities related to the teaching of World History? Work division and work assignment between the media specialist and the teachers must be agreed upon, and activities involved should be allocated between classroom and media center in the organizing process. In the example of the World History project, a first activity is selection of new materials, and teachers will be asked to review materials for purchase.

A next step in organizing is to review the unit to see what activities will involve media center staff. If production skills are needed, the supplies must be purchased. Third, a decision must be made of the materials to place on reserve, the materials to send to the classroom, and the materials to circulate to students. If additional materials must be secured from outside the school, this assignment must be made to a media center staff member to secure them and then a review made of policies and procedures in relation to these new materials. Policies and procedures for the use of materials located in alternate locations might differ from policies and procedures for school-owned materials.

Finally, decisions must be made regarding division of teaching of the unit, research skills required, reference sources, and use of materials so that the media center and the services of the media staff can be scheduled. A review of the unit as it progresses can determine the appropriate time for media staff involvement during the unit.

Directing

At the directing (actuating) phase, activities actually occur. Some decisions will be needed to determine why and how group members perform their tasks. When will the World History research paper be assigned? What media is shown to the entire class in the classroom, to a small group in the media center, or only to individual students? Task assignments again will be decided between teacher and media center staff. Decisions must be made concerning whose task it is to start, continue, or complete activities related to the unit. For example, the teacher and the media specialist choose a film to show. A clerk will be responsible for the actual showing of a film in the media center after it has been introduced by the teacher either in the classroom or in the media center. Any discussion during and at the end of the film will be the joint responsibility of the teacher and the media specialist.

In this concept, responsibility for each activity has been assigned to the appropriate person(s). Care is taken to ensure that the activities continue as planned, and that the appropriate materials and equipment are available. This stage is a matching of plan books of teacher and media specialist with media center schedule.

Controlling

Controlling is defined as evaluation of the process. Did the unit work as planned? When, where, and how are the activities being performed? And are they being performed in accordance with plans? This involves checking up and holding follow-up sessions. How well did students perform on evaluation exercises? Were sufficient resources available? What activities did teachers and students consider to be the most successful? Any final reports, comparisons to other units, costs, and projected future budget needs are fit into the context of controlling. Finally, did the activity meet the program goals?

While the above example was set in the context of curriculum, a "pure" administrative sequence can be examined. A major goal of many school library media specialists is the automation of the circulation system. At the planning stage, objectives would be written and alternative systems investigated. If the project required selling to school administrators, cost benefits would be determined. This could be done in relation to clerical time saved and reduction of error in sending overdue notices.

At the organizing level, decisions would be made as to who would input data into the system, who would be responsible for checking out materials once the system is in place, and who would generate overdue notices. The directing phase would require overseeing the circulation process in case changes were needed in the flow of work at the circulation desk. Finally, an analysis would be completed at the controlling stage to evaluate the real time savings in relation to the anticipated time savings.

Extended Projects

Planning for one week at a time is better than no planning at all. However, a school library media program can only continue to be successful and continue to improve if planning extends beyond one school year. For too long media specialists have neglected to set goals and objectives beyond a single semester. Short-term planning limits the ability to set priorities for major purchases that will continue the progress of the media program beyond a single school year.

School library media specialists should develop three-, five-, or even ten-year plans for media center operation. In this plan all components of the media program should be listed with an indication of "what is" and then "what should be," taking into account all necessary additions to the program whether they be staff, equipment, materials, or facilities. Additions or modifications to the present situation should be proposed somewhere within the first, second, third, fifth, or tenth year with a budget analysis for each activity. A sample five-year plan is shown in appendix E.

For planning large projects, school library media specialists can learn from project planners who develop a timeline. One simple timeline is the Gantt chart, named after its creator. This chart displays the tasks on the left side with the timeline across the top and bottom. The timeline itself is very flexible, depending upon the time allocated for completion of the project. The chart shown in figure 4.1 developed as a planning chart for a new elementary school's library.

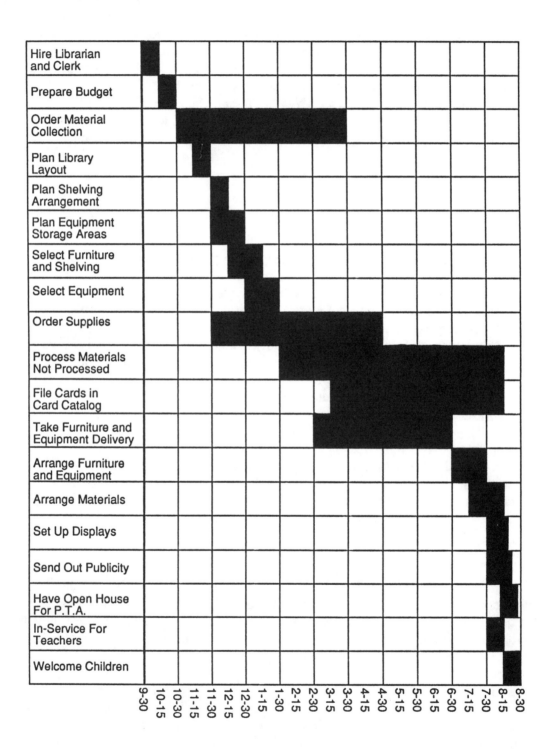

Fig. 4.1. Planning chart for opening a new elementary school library (developed using the Gantt chart technique).

The Gantt chart is very helpful because it is easy to see immediately when a project is on schedule, behind schedule, or ahead of schedule. When deadlines are not met additional resources may be allocated if the final date appears to be in jeopardy.

Final step of the chart is the *turnkey* date. At this time "keys" should be turned over and the project should be completed.

Managing the Facility

Few school library media specialists begin their jobs by opening a new facility. Rather, they must schedule the existing facility for maximum use by students and teachers—as individuals, as small groups, and as entire classes. To maximize use, scheduling and monitoring access to the media center is a major task requiring careful management of time.

Time management is a particularly difficult skill to acquire in the school situation where interruptions are commonplace rather than unusual. The school library media specialist, just as any school teacher, must plan carefully to allow for these interruptions. In fact, media specialists come to realize that the unexpected is the expected. For example, a student or small group from a classroom has an immediate need to find information. At the same time, a teacher wants to request additional materials because of an event that has just occurred. They will enter the library with great enthusiasm only to find the library media specialist conducting a storyhour with kindergarten, an activity which should not be interrupted.

Capturing the "teachable" moment involves the library media center as much as or more often than any other area of the school. Perhaps this is one of the most compelling reasons to provide free access to the media center rather than limiting access because of a rigid schedule of classes. Students and teachers with information needs must have these needs met at the earliest possible moment. Most high schools have full-time staff and large enough centers to accommodate both full classes and small groups. This is not as often true in elementary schools, and schedules sometimes present a problem.

Scheduling the Library Media Center

Many school library media specialists will argue that, unless elementary teachers are scheduled to bring their classes to the media center, they will not do so. Certainly in many school districts the elementary teachers' planning time is built around "special" subjects, such as music, art, physical education, computer literacy, and library media center. When this occurs, scheduling is arranged by an administrator, and the school library media specialist can only hope to find additional time slots for spontaneous use of the media center and its resources.

When this is the case, activities must be planned to help break this type of rigid use of the media center. It will take the endorsement of the advisory committee and detailed, careful, curriculum-related planning with one or more teachers. If a class activity has been planned for a full semester, it may be possible to exclude other classes from the media center for their regular schedule if it is to be used for a very special culminating event for that single class. This will not be easy to achieve, but if such an event is successful with one class, other teachers will want their students to have a similar opportunity. This can build attitudes in teachers that the media center is a research center rather than a free period.

At the secondary level, many students can come to the media center only when their teachers bring an entire class because they have no study halls available. Other students have so many study halls scheduled that they use the library media center as a change of scene or social gathering spot. Both situations must be addressed. Students need opportunities to use the media center at some time during the day. Homeroom might provide an opportunity. Students who are seeking something other than a study hall period of sheer boredom are a concern. Alternate activities might be used if teachers could be encouraged to help plan these activities. No one has time to waste in the process of learning for the future. Something that will fill the gap between sitting listlessly in the study hall or disturbing others in the media center would benefit all. The time it takes to plan such activities would be well spent, especially if the activities could be repeated with other students at other times. For instance, the daily newspaper provides many possibilities (perhaps multiple day-old copies could be obtained): a contest to discover the best price for bananas in grocery ads, a tracking of stock market prices for a month, and others. Some library media specialists have developed reference questions for contests. Developing a series of activities that could be used from one year to the next may help lessen student boredom and increase the value of the media center in their education.

In those schools where the media specialist has the opportunity to plan classes around the curriculum, teachers are queried often to discover their unit plans so that media center visits can be built into the unit at the appropriate time. Library media specialists who work closely with teachers will find their media centers heavily used by students who are completing class assignments requiring media center materials and the services of the media staff.

Daily Plan Books

Classroom teachers are expected to maintain a daily plan book to post the goals and objectives of the lessons, the activities, and the evaluation of progress through the units. The school library media specialist, also a teacher, should maintain a similar record, although the daily plans will be covering several classrooms of students rather than one. This plan book is a log of activities being planned, in progress, and being evaluated. It is a record of the alternatives when the original plan was revised. If timing of a unit is off the plan book shows the new schedule. In this book the library media specialist, as teacher, states goals, objectives, and activities and, finally, records progress. A sample page from a media specialist's plan book is shown in figure 4.2.

Planning New Facilities

Although the media center, as facility, exists to house the staff, materials, and equipment, its main function is to provide an environment which will encourage and support teaching and learning within its spaces. Location in the building is something most media specialists inherit, but sometimes the media specialist is able to plan a new facility.

Few library media specialists will have the chance to build a new facility, but it is possible that such an opportunity will occur. If so, visits should be made to several sites to review with other media specialists the strengths and weaknesses of their designs. What works well in one location may work well in another. What did not work in one location should be avoided if at all possible in new plans, although this is not necessarily an easy task. Collecting ideas is always helpful, and a truly successful idea can be presented to the architect as a helpful suggestion.

Next, teachers and students should be asked to help define the areas of use within the media center. Media center users will be locating information and materials. Reference areas and the card catalog or online public access catalog should be near a media specialist so that students can be helped quickly. Some areas may be designated for recreational reading, viewing, and listening, but other areas should be available for quiet study. Circulation of materials, borrowing and returning reserve materials, and requesting periodicals from closed stacks tend to be noisy areas and should be located near the entrance to the library media center.

The architects will be interested in the philosophy of service for the media center. They will also need to know the number of students and teachers to be served, the numbers of materials to be housed, and the areas that will be needed. That is, are a separate classroom area and spaces that can be darkened requirements? And what about electrical outlets for equipment, conference rooms, magazine storage, work space, and other needs?

(Text continues on page 45.)

Week of September 22-26,1986			Room Library
I 8:25 - 9:05	**II** 9:05 - 9:45	**III** 9:45 - 10:25	**IV** 10:25 - 11:05
MONDAY RESOURCE PERIOD NOTE: Meet with 4th grade teachers to discuss reading project to begin on Wednesday	202 (4) Obj: Using an overhead projector, practice identifying the 3 kinds of catalog cards (author,title and subject);Review the parts of a title page and locate those parts on a catalog card	215 (5) - Obj: Introduce almanacs and their organization-allow time for students to examine the almanac,then discuss some of the types of information found.Use almanacs to search for info.	PREPARATION PERIOD
TUESDAY PREPARATION PERIOD	209 (5) 1. Book sharing by students or librarian. 2. Book Circulation 3. Recreational Reading 4. Read aloud from the book- Where's Buddy?	217 (4) Obj: Review the parts of a catalog card-Continue working on the activity sheet- The Card Catalog Search- students are to work individually locating the parts from the catalog drawers.	CLERICAL WORK- organize magazine/journal records.
WEDNESDAY PREPARATION PERIOD	202 (4) 1. Book Sharing (by students or librarian) 2. Book selecting 3. Recreational Reading 4. Read aloud from the book- Invasion of the Brain Sharpeners	207 (4) Obj: Continue working on the Card Catalog Search-review the parts of a catalog card and practice locating them on sample cards-Use overhead proj.	Database Time- Work on requested online searches for teachers.
THURSDAY Meet with third grade teachers on new topics of study	210 (5) Obj: Begin collecting information from encyclopedias for Hist./Geog.project using 3x5 cards, students will practice note-taking steps TOPIC: National Parks and Monuments.	207 (4) 1. Book Sharing 2. Book selection 3. Recreational Reading 4. Read aloud (if time permits) from the book, Chocolate Fever discuss the character,Henry Green.	PREPARATION PERIOD
FRIDAY PREPARATION PERIOD	210 (5) 1. Book Sharing 2. Book Selection 3. Recreational Reading 4. Reading aloud from the book, Invasion of the Brain Sharpeners	217 (4) 1. Book Sharing 2. Book Selection 3. Recreational Reading 4. Read aloud from the book, Where's Buddy?	Work on plans for next week's lessons.

(Fig. 4.2 continues on page 44.)

Fig. 4.2—*Continued*

Teacher MRS. LINDA SAVIDO			**ELE D7** 662688 REV 9/83	
V 11:05 - 11:45	**VI** 12:20 - 12:55	**VII** 12:55 - 1:30	**VIII** 1:30 - 2:00	
205 (3) 1. Review the circulation rules and procedures. 2. Book Circulation 3. Recreational Reading 4. Begin reading aloud from the book-The Trouble With Magic-introduce the author, Ruth Chew, and the main characters of the story, Barb and Rick and the wizard, Harrison Peabody.	206 (3)	Clerical Chores: Shelve books and update magazine rack with new magazines		M O N D A Y
215 (5) 1. Book Sharing by students and librarian 2. Book Selection 3. Recreational Reading 4. Read aloud from the book-Invasion of the Brain Sharpeners	203 (3) Obj: Working independently, students will practice identifying Title Page parts from books found in piles on the tables-Review the parts of the Title/Copyright Pages.	Shelving Books and working on materials for new review games.	D. E. A. R TIME 2:00 - 2:15	T U E S D A Y
Database Time	203 (3) 1. Review circulation rules. 2. Book selection 3. Recreational Reading 4. Read aloud from the book-The Trouble with Magic-introduce author,Ruth Chew and characters.	NOTE: Begin working with selected 4th grade students on a Reading Project on Communication Topics.		W E D N E S D A Y
204 (3) 1. Book Sharing 2. Book circulation 3. Recreational Reading 4. Read aloud some humorous poetry from the book,The Baby Uggs are Hatching.	205 (3) Obj: Using signal cards (A=author, I=illustrator, P=publisher,PP= place of publication)students will practice identifying Title Page parts use transparencies and overhead proj.	Work on lesson plans for the next week.	DISMISSAL 2:20	T H U R S D A Y
Fill teacher requests for materials.	204 (3) Obj: Use overhead and transparencies to focus on the arrangement of the author's name-Last.Name comma First Name Middle Name-model and allow students to practice.			F R I D A Y

Fig. 4.2. Sample pages from media specialist's plan book.

Architects do not want detailed floor plans. Yet, they may wish to see the relationship of one area to another. That is, if the conference rooms need to be close to equipment storage, this must be specified. If there are to be noisy areas such as the circulation desk or reference area, the relationship to more quiet reading areas must be made clear. They must know special needs such as sinks, cabinets, carpeting, electrical outlets, plumbing.

The architects design, draw blueprints, and return with the plans for further review. It is important to understand what is shown in the blueprint. A square in the middle of the plan probably indicates a load bearing pillar. If it is placed directly in front of where the circulation desk was to be placed, rearrangement of the area may be necessary. Care must be taken to see that no blind spots are built into the furniture arrangement. Architects often attempt to beautify with balconies or exotic entrances that are not workable as a center for students.

This author is well aware of strange lighting fixtures that did not have enough light and melted when higher wattage was placed in them. Another architect built a bridge from two sides to bring middle school students directly from their open classrooms into a second floor "island." The reading room tables and chairs were directly under these two bridges. One can only wonder how many objects were dropped onto heads below before these entrances were closed, forcing students into a corridor and down outside stairs to come into the front door of the media center.

It is sometimes impossible to convince an architect to make changes. If the situation is very bad, the media specialist should ask the superintendent to intervene with the school board.

The school board will approve the plans. It may be that bids for building are far higher than anticipated and cuts must be made from the original design. It is imperative that the school library media specialist review the cuts to make sure they are made in the appropriate areas.

Some simple considerations for the novice:

1. Select shelving with backing, especially for elementary schools. It is all too easy to push books and boxes through double-faced shelving or down behind single-faced shelving which has no backing.

2. Select sufficient shelving to hold the present collection and anticipated additions for the next ten to fifteen years. It is difficult to impossible to match paint, wood, or even type of shelf with the same manufacturer after the initial order. If bids are let for new shelving and a different manufacturer is chosen, the problem is intensified.

    Capacity estimates of the number of books per three-foot shelf WHEN FULL:

    > Books of average size—thirty books per shelf
    > Reference books—eighteen books per shelf
    > Picture books, with dividers—sixty books

3. Select sufficient electrical voltages to carry present and anticipated electrical use. Sufficient outlets in planning a new facility are mandatory, and state codes may not require enough. Insufficient electrical current built into a new facility may make the new media center resemble a renovated one if additional conduits must be strung on the outside of walls.

4. Check carefully the source of shelving and furnishings. Many times bids are let for educational rather than library furniture. The author of this volume well remembers a slanting top picture book table order for an elementary school which was "custom-built" by the company furnishing the entire building. Six-year-olds could have used it for an easel, the legs were so tall. The carpenters installing the furniture were very reluctant to cut the legs to the proper size since this is very difficult to do after the furniture has left the factory.

Remodeling Facilities

Remodeling facilities can be a very exciting challenge. The end result is a new look to the library media center and, usually, added space.

In deciding how to remodel or rearrange furniture it may be helpful to place the furniture and equipment into a grid. This will help review the approximate spaces for the media center. A grid and furniture-to-scale appear in figure 4.3. While it is not necessary to make exact measurements, a fair idea can be obtained by using the grid. Following this procedure can help determine space relationships in the media center.

When remodeling is to occur, the school library media specialist should look carefully at the building. It may be better to move the media center to a new location than to try to remodel it in its existing space. Far too often the location of stairwells and restrooms impede the expansion that would be possible if the media center were relocated. The possibility of moving the media center seldom occurs to anyone, but it should occur to the media specialist. Locate the best place in the building and then rearrange so that this space can be used. The author is well aware of the transformation of one impossible situation.

The high school had two media center locations. The first was near the office area in the original building. A small reading room and a balcony to house periodicals was used as the fiction library. When an addition was placed on the building, a new area, approximately three classrooms in size, was given for media center use. The nonfiction books were housed there. The media specialist walked between these two distant locations to meet students and teachers as they planned media center activities. It was necessary to purchase two sets of periodicals to have some research capability in both locations.

The media specialist soon learned that all walls in the new building were temporarily placed and could be easily moved. The next step was to get an indication of the cost to partition the old library into three classrooms. Within one year the materials collections had been consolidated, an event the media coordinator had been striving for since the new building had been built. It is merely a task that requires careful planning and justification for the change.

Beware of the load-bearing wall. Load-bearing walls support the roof and the weight of the floors above the media center. It cannot be removed and cutting openings through it may be too expensive for the space gained. Another caution: any media specialist remodeling should ensure sufficient electrical current, surge controls to the electricity, humidity controls, telephone lines, and advanced communication lines such as fiber optic cable.

Remodeling need not always be costly. "Homemade" alterations can be carried out without major expense. The author was successful in encouraging the school carpenters to build additional shelving when insufficient funds were available to purchase shelving for remodeled facilities. Shelving was built from less expensive wood, with runners for adjustable shelving, and painted in bright colors.

School carpenters should be reminded that all shelves must be adjustable, and no shelf must be more than three feet wide. The standard depth is eight to ten inches. Oversize shelves for reference books, picture books, or for audiovisual media are ten to twelve inches. The thickness of shelves should be at least 13/16 inch. Cornices or trim is not needed and can be restrictive on the top or sides of shelves.

Elementary shelving should be no higher than five feet, junior high shelves no higher than six feet, and senior high school shelves no higher than seven feet. Adjustable runners allow variance in space between shelves to accommodate oversize books. Remodeling an existing facility may be more challenging than creating a new one. In either situation potential improvements to the program will greatly outweigh the one-time effort to pack and unpack materials.

(Text continues on page 50.)

FACILITIES EXERCISE

The following grid is to help you describe your library facility by outlining. This will provide both a floor plan and a traffic pattern. The grid is to be filled in using a scale of 1/8" to 1'. That is, each square would be 2'. It is not important that you be "architect correct," but it is important that you attempt to place your furnishings into their places using an approximate size relationship.

STEPS TO FOLLOW

1. If possible, measure your library. You may do this with a tape measure, but you may also estimate by measuring one tile (floor or ceiling) and plotting from that estimate.

2. Place tables and chairs allowing the approximate space between all furnishings and the surrounding shelves. The second sheet provides you with furniture and shelves outlined to scale. You may use it to trace in your shelves or you may cut them out and paste them down. Don't forget the chargeout desk.

3. Be sure to indicate doors and partitions and label the one entrance considered the main entrance. If you have a fire escape rather than an exit, please indicate that. These are all a part of your facilities design.

(Fig. 4.3 continues on page 48.)

Fig. 4.3—*Continued*

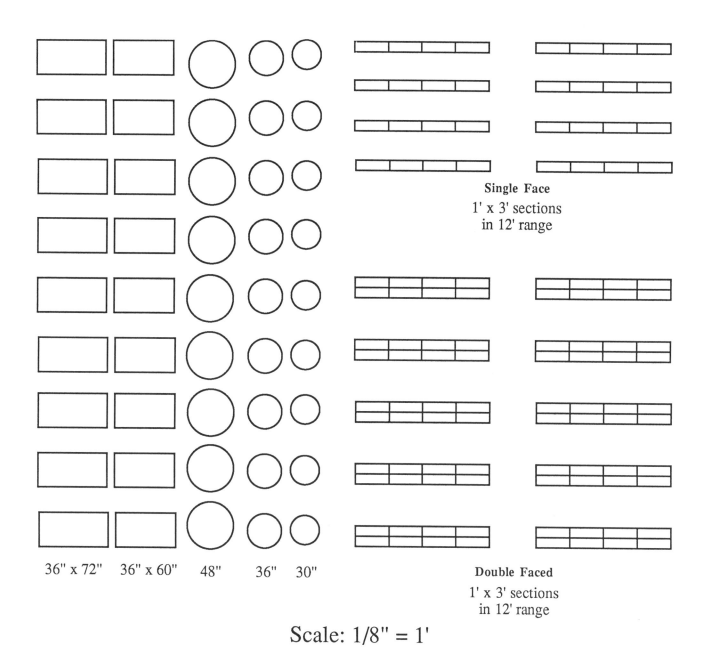

36" x 72"   36" x 60"   48"   36"   30"

Single Face
1' x 3' sections
in 12' range

Double Faced
1' x 3' sections
in 12' range

Scale: 1/8" = 1'

Fig. 4.3. Facilities grid to scale for floor plan and room arrangement.

Moving a Media Center

As school populations shift and decline from one area to another, schools close and school library media specialists are assigned the task of closing the library. This involves sending collections, furniture, and equipment to a central warehouse or distributing the collection, furniture, and equipment among other schools.

If more is needed at the other locations, the shift is planned after a careful inventory at each media center. Equal distribution may not be a case of "one for School A," "one for School B," "one for School C." Redistribution should be on the basis of need and existing collections.

Collections, furniture, and equipment to be moved should be carefully scrutinized and the old, irrelevant, and broken removed before consideration of division. Certainly the materials collection is analyzed for duplication at other schools. It may be preferable to keep materials in a central location and let interested media specialists pick only those titles of use in their collections rather than sending cartons of materials to another school and having them returned or discarded.

The administration in one school district asked each of the five librarians to work two weeks one summer to close one elementary school and move the contents to the other schools in the district. The librarians measured the time it would take to remove each item from its place on the shelf, pull the shelflist and catalog cards, pack the item into a box, unpack, reshelve, and refile cards. When the school administrators were given the anticipated number of hours the move would take, they increased professional time and added clerical assistance.

The construction work involved in remodeling an existing facility may be in progress during a school year. In this situation much of the collection may be boxed and stored. Media specialists must analyze during the preceding year the most important books and media used during the time the collection must be closed and move them to a classroom or another accessible area. The most used periodicals, microforms, and reference books should also be kept from storage. Equipment can be reassigned to storage areas or classrooms throughout the building. Again, this process takes careful needs assessment and planning.

If a new facility is projected, buying the new contents should be planned at least one year in advance, and the media specialist assigned to the new center should have release time and additional clerical assistance during this year. The amount needed should be as carefully calculated as the collection being transferred from another location and added to from new selections.

The success of any media program is dependent upon the staff and the collection. Yet, the ambiance of the facility sets the stage.

Exercises

1.   Review the daily plan book of a library media specialist. Estimate the percentage of time indicated to be spent (1) working with students, (2) planning with teachers, (3) performing administrative tasks, and (4) doing clerical tasks.

2.   Using the graph paper and furniture, draw the floor plan of an existing school library media center. See if this center can be easily rearranged to provide better access, quiet vs. noisy areas, and any other improvements you would suggest.

3. Related Case Studies: See

    Case Study 9, "Testing the Limits of the Resources and Services of the Trent Library Media Centers: Planning with Teachers for Extended Units of Study"

    Case Study 10, "What Constitutes Successful Library Media Service for Teachers? Trent High School"

    Case Study 11, "Can Flexible Scheduling Be Successful at Springs Elementary School Library Media Center?"

All of these studies are in Mary K. Biagini's *A Model for Problem Solving and Decision Making* (Englewood, Colo.: Libraries Unlimited, 1988).

Notes

[1]Daniel L. Stufflebeam. "The Relevance of the CIPP Evaluation Model for Educational Accountability," in David D. Thomson, ed. *Planning and Evaluation for Statewide Library Development: New Dimensions* (Columbus, Ohio: Ohio State University Evaluation Center, 1972), 26.

5 On the Job
Managing Personnel

For many school library media specialists, the only personnel management skills needed are interpersonal skills for communication with administrators, teachers, and students. As single managers of the library media center, they have no media staff to manage. For others, a part-time or full-time clerk may be a part of the media center staff. In very large schools the school library media center may be served by two or more professionals and several paraprofessionals and clerks. Certainly, programs to educate school library media specialists should prepare students to assume responsibility for the management of personnel within their centers and should include the skills needed to interact with others in the school.

Managing Staff

Asheim's manpower report prepared for the American Library Association described five levels of staff for the library: clerk, library media technician, library assistant, library associate, and librarian.[1] In this plan a master's degree was required for the library associate and the librarian. The American Association of School Librarians (AASL) and the Association for Educational Communications and Technology (AECT) in their 1975 standards listed media specialist, media technician, and media aide.[2] Chisholm and Ely included generalist, specialist, technician, and aide.[3]

At times school administrators have discussed differentiated staffing models. In the team teaching setting, divisions were proposed between master teacher and staff teacher. The staff teacher would need only a bachelor's degree unless permanent certification in a state required education beyond the bachelor's degree. The master teacher would hold a master's degree and would work on an extended-year contract. A teacher specialist would be available at the large school or district level for curriculum areas.

If differentiated staffing exists, the school library media specialists who are directors of the library media center should be on a level with the master teacher working with an extended-year contract. Other media specialists would be in the category of the staff teacher, tenured with experience. District directors of library media programs would be considered teacher specialists.

Within the media center the staff may include one or more professional library media specialists and one or more clerical staff to be managed by the director. Chisholm and Ely list seven competencies in the personnel management function.[4] The following would be a part of the job description of the media center director.

Writes job descriptions for recruiting and hiring personnel.

Recruits, hires, and terminates personnel.

Conducts training for staff.

Assigns job responsibilities to specific personnel.

Supervises personnel.

Maintains job satisfaction of personnel.

Evaluates employee performance.

These competencies relate directly to the personnel working within the media center. The degree to which any library media specialist may participate in any of these functions is a product of the organization of the school district and the contracts binding upon personnel within that school district. A building-level media specialist might be asked to create the job description for other professionals and the clerical staff, although this might be done at the central office level.

Centralization of job descriptions at the district level eases uniformity in operation through all schools. When tasks in one media center are different from another, this must be taken into consideration. For instance, if a clerk is searching on a bibliographic or other online database, this becomes a part of the job description even though the service is limited to one school.

When staff leave the school district, a job description should be provided for applicants for the replacement. Job descriptions are also necessary for any new positions that have been created.

While there may seem to be little need to prepare a job description until funds have been allocated for the position, the media specialist must clearly analyze the need for additional staff. A first task may be to sell administrators on the need for a new or expanded position. If so, the foundation established in the job description may become the justification for funding.

In order to approach an administrator with the need for additional or continuation of staff, an analysis of the tasks currently being accomplished, and those not able to be accomplished because of lack of staff, must be presented in such a way to convince others that a need is not being met. To couch the request in, "I don't have time to write overdues," or "The books don't get shelved very fast," probably won't get an administrator's attention. Calculating actual cost for clerical tasks in relation to professional salary is presented in chapter 7.

Writing job descriptions for recruiting and hiring personnel is not an easy task. One document which might be useful is the 1975 AASL/AECT standards, *Media Programs District and School*, mentioned above. Duties of each library media center staff member have been described, and these could be adapted to the local situation. If fewer staff are available in a school, some duties can be moved from one or more position statements to describe a single job. Care should be taken to make sure administrators recognize the division between clerical tasks and professional tasks.

The recruitment of personnel may be accomplished at the district level through a personnel office rather than by the individual media center directors. Skills tests or assessment of credentials to meet employment standards are done centrally, and persons meeting qualifications may be assigned to a building with the library media specialists having little or no control over the selection. When selection is at the individual school, the members of the Advisory Committee should be asked to help interview additional professional and clerical staff to ensure the selection of the best candidate.

The competency, "conducts training for staff," will be discussed in more detail in the section concerned with providing services for teachers and students (see chapter 8). Inservice training of staff, teachers, and students is considered in depth there.

Assigning job responsibilities is a management task which must be undertaken with great care, because appropriate task assignments can make the difference between a successful and an unsuccessful program. Certainly the division of the program into discrete tasks and assigning each task to the best person to accomplish it is the only way that the program will function efficiently.

It is better if most tasks can be shared by all. Obviously, personnel must be assigned to tasks for which they are qualified and trained and that they are willing to do, but all members of a staff as small as those assigned to most school library media centers should understand all basic operations. If only one person understood how to operate the circulation system, the media center would close if this person was absent.

Motivating staff is another responsibility for the media specialist. Once upon a time the author's father suggested that she should never ask anyone to do something she was not willing to do herself. This is true of library media specialists. It is often media center directors who must not only say they are willing to do any task, but also to demonstrate their willingness by doing the task. Clerks, students, and volunteer parents are much more willing to shelve books and read the shelves if the library media specialist is seen working at tasks such as these that are considered to be particularly dull and tedious. That is not to say that clerical tasks are appropriate for professionals, but that professionals should not appear to be too important to do them. That attitude does not enhance the task nor the self-image of the student or the volunteer. The feeling of students helpers and volunteers that their assistance is critical, and it is, can only be enhanced if the media specialist demonstrates the importance of the unpleasant as well as the more pleasant tasks.

Supervision of personnel is the process of dealing with the persons who have been assigned the job responsibilities discussed above. Some supervisors view this role as one of "boss" who must monitor behavior. The other end of the continuum is where the supervisor is a colleague with the staff to accomplish the task. These two concepts can be discussed in relation to Douglas McGregor's Theory X and Theory Y.[5] In Theory X, management is responsible for organizing the work and directing the efforts of those involved to get the work accomplished. The Theory X manager believes that staff will work as little as possible because they are lacking in ambition, that they dislike responsibility, and are self-centered and indifferent to the needs of the organization. The Theory Y manager believes that staff can assume responsibility, and that it is the responsibility of the manager to arrange the situation so that those working within the organization can direct their own efforts toward the objectives of the organization.

In order to be a Theory Y manager, the director of the media center must work with all staff to determine the tasks to be done and to solicit input as to the best methods to accomplish the tasks. A regularly scheduled staff meeting can be used to discuss progress toward the mutually set goals and objectives for the media program, to discuss the media center schedule for the week, and to divide duties among the staff. Any items which may have been overlooked can be added, and any activity that will relate to another can be determined. That is, the media center classroom may be used by only one group at a time, and inadvertent double booking would be disturbing to all.

Maintaining job satisfaction in the library media center should be an easy task. If staff have been queried as to the best method to accomplish a task, and their suggestions implemented whenever possible, they should consider that they have worth within the organization. They must also feel they have the opportunity to develop on the job.

Staff development depends upon two conditions. The first is *group relationships* that contribute to productivity and achievement of organizational goals. The second is *climate*, the work situation that helps individuals to grow, create, produce, and to give themselves enthusiastically to the work for which they are responsible.[6]

Job satisfaction exists in the library media center when (1) the facility is appealing, (2) staff appear to understand their jobs and are doing them, (3) an efficient operation is in place, and (4) the library media center director is not a boss but a facilitator.

Evaluating Personnel

In many school districts and in many states, personnel evaluation is no longer by choice but by necessity. In some states, evaluation is mandated by the state department of education.

In the case of professional staff, the school district requirements include evaluation of performance to determine reappointment or tenure. The evaluation steps to reappointment and tenure were suggested as information to be gathered before accepting a position in a school district. Since many persons seeking positions do not always know exactly what questions to ask, after they begin their school year they need to understand this process more fully. The principal, the district library media director, and the personnel office in the school district should be good sources of help for information about securing permanent certification and in earning tenure. It is essential that correct information be obtained. While many teachers may think they understand this process, they may not be up-to-date on the latest policies or requirements in the state or district. Once teachers have been tenured, they are less interested in the process. Since they do not need to know, they may have incorrect concepts. It is better to get this information from the district office and thus confirm any suggestions from other teachers and media specialists. In the media center with more than one professional, directors must keep current on tenure policy because they will be part of evaluating personnel.

Evaluation may be required even after tenure. Forms developed by the state department of education are provided to school districts to evaluate the teaching and clerical staff. These forms seldom cover the unique tasks of the school library media specialist. One of the more often heard complaints is that school library media specialists are judged with the same descriptors as the classroom teacher when, in fact, their roles and tasks are very different. In some states, the evaluation form is developed by the state board of education for the evaluation of all education personnel. If this is the case, the library media specialist may help the principal by defining the evaluation criteria in library media terminology. The author is reminded of a situation when a library media specialist requested release from a sabbatical commitment. Unfortunately for all concerned, the sabbatical replacement had been inadequate. The substantial extra salary cost for the returning media specialist was borne by the school district simply because the administrators did not understand how to define, monitor, and correct a bad situation in the media center when they were very well aware of methods to improve the classroom teacher's (but not the media specialist's) performance.

Evaluation forms can be developed by the state library media organization. This group, often in cooperation with the state department of education's school library media director, may provide a better form for the evaluation of performance of the building-level library media specialist.

The most efficient form of evaluation is direct observation. Direct observation of performance is usually uncomfortable for all concerned. Students are uneasy because the media staff person being observed is uneasy. It is difficult for the observer to be at ease because this is an evaluation situation. The performance is strained, and the process seems contrived. However, evaluation must be made of the ability of media professionals as they interact with students and teachers. If this is not to be an arbitrary decision, it must be based upon concrete facts. One method to get these facts is through direct observation.

As school administrators revise their expectations of performance, evaluation changes. In other words, as they recognize that the job of the media specialist is similar to, yet quite different from, that of the classroom teacher, they will better understand how evaluation criteria must also be different.

Unfortunately, media center directors may be asked to help with the review of a less efficient employee, and evaluation may involve keeping a detailed record of inefficiency to support dismissal. School library media specailists hope that they will not need to dismiss personnel, but when the situation does occur, the principal and the district library media director should be consulted to establish the appropriate procedures. Dismissal requires a carefully documented record of tasks done incorrectly and those not done at all. It is not a pleasant assignment, yet it is irresponsible to allow inefficient, ineffective, and even harmful employees to remain on the media center staff when the education of students is at stake.

Since clerical or technical staff are seldom tenured, evaluation determines salary increase and continuation of position. Records must be maintained at all levels. Efficient staff must be rewarded, and merit pay raises often must be documented as carefully as refusal to grant merit pay raises. The dismissal of inefficient clerical and technical staff requires careful and thorough documentation just as in the case of professional staff.

Managing personnel may also be defined as getting along with the clientele. In the next sections, suggestions for managing with administrators, teachers, students, and volunteers are offered.

Managing with Administrators

This section might be subtitled, "How to get along with your boss." Certainly, managing with administrators is getting along with those in authority in the school district. The focus will be on the building principal, but the methods and the suggestions for activities are equally applicable to the director of the library media program and the district superintendent. The first method is the planning phase. The school library media program will prosper if the media specialist learns to plan with the principal.

Planning with the principal does not mean discussing the titles of periodicals to which to subscribe. That is a professional task for which the media specialist has had training. Rather, the planning with the principal should include such topics as the costs of reference services and the reference materials needed—books, periodicals, and databases—to increase student potential in the school. This is a very broad and somewhat different approach to the relationship between principal and library media specialist. Pat Mautino, of the Oswego BOCES, in Mexico, New York, sees the relationship between these two educators as a peer relationship. They both touch the educational lives of every student through their interaction with students and teachers. Discussion of the learning needs of students as they are reflected in the library media collection is a continuing topic.

A second management method is reporting to the principal. Regular reports, which detail successes as well as needs, will help present the media center program in such a way that the principal can brag to other principals. Too often in life the complaints outweigh the compliments, and complaining is not the way to win friends or influence the principal. Regular monthly reports detailing the use of the media center and the positive experiences of students should outnumber the list of needs, great though they may be. Media specialists should also plan to submit a yearly report, which is a compilation of the monthly statistics. If the media specialist has developed a three-, five-, ten-, or fifteen-year plan with the principal, this yearly report will cite progress toward each of the goals, point out what has not occurred, and present the plan for fulfilling this objective in the next one or two years. The year-end report should be attractive and easily understood.

The principal who participates in activity planning will better understand the role of the media specialist and the amount of responsibility involved in managing a media center. In evaluating performance the principal must clearly recognize the dual role of the media specialist—as teacher and manager—and adjust the method of evaluation accordingly.

Finally, the school library media specialist has full responsibility for accomplishing as much as possible in the education of each student. Testing, recording, and reporting the role of the media center in the educational progress of students will ultimately make the principal look good, the best of all possible results in managing with the administrator.

Managing with Teachers

Management with teachers is easily accomplished when the media specialist is constantly available for curriculum assistance. Striving to reach level ten within the taxonomy will provide teachers with the help they need as they plan their classroom activities. Accessibility of resources at the time they are needed is essential. Media specialists should encourage teachers to plan ahead as regards their media needs, but instant help must be given willingly, not grudgingly.

Another proposed method of managing with teachers is to put as few restrictions as possible on media center access. Under this method, the media specialist allows as many students as possible access to the media center from the classroom and works with teachers to ensure the best possible experiences for their students while they are in the media center.

Determining the services teachers prefer and attempting to offer them is another excellent way to manage with teachers. "Success" can often be defined as doing what teachers think should be done. Asking which services teachers want and then offering those services will appear positive.

One way to help teachers understand the role of the media center in the instruction of students is to provide inservice for teachers in information sources, research methods, research in the field of education, and new additions to the media center. Also, the media specialist can provide inservice that will help teachers gain technological skills they may be lacking.

Helping teachers expand their skills, without indicating that they do not have the skills, is a successful management method. Overcoming teacher resistance is possible when teachers have been involved in the planning of the inservice activity. That is, the program will be based upon teacher-developed needs.

Finally, the media specialist should be willing to assist with extracurricular events. When the music teacher needs someone to go to the city choral festival with the school choir, the media specialist should volunteer rather than be drafted. The author of this book spent many hours helping the music teacher with costumes, helping the drama coach backstage, and making hats for a physical education demonstration. As sponsor of the cheerleaders for three years, she attended the athletic events. At intervals she also was responsible for the publishing of the school newspaper and helped the English and art teachers with the school magazine. These tasks were not in the job description of the media specialist, but they were activities requiring a teacher-sponsor. Ignoring the opportunity to assist the teachers would have made managing more difficult later when teachers used the media center.

Managing Students

Providing an orderly library media center is the first task of the media specialist in managing students. Letting them know what is expected in behavior in the media center, in their conduct in other libraries they may use as they gather research materials, and in their care of the media center materials is a major responsibility of a media specialist. Very few books exist to help the teachers manage the classroom and even fewer exist that treat the management of students in the media center.

Discipline is much easier if the traffic flow of the media center is under control. Locating the probable noisy areas near the entrance is one way to begin to control. Rearranging furniture so that contact between students is lessened is another. Placing shelves for visibility is a third. Once the facility is arranged, attitude toward students must be assessed.

> For some students, and in certain schools this may be many students, the only library skill that they should have to acquire is an awareness imprinted indelibly and happily upon them, that the library is a friendly place where the librarians are eager to help.[7]

This friendly attitude and demonstrated willingness to assist is often far beyond that which a public librarian or an academic librarian is required to exhibit. When the author once told a class of aspiring media specialists that school library media specialists worked harder and happier than any other teacher, a student said, "I resent your implication that we must work harder. We aren't paid more." However, the freedom which should exist in the media center to allow students to explore their environment, to learn from one another, to read or view or listen to materials recommended by their fellow students poses a difficult situation. Knowing when this interaction moves from exploration and encouragement into mischief is a skill that may take practice to acquire. The only suggestion is to continue to seek ways to allow students the freedom to explore.

The media center is the only room in the school where no student need fail. Students with reading or math problems find frustration in the classroom. Asking for teacher help may be perceived by other students as a lack of ability to accomplish a task the other students in the classroom seem able to do easily. For students who are tone deaf, cannot sing or play an instrument, and cannot read music, music class is an uncomfortable situation. If students are color blind, the art room may be a greater challenge than they wish to attempt. Certainly many students are uncomfortable with physical activities, especially if they are chosen last for team sports.

In contrast, the library media center has no chosen sides. It should have information at all levels and to satisfy all interests. The media specialist should be available to give individual assistance to the students without drawing attention to the process. All students ask for help finding materials they would like to have, and all students find something with which they can work.

Media specialists, when they assume the role of teacher, must follow the prescriptions given for classroom management and effective teaching. For example, one principal suggests:

> A well-prepared lesson plan is your most important tool for effective teaching and classroom control. It will give your students a feeling that your class has structure and direction and it will give you confidence.[8]

He goes on to suggest that "good teaching is hard work, only bad teaching is easy." Good teaching will occur when the unit is planned and understood by the media specialist. It is impossible to fool an audience of strangers for very long. Students are very astute. They will be annoyed by busy work. Set objectives and share these objectives with students. It will not be busy work if they understand the reasons behind the exercise.

Units should be planned with a variety of activities, some lecture, some discussion, some viewing of media, some exercises that are active and allow them to move around. No one really enjoys sitting for long periods of time, and the media center is one room in the school that truly invites browsing and moving from one place to another.

Certainly not all students will earn affection, and in many it may be very difficult to find redeeming qualities. However, it is the responsibility of media specialists to like students and to let them know it.

Managing Parents and Volunteers

Much literature on the parent and the volunteer is available, especially on the parent as volunteer. Volunteers can be very helpful. Two cautions are in order:

1. The media specialist does not monitor the volunteer process.

2. Care must be taken to keep confidential information about students confidential in the presence of volunteers.

A volunteer chairperson is essential to maintain the regular service of volunteers. Since they are volunteers, more important events—a sick child, an unexpected errand—will cause them to miss their scheduled time. The media specialist cannot take time to make the telephone calls to get another volunteer for that day. This is more appropriately the task of a volunteer chairperson.

It is almost impossible to expect volunteers to remain silent about interesting events in the media center. However, for one parent to see the record of another child and report it to a third parent might be open to legal action.

Also, great care must be taken not to leave a volunteer in charge of a group of students. The legal responsibility for students in most states lies with a professional with teacher certification. A student injured in any way while the professional is away from the media center could cause a great deal of difficulty and perhaps legal action.

Volunteers, who are of great help in the media center, can become excellent advocates. They must, however, be carefully managed. Some forms that may be helpful in the management of volunteers are found in appendix F.

The parent as parent is a separate issue. Media specialists may think that they will see few parents since they are not classroom teachers, but this is not the case.

The media specialist must be ready to listen to the parent who comes into the library media center to discuss the child. This may range from a complaint about a book to a concern that the child isn't reading at grade level to a request that the child be permitted to take home the unabridged dictionary. The parent may also be interested in helping the media program and may be an advocate for the next budget request or the next effort to update materials or equipment.

Friends of the Library

Library media specialists may be aware of, and even members of, the Friends of the Public Library in their town. The national organization, Friends of Libraries USA (FOLUSA), has been very interested in encouraging Friends of School Libraries. A media center Friends organization extends beyond the local parent and teacher organization within the school and may include other members of the community. In some schools, these "friends" help with programs such as Junior Great Books, while in other schools they act in the same fund-raising capacity as they do in the public library domain. More information about FOLUSA is available from the American Library Association.

One media specialist recruits his Friends group from students within the school in much the same way Friends of public libraries are the users of the public library. These students are his library helpers, for he has a very large school with a twelve-month program and no clerical assistance.

Exercises

1. Discuss with media specialists the greatest problems and the greatest joys they have experienced in each of the following categories. Then see if you can plan practical solutions to the problems.
    Managing staff
    Evaluating personnel
    Managing with administrators
    Managing with teachers
    Managing students

2.   Related Case Studies: See

Case Study 6, "A Vital Link: Communicating with Trent Principals"

Case Study 9, "Testing the Limits of the Resources and Services of the Trent Library Media Centers: Planning with Teachers for Extended Units of Study"

Case Study 10, "What Constitutes Successful Library Media Service for Teachers: Trent High School"

Case Study 14, "Encouraging Independent Student use of Laurel Junior High Library Media Center"

Case Study 26, "Are Trent Library Media Specialists Teachers, or ... Something More? Performance Appraisal"

Case Study 27, "The Trent Library Media Specialists Burn Out: The Effects of Stress on Job Performance."

All of these studies are in Mary K. Biagini's *A Model for Problem Solving and Decision Making* (Englewood, Colo.: Libraries Unlimited, 1988).

Notes

[1]"Library Education and Manpower," *American Libraries* 1 (April 1970): 341-44.

[2]American Association of School Librarians, American Library Association, and Association for Educational Communications and Technology. *Media Programs District and School* (Chicago: American Library Association, 1975).

[3]Margaret E. Chisholm and Donald P. Ely. *Media Personnel in Education: A Competency Approach* (Englewood Cliffs, N.J.: Prentice-Hall, Inc., 1976).

[4]Ibid.

[5]Douglas McGregor. *The Human Side of Enterprise: 25th Anniversary Printing* (New York: McGraw-Hill, 1985).

[6]Howard F. Shout. In Elizabeth W. Stone, ed. *New Direction in Staff Development: Moving from Ideas to Action* (Chicago: American Library Association, 1971), 58.

[7]Francis Henne. "Learning to Learn in School Libraries," *School Libraries* 15 (May 1966): 17.

[8]Norman Koslofsky. "Planning and Behavior: Two Factors That Determine Teacher Success," *NASSP Bulletin* 68 (September 1984): 101.

6 On the Job
Managing the Collection

Collection management is presented in four segments: circulating materials, selecting materials, and acquiring and cataloging them. Circulation of materials is a first consideration in adding to and maintaining the media center collection. The collection is provided for use by the school community. Materials must circulate with minimum wait for patrons at the chargeout desk, records of borrowers must be maintained, and a system must be in place to track missing books and media when they are not returned.

The second part of managing the collection is the selection of materials and equipment. The problems of censorship and some proposed solutions are described as well as methods to employ to maximize choosing functional equipment that will survive heavy use. The third part includes methods for acquiring and deleting materials and equipment. The fourth segment of collection management is organizing the collection. Many choices for cataloging and processing materials are available, and the best choice for a given situation should be based upon full information.

Right to Privacy

Traditionally, users signed bookcards or slips when they checked out materials from the library media center. Replacing the bookcard or destroying the slip when the material was returned completed the transaction. As collections expanded and use increased, students and teachers were issued identification cards to speed circulation. However, these methods permitted the recognition of persons who had checked out any items, and this has been interpreted as a violation of individual privacy. The American Library Association policy on this follows.

Confidentiality of Library Records

The American Library Association strongly recommends that the responsible officers of each library, cooperative system, and consortium in the United States (1) Formally adopt a policy which specifically recognizes its circulation records and other records identifying the names of library users with specific materials to be confidential. (2) Advise all librarians and library employees that such records shall not be made available to any agency of state, federal, or local government except pursuant to such process, order, or subpoena as may be authorized under the authority of, and pursuant to, federal, state or local law relating to civil, criminal, or administrative discovery procedures or legislative investigatory power. (3) Resist the issuance or enforcement of any such process, order, or subpoena until such time as a proper showing of good cause has been made in a court of competent jurisdiction.[1]

Librarians must protect each user's right to privacy with respect to information sought or received, and materials consulted, borrowed, or acquired.[2]

These policies were expanded with the following:

> The members of the American Library Association, recognizing the right to privacy of library users, believe that records held in libraries which connect specific individuals with specific resources, programs, or services, are confidential and not to be used for purposes other than routine record keeping: to maintain access to resources, to assure that resources are available to users who need them, to arrange facilities, to provide resources for the comfort and safety of patrons, or to accomplish the purposes of the program or service. The library community recognizes that children and youth have the same rights to privacy as adults.

> Libraries whose record keeping systems reveal the names of users would be in violation of the confidentiality of library record laws adopted in many states. School library media specialists are advised to seek the advice of counsel if in doubt about whether their record keeping systems violate the specific laws in their states. Efforts must be made within the reasonable constraints of budgets and school management procedures to eliminate such records as soon as reasonably possible.

> With or without specific legislation, school library media specialists are urged to respect the rights of children and youth by adhering to the tenets expressed in the Confidentiality of Library Records Interpretation of the Library Bill of Rights and the ALA Code of Ethics.[3]

Pennsylvania has passed legislation which prohibits access to library records. The PA Act 1984-90, Section 428, reads:

> Library Circulation Records.—Records related to the circulation of library materials which contain the names or other personally identifying details regarding the users of the State Library or any local library which is established or maintained under any law of the Commonwealth or the library of any university, college or educational institution chartered by the Commonwealth or the library of any public school or branch reading room, deposit station or agency operated in connection therewith, shall be confidential and shall not be made available to anyone except by a court order in a criminal proceeding.

The need to maintain the privacy of students' use of materials has been one strong justification for automating the circulation system.

To Automate or Not to Automate

Many school library media specialists have been able to renew or expand the interest of their administrators in the media program through the careful presentation of facts that will lead to automation of the library media center functions. To many administrators, implementation of high technology is desirable even if such implementation is little understood and perhaps not even worthwhile. The decision to automate is one which must bring with it the need to justify increased funding; and the amount needed will be determined by the type and level of automation selected. Additional funds for automation are usually not immediately available to the school library media specialist, and approval must be sought from administrators and the school board if more money is to be made available.

If approval has been granted for additional expenditures, the question then becomes what and how much to automate. In the view of many, microcomputers provide the necessities for automation, while others favor programs requiring use of the district minicomputers or mainframes.

The storage capability of the microcomputer is not as large as that of the minicomputer or the mainframe. However, the storage capabilities are sufficient for many activities, and care must be taken not to store unnecessary information simply because records can be maintained. These records should be essential to the operation of the media center. One example of overkill is the media specialist who kept an inventory of publishers' catalogs on a floppy disk. This meant having to retrieve the disk and to have access to a microcomputer on a regular basis. Looking in a file drawer would be as efficient, particularly since updating the list on the microcomputer was time-consuming. In some cases, a new catalog would be filed and not retrieved until the newer catalog arrived. Perhaps consideration should have been given to a database which would have listed the products of the vendors rather than just their names. Other media specialists input each day's circulation manually so that overdue notices can be written. Since a very small percentage of the materials checked out became overdue, time would have been saved if input had occurred when the materials became overdue. However, one of the first priorities for most media specialists is a circulation system to help control overdues.

Circulation Systems Decisions

A wide variety of circulation systems exist and choices must be carefully made. Five major considerations are cost, scope, compatibility, choice of record, and method of retrospective conversion.

The first consideration, albeit not the most important, is cost. Circulation systems may range from $1,000 to $100,000. Cheaper is seldom better, and too cheap may appear to be less expensive in the initial stages, but it may become much more costly later.

The second consideration should be the scope or breadth of the circulation system. Will it merely record circulation of materials, or can records be used for online public access catalogs? Expending clerical or volunteer time to input records which will serve only for circulation should be reconsidered. This system will continue to require the input of new records throughout the life of the system. Is circulation truly such an onerous task, or would it be preferable to delay until sufficient funds are available to have both circulation and an online public access catalog? Can the system be used for acquisition or serials control?

A third consideration is compatibility, and the question is: With whom should the media center circulation system be compatible? An in-house circulation system which offers no opportunity to share with another location is a very narrow point of view and one which is already dated. Compatibility is directly related to a standard record of materials in the system. Therefore, the next consideration is a major one.

The fourth consideration is choice of record to use for the system. To ensure that one media center's catalog is uniform with most other libraries, records should be input using the MARC bibliographic and authority records. As mentioned in chapter 1 in the discussion of online card catalogs and circulation systems, MARC stands for Machine Readable Catalog and is the format established by the Library of Congress. MARC records contain the necessary information and the format required if systems are to "talk" to each other. Some circulation systems do not have enough storage to accommodate the MARC record, and while it can be argued that few media specialists need everything in the MARC record, use of this standard form ensures compatibility later. Some systems are using an abridged MARC record.

A fifth consideration is the method of retrospective conversion, defined in chapter 1 as the transfer of a paper record of the media center holdings into a machine-readable records. If a record is input from the shelflist in the media center, this record may be inaccurate. If the record is to be used later for the online public access catalog, it may not have appropriate subject headings. Misspelled author's names, incorrect titles, and insufficient subject headings will greatly decrease the possible uses of the materials later. Some media specialists have input their collections on MARC records through a national utility. Can these records be downloaded into the circulation system under consideration?

Additional queries must be made when selecting a system. As with any piece of technology, an important consideration is the service available. What happens when the system goes down? Many library media specialists have retained the bookcard and book pocket to use in case of equipment failure. Certainly swift service is a necessity.

Software providers are constantly revising their systems. If a major revision occurs, what is the responsibility of the vendor for the systems sold in the past. Will the new system accommodate the old records? Will the school library media specialists be given a free update or at least a chance to purchase at a reduced cost?

With this particular technology, training in the use of the system is extremely important. How many training sessions are provided free of charge with the purchase of the system? Is additional training provided if additions are made to the system?

Some of these questions can be answered in the literature. The American Library Association's *Library Technology Reports* published an assessment of microcomputer circulation control systems in their January/February 1986 volume. Dated almost as soon as it was published, the format of the information can be used as a model for questions to be asked in choosing a system.

Selecting Materials

Persons working in school library media centers are the most important component of the program. Their enthusiasm, willingness to be helpful, and their open invitation for students and teachers to use the center are the keys. Once the clientele have arrived, adequate and carefully selected materials and equipment must be available for use or the eagerness to find information and resources generated by the library media specialist will quickly die. Selection of resources is a high priority activity for the media program, but it is not totally the responsibility of library media specialists.

Materials should be suggested and selected for placement in the school library media center not only by media center staff, but also by other library media users, including administrators, teachers, students, and parents. Library media specialists who select a collection with little or no input from media center users may find that the choices appeal to a single person, the library media specialist, who chose the items.

Several methods are available to encourage teachers and others to make selections. Some of these will be discussed in chapter 8 because suggestions for purchases are made at the beginning and end of unit planning for teachers. At other times, teachers should be encouraged to make choices by sharing any bibliographies of materials which might be of interest. Students can be encouraged to suggest titles for inclusion. Preparing a justification for purchase of an item seen or read in another library can help develop students' writing skills. Students might also enjoy reading reviews of new materials in *Booklist* or *School Library Journal* and completing an order form for any titles that appeal to them. If students are assigned to the media center for work study or as library media center aides, their opinions should be actively sought in the selection process, and review of materials should be a part of each person's assignment. All involved in selection must be made aware of the selection policy criteria.

All materials selected should meet the criteria of the library media center selection policy. If no selection policy exists, library media specialists should write one that conforms to the ALA Intellectual Freedom Policy (number 53.1 through 53.1.11) with the AASL expansion. Both documents are found in appendix G. Selection policies are essential because they explain the process followed and the priorities established before any material is purchased or accepted as a gift and placed in the media center collection. The policy also communicates the selection steps followed to anyone who questions a purchase or an item found in the media center. The policy is based on and guides actual selection practice. It should include a statement of the goals and objectives of the library media center, cover the needs of the clientele in the building, and describe any unique needs such as special programs of study.

Readers of any selection policy should be told the grade levels and ages of students the collection will serve, the formats of materials to be included, special geographic needs (e.g., schools on either coast will need more materials on the ocean than perhaps students in the Middle West). A statement may be included regarding the availability and use of materials in neighboring libraries.

A final section of the selection policy should contain the procedures to be followed when a grievance is filed. This procedure must be carefully described and must cover as many contingencies as can be predicted.

Selection policies should be reviewed by and approved by the school board. While some states require that school districts have a written selection policy before state funds are distributed to school library media accounts, others do not. When school boards approve selection policies, they should cover all the schools in the district rather than a single building.

If no policy exists, school board members may consider that the process of approving a policy may open a can of worms, and they may be reluctant to discuss the issue. Regardless of whether the school board approves a statement, school library media specialists should prepare one to show their priorities and methods of selecting materials.

School library media specialists who have been unfortunate enough to have materials questioned will admit that the experience is frightening. In most media centers a single person is in charge, and that person feels very isolated when a parent, community member, or fellow teacher questions the availability of a certain item for students. Having a selection policy available for the complaining person to read as well as a procedure to follow should allow time to notify the principal of the situation. The principal may need to be reminded that the superintendent should also be told that a book, film, filmstrip, or other material is being questioned and by whom.

The American Library Association's Office of Intellectual Freedom has staff trained to respond to inquiries from school library media specialists who have censorship problems. This office will respond quickly to any question, and will even accept collect calls when a library media specialist feels beleaguered.

The selection policy will cite the selection aids used in choosing materials. A variety of selection aids (bibliographies, lists, etc.) review new publications. A first source of information would be in the category of aids to aids, or lists of those publications that serve as selection aids. One such list is "Aids to Media Selection for Students and Teachers," originally published in 1971 by the Office of Library and Learning Resources of the Bureau of Elementary and Secondary Education in the U.S. Office of Education. The original was followed by several reprints and two revisions, in 1976 and 1979. The update of the 1979 volume is now available from the National Association of State Media Personnel (NASTEMP), distributed through Libraries Unlimited, Englewood, Colorado. A bibliography such as this will help the school library media specialist choose which source to purchase and, if budgets are very limited for professional materials, which sources to locate in the immediate area.

Standard selection tools are useful in developing a core collection and in reviewing that collection for retention or removal. These tools represent research and professional experience by experts in the school library media field. They are accepted as reliable guides for selection and can be used to confirm choices.

Selection aids may include a variety of formats, or they may concentrate on one. The H. W. Wilson lists, *Children's Catalog, Junior High School Library Catalog,* and *Senior High School Library Catalog,* are published in hardbound volumes with paperback updates. These lists provide only book titles while the Brodart publication, *Elementary School Library Collection,* contains books and other media. These hardbound volumes, with their carefully selected entries, can be very helpful to media specialists in establishing a core collection and in reviewing materials for retention or discard. However, they may not be as useful for selection purposes because many of the materials listed are out of print when the volume is published.

School library media specialists may rely on bibliographies provided by professional associations, if these are current, and by the periodical literature. *Booklist* and *School Library Journal* review both books and media while *Bulletin for the Center for Children's Books* reviews books only.

Providing a core collection is the first step in collection development. More important is selecting the remaining materials, which must be chosen to fit the school's curriculum. This was discussed briefly in chapter 3 and is only reviewed here.

Meeting curriculum needs is a major criterion for placing items in the collection. Library media specialists can begin to address this task by carefully reviewing the textbooks used by each teacher, by finding out the length of time any unit is taught and to how many students, and by discovering what teaching method is used and what the research assignments are likely to be. Next, a bibliography of available materials in the media center can be obtained by searching the Dewey Decimal Classification numbers in the shelflist or online catalog and by conducting additional searches for specific subject headings in the card catalog. If the resulting bibliography does not appear to have relevant titles or titles at the ability or interest level of the students in the course, additional materials must be purchased. As a temporary measure, materials may be requested from other libraries in the area, but this is, at best, temporary.

David V. Loertscher has designed a method to ensure the thoughtful addition of materials to a school library media collection. His evaluation strategy for collection development is called *collection mapping*, and he suggests that school library media specialists do not build the collection as a whole. Rather they should create a collection that is tailored to the specific needs of a school, for it is essential that the collection be built piece by piece. He divides the total collection into three segments:

1. A basic collection designed to serve a wide variety of interests and needs. This collection provides breadth.

2. General emphasis collections, which contain materials that support a whole course of instruction such as United States history or beginning reading. These collections provide intermediate depth in a collection.

3. Specific emphasis collections, which contain materials that support units of instruction such as "Civil War" or "dinosaurs." These collections provide full depth and support as advocated by the national standards.[4]

A discussion of the process and product of collection mapping can be found in the Spring 1985 issue of *Drexel Library Quarterly*. This includes research into the process, the relation to collection development in one school district, and the techniques which can be used to improve communication with teachers. The complete system has been published in *Computerized Collection Development for School Library Media Centers*.[5]

Defending the Collection

Defending the collection is an obligation of the school library media specialist. Materials have been carefully selected to meet the needs of teachers and students in the school. One, two, or more persons lodging complaints about items should not be allowed to prohibit use by others in the school. Parents may request that their child not be allowed to read, listen to, or view materials on evolution or holidays, but the materials should not be removed from the media collection. If steps have been taken to ensure that a selection policy is in place and that there is a procedure to follow in case of complaint, responding to pressures can be more organized and less harassing.

Selecting Equipment

Selection of equipment is a further responsibility of many school library media specialists, and some may feel inadequate to make these choices. It is important to keep in mind the user of the equipment, the quality of equipment, compatibility, warranty, maintenance and repair. The first consideration, as with all items in the media center, is the user. If the user is someone who does not use the equipment frequently, it must be easy to use and difficult to misuse. The self-threading 16-mm film projector is an example of an easy-to-use piece of equipment. Veteran projectionists prefer the manual-threading machine because the film can be removed easily if only a portion of the film is to be shown. Use of equipment is no problem at all if an operator is sent to the classroom with each piece of equipment. However, this is seldom possible.

The quality of the equipment is a major concern. Many media specialists consider the lower price of the home-use equipment in comparison to the commercial-use machines. This is a false economy because home-use machines are not designed to withstand the use given to equipment in a school.

Compatibility is very important from two perspectives: matching what the school owns (Beta or VHS) or matching two types of equipment, such as microcomputers. Deciding between ½-inch and ¾-inch video machines as well as brands of video have been concerns. Many school districts were stuck with less expensive microcomputers that were supposedly compatible to a more expensive machine only to find that not all of the software would work. Moreover, often the company producing the clone went out of business.

Warranty for the entire piece or parts of equipment should be considered. If the supplier is reluctant to give any warranty for the equipment under consideration, it would be better to look elsewhere.

Finally, maintenance and repair are extremely important. If a much-used piece of equipment must be sent away for an extended period, a replacement piece should be available during repair. The repair shop should be in the immediate vicinity rather than 200 miles away.

Acquiring Materials and Equipment

Many methods exist for acquiring resources for the library media center. While some gifts are given to the media center, most additions to the materials and equipment collection must be selected, ordered, received, and paid for. A first step in the acquisition process is to select a source for purchasing an item.

In many states, selection of a purchase source is based upon a bid process when an item costs a specified amount, e.g., all items over $100 must be placed for bid. This means that suppliers bid to provide the material or equipment and the lowest bidder receives the order. This is often true of the jobber chosen to supply library books.

A jobber is a supplier who buys from a wide variety of publishers so that the library media specialist may send one order for most book materials selected for the media center collection. On the other hand, an even better discount may be given by the individual publishers, but this means that individual purchase orders must be sent. Chapter 7 will include an explanation of why business managers prefer to order from a single source rather than send multiple orders to individual suppliers. Once materials and supplier have been determined, a purchase order is written. A sample of a purchase order is shown in figure 6.1.

The purchase order may be issued (1) when a requisition has been submitted by the library media specialist to the business office, (2) by a designated secretary in the principal's office, or (3) by the library media specialist. A purchase order is a legal document which obligates the school district to pay for the materials ordered. For this reason, great care must be taken in completing the purchase order form.

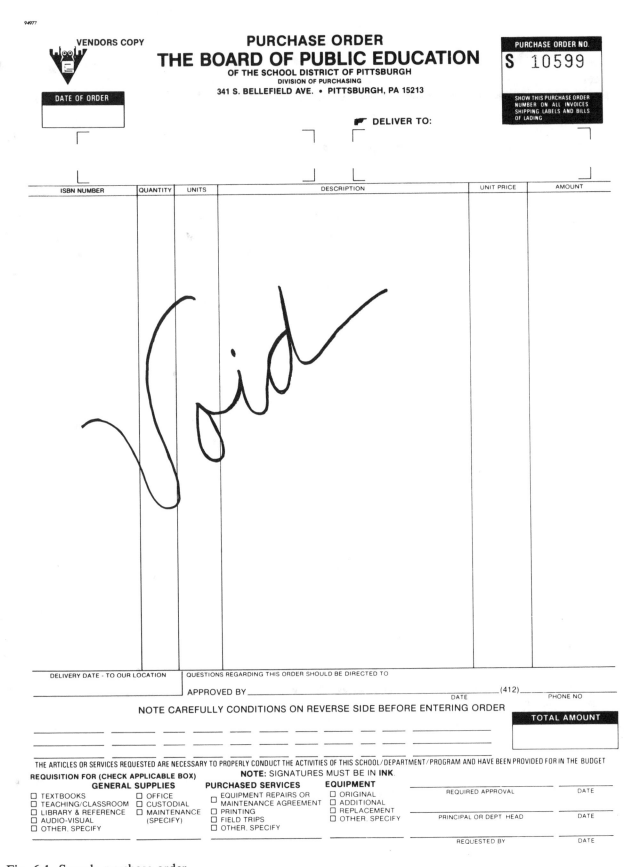

Fig. 6.1. Sample purchase order.

The library media specialist should be aware that book jobbers are now offering electronic ordering. They will provide electronic devices for the library media specialist to key in a number, usually the ISBN; the availability of all titles ordered will be confirmed, and the books will be shipped and billed immediately. Many school district purchasing officers may be reluctant to permit this because they will not be issuing a signed purchase order. However, business managers can set a total price limit beyond which the jobber should not send further shipments. This ceiling on purchases can allow the library media specialist to use such quick-order opportunities.

The materials have been selected, orders written, and the shipment has been received. The purchase order must be checked against the shipment, any missing items must be noted and letters written, and acknowledgment must be sent to the business office.

School district business managers do not always understand the idiosyncrasies of the library media world and will welcome assistance in the selection and ordering process. That is, they may need help in selecting suppliers of materials especially when they are not the more familiar sources of other educational items; in writing specifications for equipment; and in confirming that the products ordered have, in fact, been received. This is one way to make friends with those who handle funds for library media programs.

Making friends with the business manager is as important as making friends with the administrators in the building and with the custodial staff. Remaining friends with these persons is easier if care is taken to make their job easier. One excellent way to make their jobs easier is to return purchase orders or requisition forms indicating the items that have been received. This enables full or partial payment to be made to the supplier. If this is not done in good time, the supplier continues to send bills to the business manager, and no one likes to receive second or third notice of unpaid bills.

De-Selection of Materials (Weeding)

Perhaps as important as selecting materials for a collection is discarding materials no longer of much value to students and teachers. This may be a temporary loss of value due to a change in focus, or it may be a permanent loss due to curriculum change. Reasons for removing items may be age, lack of relevance, or wear and tear. A smaller, more attractive collection of relevant, up-to-date materials is more important to students and teachers than a large collection of mostly useless materials which will be ignored by all but the most aggressive students. Many school library media specialists find themselves with inadequate shelf space, and their collections must be reviewed frequently to provide space for new additions.

Many library media specialists use the excuse that state standards dictate that a certain number of materials are required by state law. This is true, but few states have such high standards that collections in present schools cannot meet the quantities required. Useless materials on the shelves do not provide quality and should be removed. If the school administration insists that an unusually large number of materials be maintained, a separate drawer of the shelflist could house *all* catalog cards for these useless materials. They would still be a part of the collection, but they could be stored out of sight.

Collection reevaluation and de-selection can be justified because:

1. changes in the curriculum revise the focus of the collection;

2. materials must be repaired or replaced if in poor condition;

3. the media center shelves should appear attractive and inviting to the user;

4. numbers of items counted as holdings should represent useful resources rather than appear to be a larger total number including many unusable items;

5. students and teachers should be provided with the best possible collection of materials for their use.

De-selection is a continuous process. Each item that circulates should be reviewed by each person who handles the item. It is as much the responsibility of students and teachers as it is the library media center staff to evaluate materials regularly. Students are very able to judge if the material was helpful to them and if not, why not. Interested teachers who are subject area specialists can be most helpful in evaluating their special areas within the collection. The media center staff will conduct a thorough evaluation of the entire collection at least once every three years.

The school library media specialist is responsible for reviewing the collection to see that it complies with the selection policy. As with the selection process, de-selection must be regulated by the selection policy, not by personal bias.

In general, four categories of materials are taken from the shelves: (1) materials to be stored until needed, (2) materials to be sent to another school media center for younger or older students, (3) materials in need of repair or replacement, and (4) materials to be discarded.

Materials to be stored are of good quality and accurate, but treat topics temporarily not being taught. They are unlikely to become dated and are attractive and at the appropriate level for students in the building.

Materials that are judged to be below or above the reading levels of students in the building, or treat subject areas shifted to another grade level, may be sent to another building. Retaining titles that might be useful some time in the future is usually not a good plan. It would be easier for the receiving school to return the materials if the situation is reversed.

Materials in need of repair or replacement should be carefully evaluated. Books may be sent to the bindery if the paper is of good quality and the information they contain is important. Parts of media kits are often lost, and missing items should be reordered if the kit is useful and the missing item is important to the information presented. In-house repair of materials must be carefully reviewed to see that the time of the person making the repairs, added to the cost of the materials needed for repair, do not exceed the cost of the item being repaired.

Finally, materials must be evaluated for retention or withdrawal. Old, worn-out materials must be discarded. Any material that is out-of-date should be removed unless it has great historical benefit. Duplicate titles may be reassessed if the need for multiple copies has passed, yet one title would be useful in the collection. Biographies of persons unknown to the present generation should not be retained.

Outdated materials may be almost anything in science and technology with a copyright date that is more than five years old. Psychology, history, business, and education become dated in ten years. In the fiction area, certain authors and certain topics may lose their appeal to an age group. An author read by high school students fifteen years ago may be devoured by elementary students today.

In the case of a core collection, a title may be matched to a selection tool. Materials listed in a selection tool should be carefully considered. It may be that the item should be brought to the attention of students and teachers. It may be that the item should be removed, although it appears in a recommended list.

Reference books, especially, have to be reviewed. Encyclopedias need to be replaced every five years, and the old copies should *not* be sent to the classrooms. Inaccurate information has no place in a school library media center or in the classroom. Because encyclopedias are so expensive to purchase, retaining copies seems to be considered an asset; it is, however, a great liability.

Figure 6.2 lists considerations for retention or discard of materials.

Dewey
Decimal
Class No.

000 New editions of encyclopedias are needed every five years.

100 Information in this category is judged by use of material.

200 Religion books are also retained depending upon use. The media center collection should contain basic information about as many sects and religions as possible, and all issues should be as well represented as possible.

300 Controversial issues must be well represented from all points of view. Almanacs and yearbooks are superseded by each new volume. These are seldom of much use after five years although some library media specialists retain back issues to use in teaching about the almanac. During instruction, facts can be compared to show the changes in the information. However, older volumes should not be on the open shelves. Books dealing with historical aspects of politics and economics are determined by use. Timely or topical materials are discarded after five years. These should be replaced with new editions when available. Books on government should be replaced after ten years. New material on government should supersede older materials.

Nonhistorical concepts in social welfare become dated within ten years. Historical materials in education and commerce should be retained if they are used. Nonhistorical materials in education and commerce should be replaced within ten years.

Basic materials in folklore should be retained. De-selection depends upon use. At the elementary level, fairy tales represent a popular area of the collection.

400 Basic materials on languages should be retained based upon use.

500 Pure science books, except for botany and natural history, are out-of-date within five years. Collections must be kept current.

600 Information on inventions and medicine are dated in five years except for basic or historical materials on inventions and basic information about anatomy. Applied science and mechanics become dated within five years unless they have historical information.

Radio and television materials are dated in less than five years. Information about gardening, farms, farm and other domestic animals do not become dated as quickly as other sections of the 600s.

Home economics books are evaluated based upon use; however, most cookbooks are retained until they wear out. Business information becomes dated in ten years while chemical and food product materials should be removed in five to ten years, depending upon contents. Manufacturing and building information should be removed after ten years except for books on crafts.

700 Basic art and music materials should be retained. These items are preserved according to their use.

800 Basic literature materials must be retained. Evaluation is based upon use.

900 General history materials are evaluated depending upon their use and the curriculum requirements. Accuracy, relevancy, and variety of interpretations are of primary concern.

Materials about countries and geography books must be replaced as soon as new editions are available. These materials are very likely to provide misinformation.

Biography materials, unless the person has a permanent place in history, should be discarded as soon as use diminishes. Older biographies of mediocre value should be replaced as more literary efforts are available.

Fig. 6.2. Discard criteria.

Newspaper and magazine files should be kept up to five years if storage allows. Microfiche is an easy-to-store format that does not occupy as much space as paper products do, and it will not disintegrate as quickly as newspapers.

Pamphlet materials are always a concern because this file is supposed to be the most up-to-date in the media center. Media specialists should stamp a date on each item placed in the vertical file since most items are not dated. Topics should be carefully reviewed once each three years and all folders reviewed before items are circulated to students or teachers.

Equipment can be evaluated with two criteria: use and repair record. Equipment may no longer be used by teachers or students because of lack of appropriate software and should be removed from the storage area. Equipment should also be removed when the repair costs exceed the replacement costs. Knowing the repair record of each piece of equipment is very important. A simple method of recording equipment repair is to enter the date of purchase and the type of equipment. Each time the equipment does not function, a record is made of the malfunction. If a repair was required, the nature and cost of the repair should be noted. In this way, a record of the number of repairs made on equipment is available.

The final section of this chapter will discuss methods to organize materials for easy access. Options for cataloging materials range in time and effort from original cataloging and preparing cards on a typewriter to receiving cards from a bibliographic utility.

Options for Cataloging

The school library media specialist should always keep in mind that the process of organizing the media center collection is to provide access to the contents for the users of that collection. Many times, cataloging and classification courses are taught in library science programs with a major emphasis on such details as the number of spaces after a punctuation mark; and the process becomes more important than the product. While the organization of a collection should be consistent with the national standard, such as the use of AACRII for cataloging rules and the use of the MARC format for machine readable records, these must be adjusted to the situation. For example, it is a rare elementary school library collection that needs Cutter numbers to identify author.

Until an automated circulation system and online public access catalog are in place, school library media specialists must continue to find methods to catalog, classify, and process materials. The first level is to provide all cataloging in-house. In this situation, the media specialist prepares a copy slip, using Cataloging in Publication (CIP), the cataloging prepared by Library of Congress from galley proofs and most often found on the verso of the title page, or original cataloging. The cards are then typed on a typewriter, on a memory typewriter, or on a microcomputer, using a card preparation program.

A second level is to buy catalog cards and pockets from a supplier who will send the book pocket and catalog cards. Choices are available between Library of Congress classification numbers or Dewey. Book pockets are then pasted into the book in the media center.

School library media specialists may choose to purchase partial or complete cataloging and processing from the jobber who supplies the items ordered. Kits containing card, pocket, and catalog cards may be ordered with the book and media order. Final processing is completed in the media center, or full processing, including plastic jacket covers, may be ordered. Jobbers who provide full processing send book pockets and spine labels attached and plastic jackets placed over the paper book jackets. Location labels are placed on media items. Most jobbers allow some flexibility, such as whether to use FIC for fiction books and 920 or B for biographies, or whether to paste the book pocket into the front or into back of the volume.

Another source for securing cataloging and processing services is school districts or intermediate units with centralized processing centers. Materials are ordered centrally, shipped to the processing center where catalog cards and pockets are prepared, and then shipped to the individual buildings. In this case, the cataloging record will conform to the district rules which may or may not allow for individual choices at the building level.

The final method of acquiring cataloging information is through a bibliographic network. Costs for this service were discussed briefly in chapter 1 and will be discussed more fully in chapter 11.

Exercises

1. Review *Library Literature* for an update of information concerning circulation systems available. Interview one or more school library media specialists who have automated their circulation systems and get their opinions of strengths and weaknesses. Analyze these in comparison to any information you have located in the literature.

2. Related Case Studies: See

    Case Study 17, "Why Have These Materials Been Chosen? Developing a Materials Selection Policy for the Trent Public Schools"

    Case Study 18, "Updating Trent Collections for Currency"

    Case Study 19, "What Are the Purposes of Collections for Young People? Cooperating with the Trent Public Library on Collection Development"

    Case Study 20, "Teachers Trade Film for Video: How Changes in Teaching Affect Collection Development and Use"

    Case Study 21, "A Clash of Values: Handling Challenges to Trent Library Materials."

All of these studies are in Mary K. Biagini's *A Model for Problem Solving and Decision Making* (Englewood, Colo.: Libraries Unlimited, 1988).

Notes

[1] American Library Association Policy 52.5.

[2] American Library Association Policy 54.15.

[3] Unpublished interpretation of ALA Policies 52.5 and 54.15.

[4] David V. Loertscher. "Collection Mapping: An Evaluation Strategy for Collection Development," *Drexel Library Quarterly* 20 (Spring 1985): 10-11.

[5] David V. Loertscher and May Lein Ho. *Computerized Collection Development for School Library Media Centers* (Englewood, Colo.: Hi Willow Research and Publishing Co., 1986).

7 On the Job
Managing the Budget

Introduction

School library media centers expand or disintegrate depending upon the amount of money allocated to the purchase of needed resources, new materials and equipment. The district budget, developed by district administrators, is presented to and approved by the school board. The type of budget presented is usually dictated by the state education department and may be directly related to some trend outside education, but it is adopted by educators. Education has responded to Program Planning Budgeting Systems (PPBS), originated by Robert McNamara to assess success in government. This system of zero-based budgets, whether in business, government, or education, is designed to make each person justify each expenditure in every department or area. Whatever the model used by the school district, school library media specialists must conform to that model whenever they have input in the budget process. Whenever school library media specialists respond to requests for budget input, they should show they have made a needs assessment, and that the budget covers proposed activities for a year, with the supporting rationale for each activity.

Conflict situations are created because of the realities of the financial situation in the school district, usually defined by level of local taxation, and the practical need to provide a wide variety of materials for students and teachers. These conflicts can occur at the district level (when the library budget is distributed from a central library budget) or within each school, if district funds are distributed to individual buildings. Since budget items for the library media program are a part of the total school district budget, the funding requested comes into competition with other units such as the academic requirements, art, athletic, and music programs. Budgets distributed within the local school will find school library media specialists in competition with the classroom teacher's requests as well as with requests from other special programs.

Annual budgets for school districts are prepared early in one fiscal year for the next year's expenditures. The superintendent, usually with assistance from others who may be asked for input into the process, makes the final decision of items and amounts which will be presented to the school board for approval. Principals, as well as the superintendent's central office staff, are usually included in the budget discussions; however, other participants may be included by demand rather than by request. An example of this would be the negotiators for the teachers' bargaining unit who may oversee the preparation of the budget to make sure no budget decreases will necessitate personnel reductions and to confirm the inclusion of a provision for salary increases and other benefits.

Once the budget is prepared, it is presented to the local school board for approval, or, in some states, it is the state board of education members who grant final approval. In other states, voters are asked to pass a referendum for funding, and budgets can be voted down by the community. The amount of control exercised by local or state boards of education, or the voters during a referendum, is in direct proportion to the amount of funds they control. In states where the major portion of funding for education comes from state support rather than local dollars, state officials maintain closer control over the local budget process than in states where control is the responsibility of the local school board. Lack of support for schools has been critical in the late twentieth century.

Public schools can be defined as service institutions, and measuring the quality of their services can be very difficult. Recently, public schools have not been perceived as performing well in the education of students. According to Peter F. Drucker, one reason given why service institutions do not perform well is that they are given budget allocations rather than having to earn the income to exist.[1] In the past, funding for schools has come from the automatic allocation of dollars collected from property taxes. A minimum level of funding was designated by state law. Communities were subsidized by the state when their tax base was insufficient to provide minimum funding.

Seldom was there any performance evaluation. Educators did not appear to be concerned if performance was good, bad, or indifferent because they were not faced with a necessity to provide "cost-accountable" educational experiences for students. With reduced funding, the picture has changed. Educators are now faced with a public demanding test scores at and above the national average, merit review for teachers, cost accountability for expenditures, and confirmation that the educational program is meeting the objectives set by school personnel. The plight of low funding for education directly impacts the level of funding for the school library media center.

States may mandate a minimum amount that must be spent for school library media materials. This amount is usually based upon a per-pupil allocation calculated by average daily attendance in the individual schools called "attendance centers." If the amount is not specified, the local education agency or school district may grant a specific amount to be spent per pupil. In other districts, principals may be given a sum for the total program in their building, and they decide how much will be allocated to each teacher or classroom program. In other situations, the library budget is allocated through the supervisor of the library media program.

In situations where a sum is specified by either the state or the school superintendent, it is much more difficult for the individual building-level school library media specialists to affect the amount they receive. When the budget is given to the district library media coordinator for reallocation, the needs of each school may be assessed; school library media specialists present their needs in relation to the possible allocation of funds. A similar case must be presented to the school principal if the library media specialist must justify budget from a central allocation to the individual schools. Whatever the division of budget, school library media specialists should understand the method of budget and the placement of funds in each category. An understanding of the school district budget begins with a look at that budget.

While each state may have a different format for placing budget items, most states use line item budgets. This means that each item of the budget is placed on a line next to the account number and description of that item. Usually the budget begins with the revenues accruing to the school district.

Most school districts are funded by property taxes, and the major revenue is from this source. Added to this will be any funds from the state or national government, proceeds from bond sales, sale of property, interest from investments or trust funds, and rentals from facilities.

The next pages of the budget contain the expenditures. Most school budgets reflect the past year's budget with actual expenditures, the current year's budget with actual expenditures, and a column to project the next year's budget. That is, if the budget were being prepared for 1991, the first two columns would show the budget for 1989 and the actual expenditures against that budget. The middle two columns would show the budgeted amount for 1990 and the expenditures against that amount at the date of budget preparation. The final column would show the anticipated budget for 1991.

The numerical sequence for the Pennsylvania budget is shown in figure 7.1.

1000 INSTRUCTION
 1100 Regular Programs-E(lementary)/S(econdary)
 1200 Special Programs-E/S
 1300 Vocational Education Programs
 1400 Other Instructional Programs-E/S
 1600 Adult Education Programs
 1700 Community/Junior College Education Programs

2000 SUPPORT SERVICES
 2100 Pupil Personnel
 2200 Instructional Staff
 2300 Administration
 2400 Pupil Health
 2500 Business
 2600 Operation and Maintenance of Plant Services
 2700 Student Transportation Services
 2800 Central
 2900 Other Support Services

3000 OPERATION OF NONINSTRUCTIONAL SERVICES
 3100 Food Services
 3200 Student Activities
 3300 Community Services
etc.

The 1100 INSTRUCTION for regular programs number is further divided as follows

100 Personal Services-Salaries
200 Personal Services-Employee Benefits
210 Group Insurance
etc.

Fig. 7.1. Numerical sequence from sample school budget.

That is, teacher salaries would be under 1000-100 and teacher benefits would be found under 1000-200. The supply account number is 600, with books and periodicals under 640. Therefore, the purchase of books and periodicals from the regular instruction account would be charged to 1000-640.

Items have been shown as they exist in one state. Budget processes as well as numbering vary from state to state. School library media specialists should locate the appropriate person who can help with questions. This person may be a secretary or accountant in the school itself, or the business manager in the central office.

The Fiscal Year

One of the first questions to ask this resource person is: what is the fiscal year? School districts usually match the state government pattern. That is, if the fiscal year is from January 1 through December 31, all materials must be ordered, received, and paid for no later than December 31 or the expenditures will be charged against the next year. If the fiscal year is July 1 through June 30, the closing of the books will be June 30, and all expenditures not cleared by that date will be charged to the next year's budget.

Business managers often require that all purchase orders be issued in enough time to receive the merchandise, confirm the shipment of the appropriate items, and issue payment before the end of the fiscal year. In some cases, no purchase orders will be issued within four months of the end of the fiscal year so that orders will be completed in ample time before closing the books. Library media specialists seldom have large budgets, and any loss of funds can be crucial. Items that require longer times for shipments should be ordered early in the budget year, if at all possible, to allow maximum time for receipt. Also, equipment that might require testing before payment should be ordered as early as possible in the budget year. Moreover, library media specialists should be aware of what happens if a shipment is NOT received before the books are closed. It may be charged against the next year's budget, costing "double." This is because funds were lost from one year, and an unexpected purchase was added to the next year decreasing that budget by that amount. Much of this type of error can be avoided if the fiscal officer is aware of the interest of the media specialist.

The need to handle fiscal matters promptly is one of the reasons fiscal officers sometimes wish to limit the number of orders from the media center to one or two book orders each year. Limiting the ability to order when needs arise impacts seriously on the ability to provide materials for students and teachers. Working closely with business managers and clerical staff in the offices can help overcome this problem.

It is well to be as supportive of the fiscal officer as possible. Most library media specialists will present necessary buying information to the purchasing agent by submitting order cards, special order forms, school or district requisitions, or purchase orders. All forms must be completed accurately, from correct spelling and address for the supplier through correct spelling of author, title, and publisher for books, accurate item numbers for supplies, accurate model numbers for equipment, and accurate quantities desired, unit item costs and item totals. Any erroneous information on an order may cause an incorrect shipment or incorrect billing which will result in additional correspondence from the business office for the return or exchange of items. This will be costly in use of staff time in the accounting office and may mean that the business manager will restrict the media specialist's freedom to issue a requisition or a purchase order.

As technology continues to emerge for handling routine ordering, it may be that orders will be submitted through terminals or hand-held recording devices directly from the supplier. Whatever the method, the school library media specialist should be sure that item numbers, addresses of sources of supply, quantity desired, and other information are carefully submitted so that errors are minimized. Orders must also be checked to see that the item supplied meets the written specifications.

Writing Specifications

Specifications are written to ensure the delivery of materials and equipment to meet the stated need. If the media specialist wants only playback equipment, the specifications will read "tape player." If recording capability is preferred, then a "tape recorder" will be specified. This is a simplistic example, and for major purchases the specifications may be a half page. A "how to" book on writing specifications was published some time ago by the Educational Products Information Exchange (EPIE) Institute.

Educational Product Report 28, *Writing Equipment Specifications: A How-To Handbook*, explains the problems of purchasing instructional hardware, the central problem being developing purchase specifications. "The fact that the user must write a specification and then go through an extended, complicated purchase procedure is just one more frustration of being an educational administrator."[2] However, preparation of good specifications can ultimately "provide better educational systems, at lower cost, for a school or school district," and such a school will give status and credibility to the astute library media specialist.[3]

Purchase specifications

1. must communicate the desires of the buyer clearly to the potential supplier;

2. provide more than information about the product or system;

3. set forth the conditions that govern the purchase;

4. set forth the purpose for which the equipment will be used;

5. set forth the results the user desires;

6. contain definitive requirements as to the expected performance of the delivered merchandise;

7. state how the equipment is to be installed, where it is to be installed, and the standard of workmanship expected, and

8. state to whom the equipment is to be delivered.[4]

To order technical equipment to meet performance standards, media specialists may wish to consult with others before beginning to write the specifications. Collecting suggestions from knowledgeable media specialists concerning the best product to meet the need is beneficial in making sure that specifications cover all contingencies.

Another source of information for developing specifications is *The Equipment Directory of Audio-Visual, Computer and Video Products,* a publication of The International Communications Industries Association (ICIA), formerly National Audiovisual Association. Located in Fairfax, Virginia, this organization publishes a new edition each year. Photographs of equipment are accompanied by the specifications for that piece of equipment.

Business managers, building principals, and others involved in purchase will usually welcome assistance in writing specifications for materials or equipment with which they are not familiar. Assistance in checking the returned bids to see if the product being offered meets specifications is essential. When it does not, the reasons for rejection must be outlined or the supplier may demand acceptance of the low bid, and an inferior product will be delivered just because it meets the written specifications. When the product is received, it again must be carefully checked to see that the specified item was shipped, and that it meets the specifications described in the bid. If not, it should be returned and another bid used for the order. When an item is returned, its deficiencies must be carefully described in writing because the school district will be rejecting a "contract" for delivery after the bid has been accepted. This is even more difficult than rejecting the initial bid because the product as it was described appeared to meet the bid specifications.

Demanding quality products for the media center is one step in being cost-accountable to the taxpayers or the sponsors of the schools. The section that follows describes cost accountability in the media center.

Cost Accountability and the Media Specialist

Placing a dollar amount on components of a media program is not an easy task. Costing out services is a process of estimating labor as well as materials used. Often the cost of time, whether volunteer, staff, or professional, is overlooked. After all, the library media specialist is on the job anyway. Placing the cost of any service in terms of the time necessary to conduct the service divided into the salary for the person conducting the service will give one cost figure. To this must be added the cost of any materials, supplies, or equipment being used in the project. How to build these cost figure estimates, basing them on careful analysis, will be shown below.

Human costs include professional and clerical staff in the media center. If the annual salary of the media center director is $30,000 and this person works 180 days per year and seven hours each day, both daily wage and hourly wage are easily calculated. To calculate the daily wage, divide the days worked per year into the yearly salary. This indicates that the director earns approximately $160 per day. Calculate the hourly wage by dividing the hours worked per day into the daily rate. This person's hoursly wage is approximately $23 per hour. If the director of the media center spent thirty minutes to catalog a book, the cost would be $11.50. This would not be cost-accountable since complete processing from the book jobber would cost $2.00 per title.

To calculate the cost of equipment use, list the pieces of equipment and their purchase price. Divide this by the number of expected years of service by number of days of possible use and then the days by hours of expected use and arrive at a "use-per-hour" figure. This figure will *not* reflect any repair over the lifetime of the piece of equipment. However, unless a piece of equipment is in constant use, the downtime for nonuse should help cover anticipated additional expenditures for repairs.

Materials are calculated based upon their average cost, which rises with inflation. It is wise to use the estimate given yearly in the *Bowker Annual* (New York: R. R. Bowker Co.). Thus, the average cost of a book multiplied by the number of books that were lost, missing, or stolen from the media center can show the replacement cost. This approximate replacement figure can be used in two ways. The first is to show the total replacement value of the media center and the amount of materials and equipment the manager oversees. If a media center has 20,000 items and it would cost an average of $12 per item to replace, the director of the media center oversees $240,000 in materials. Adding the cost of replacing equipment greatly increases this amount. Book, media, or equipment estimates can also be used to show students how valuable the media center is to them. That is, if books average $12 and 200 are circulated each week for nine weeks, students and teachers have borrowed 12 x 200 = 2400 x 9 = $21,600 worth of books.

Media specialists in single-person centers are usually concerned about the clerical tasks involved. When a $23-per-hour person spends an hour shelving books, the cost to the district is very high compared with the $6 it would cost for clerical staff to do that job. If it takes one hour to gather items for a bibliography for a teaching unit and one hour to produce the bibliography, the cost to the school district is $46 in the single-person center. It would be $29 if a clerk produced the bibliography. Selecting appropriate items to meet the content of the unit and match the reading and interest levels of the students is a professional task. Producing the bibliography is clerical.

For some media specialists, clerical tasks have some reward in that clerical tasks have a beginning and an end, while media management is ongoing. The sense of accomplishment is seldom one of task completed, but rather of a never-ending challenge briefly met as another challenge arrives to take its place in the queue of unfinished work. It is also the excitement of being in the media center, and being able to attack the tasks with few clerical interruptions. This is a situation worth striving for by demonstrating to those responsible for budgeting the loss to the district that occurs when the media specialist is spending time at clerical tasks.

The greater loss, and even more difficult to show, is what is not being done when a professional is not available to plan with teachers. A media professional who is preoccupied with clerical tasks cannot help students find materials or assist teachers in locating teaching aids. Certainly a stronger case can be built for clerical assistance in the media center than has been made in the past.

Developing budget requests may not be perceived as a function of the school library media specialist. For many, little opportunity is given to plan a budget or to request funds. School library media specialists must assume a more aggressive role and plan for their programs, establishing a dollar amount for each facet. This process takes into account the present, the immediate future, and long-range planning for the distant future. Unless the school library media specialist begins to plan for the future, carefully detailing the anticipated costs for offering necessary services, principals, supervisors, and other administrators will remain unaware of the costs to provide for the information needs of teachers and students. Needs and objectives are established and proposed expenditures are clarified. Success is more likely if the requests are presented in a structured format.

Writing Proposals to Expand Programs

Many school library media specialists would like to expand their services. In order to do this, a carefully thought out and documented proposal must be developed. It may be that this proposal will stay within the school district and that the school administration and school board will accept the proposal and fund the project with local funds. At other times, the school district budget is truly inadequate to do this, and the school library media specialist, with school board approval, seeks outside funding. Whether the project remains within the district or is sent to an outside agency, a proposal is developed.

A proposal for a project should include the following elements: statements of need and of goals and objectives, a plan of action or activities and procedures, an evaluation plan, comments about facilities and other resources available, and a carefully prepared budget. Additional items may be required if the proposal goes beyond the school district. These will be discussed later.

Developing the Statement of Needs

Few individuals are willing to allocate money without a needs statement. Even children are required to justify additional allowance from their parents. School library media specialists cannot expect additional funding without a strong case for why it is needed. Needs can be defined in a variety of ways, but defining needs is much more effective if it is done by a group rather than by a single individual. While a school library media specialist can say that the library media center collection is inadequate, the statement is much more powerful if teachers have reviewed the collection in their areas and have found it inadequate, or if students have written lists of missing topics or inadequate materials for assignments they have researched. Certainly it is very important that the assessment of needs involve those persons who are directly or indirectly affected by the proposed project. It would be foolhardy to ask for an expanded collection of art books if the art teacher did not plan to use the books or make assignments that would require students to do research from them. To confirm the participation of others in establishing needs, the proposal writer should list all meetings held and who was present, tests that were administered and the results, and any other relevant details. Participation may also be confirmed by letters of support for the proposal, which will be appended to the body of the proposal. Once the need has been established, a goal should be stated and objectives for the project developed.

Preparing Goals and Objectives

A goal is a broad, general statement and it is *not* measurable. Since a goal is such a broad statement, it is not always required for a project proposal. When a goal is required, it should be realistic. Trying to overcome reading problems in an elementary school in a single year might be an unrealistic goal. If children are reading well below grade level, if reading at all, a few books and magazines added to the library media collection is not going to alleviate the problem and the goal cannot be met.

Objectives, on the other hand, must be measurable. They are designed to help solve the needs that have been determined, and they should state the precise level of achievement anticipated and within what length of time. Objectives must be an outgrowth of the stated needs and should describe where the school library program should be in this time frame in relation to where the program is currently and who or what is involved in the project. The better written the objective, the easier it will be to handle the evaluation later.

Goals and objectives themselves may be evaluated. Context evaluation is the assessment of the goals and objectives to see if they are written in terms of the constituency to be reached by the project. This evaluation reviews the number of students, by category, who will benefit from the project, for they should be a part of the stated objective. Funding agencies are particularly interested to see if those to be served by the project helped identify needs and if those identified needs were used to help set the priorities. As stated earlier, proposal writers may cite the persons involved in the needs assessment process.

Objectives are often confused with activities. Rather than state the expected outcome, novice proposal writers often list the methods to achieve an outcome. These methods are activities rather than stated objectives.

Establishing the Plan of Action

The section of the proposal that states the plan of action, or proposed activities, describes the methods to be employed to meet the stated objective and alleviate the needs that have been determined and described. A general statement may be made of the overall design of the project, including what population is to be served, how that population will be selected, and how the project will be managed. But the activities themselves must be directly related to objectives, and that relationship must be clear. Procedures to attain the objectives must follow from the objectives. If the relationship between objective and activity is ambiguous, persons reading the proposal may not consider the project suitable for implementation. Funding agencies and school administrators prefer projects which have a step-by-step plan of realistic activities to meet the objectives and alleviate the need.

When a project planner is unsure that proposed activities will meet objectives in the anticipated time frame, consideration of alternative plans of action may be presented. A rationale for each possible alternative may include a brief statement about why the first plan of action was proposed and how, when, or why it will be decided to use the alternative plan. Whenever possible, proposal writers should include relevant research which supports their choice from the array of possible activities.

As the project activities are stated, a timeline covering the length of time for each of the activities may be presented. Such a timeline shows the proposal reviewers the sequence of separate activities—what has gone before, what is currently in progress, and what will be done in the future. This helps the reviewers understand the relationship of the activities, that is, if and when the initiation of one activity is dependent upon the completion of another, when activities overlap, and the progress necessary for project completion.

Planning for Evaluation

After the activities have been designed, proposal writers must then determine the best methods to evaluate the activities to see if they are, indeed, meeting stated objectives. To do this, two kinds of evaluation will be helpful: formative and summative. Formative evaluation processes occur throughout the life of the project. At each step of the project, an evaluation may be made to see if the activities being implemented are successful in making the planned improvements. If the project does not appear to be successful, an alternate plan of action may be put into place. Progress using the new activity will then be evaluated to see if it shows more success than the previous plan. Formative evaluation further determines if project progress is within the anticipated time period outlined.

At the close of any project, a final evaluation is conducted. This is called summative evaluation. At this time, each activity is evaluated to determine the degree of progress made to meet the stated objectives. Proposal writers must detail the means by which they or their agency will verify for the funding source that the project has accomplished the objectives as stated and the degree to which the objectives have been met. Information to be collected must be described, methods used to analyze the information must be outlined, and the degree of success which should be expected must be stated. This is not an easy task, and many proposal writers seek help from persons in tests and measurements offices in colleges and universities and in local or state agencies to help define the evaluation procedures to be used after the project begins.

Many funding agencies prefer that summative evaluation be conducted by an outside evaluator. This is an attempt to eliminate or modify the possibility of bias from the evaluation process and add validity to the evaluation statements. When project funding is sought from outside agencies, it is possible that the choice of the outside evaluator, especially when the funding agency is familiar with the reputation of this person, may place the project in a more favorable position to be funded. Someone not directly related to the project may be better able to measure the degree of success. Certainly the evaluation proposed is one of the most important aspects of project planning and should be given full attention.

Deciding on Dissemination

While outside funding agencies may not ask about the dissemination planned to present the project and its outcome to the general public, the school library media specialist should be prepared to share the results of any project with the appropriate audience. Just as government agencies and foundation staffs will need to know the degree of success of their investment, they anticipate credit for the contribution they made to the project. For locally funded projects, the school library media specialist will report project success to the superintendent and the school principal. They should be given material they can use for publicizing a successful project. It is no virtue to hide project success.

Just as many funding agencies need good publicity to continue being able to award appropriations for projects, the school library media center will be more likely to be awarded additional funds when the outcomes of successful projects are reported in the media. Therefore, care must be given to the selection of ways to present information to appropriate audiences beyond the immediate location of the project. It may be sending letters home to parents, or it may be full coverage in the news media—both newspapers and television. The school district may have a person in charge of public relations who will be responsible for publicity, or the library media specialist may need to send out press releases and appropriate copy to reporters.

Information presented for publication must be well written, accurate, and complete. Care must be taken to secure permission from students if photographs are submitted.

Finally, successful school library projects should be reported to the school library community through articles in the professional journals and through presentations at conferences and workshops. The outcomes of projects must be shared with the field so that successful activities can be replicated in other school library media centers. A list of publications of special interest to school library media specialists is provided in appendix H.

Describing Local Resources

Project proposals should also describe the facilities in which the project will be conducted. If the school or school district has excellent facilities in place to support project activities, there is a greater chance for success and less chance for failure. That is, if an elaborate program is described, but the school does not have adequate space for the program, it will appear that there is a good chance for project failure. Describing facilities and additional resources available, human and material, will help the funding agency realize that the school library media specialist has a better chance of conducting a successful project. If special equipment is needed for the project, the equipment must become a part of the project proposal, or the method of securing this equipment must be shown in the project narrative and budget as in-kind contribution.

Proposal writers should list all resources that add credibility to what, or who, is being proposed. If a school library media specialist lacks long experience in the library media world, it may be that assistance is available from a district level coordinator. The community may be supporting the school library media specialist in some unique or special way, and this should be explained. Additional funding may be available for the project from other funding sources – the community, individuals, or the state department of education. This support should also be cited.

Personnel who will work on the project must be listed. If they are available as in-kind contribution to the project, this means that the school district will pay the salaries of these persons and their salaries will not be a part of the cost assigned to the project budget. All personnel to be added to staff must be listed. Job titles, job descriptions, numbers to be added, qualifications expected, and length of time assigned to the project are all items which must be described. Résumés should be attached for all persons who have been identified as part of the project staff. This includes project director, coordinator, consultants, clerical and technical staff, teachers, and evaluators. These résumés must be very brief, and the activities and positions described in their backgrounds should be only those that will show their skills as they relate directly to the project.

Before submitting a person's name as a part of any project staff, proposal writers must secure permission from that individual. It is very annoying to most people to find that their name has been submitted without permission. Often, an implication exists that these proposed project consultants or staff have approved the proposal in principle, even if they did not actually participate in writing the proposal. Also, the danger exists of including someone's name in a proposal when this person is writing a project proposal in response to the same request for proposal. In this instance, it should be clear to proposal writers that some potential staff may be unaware of their inclusion.

When competing for limited funds, the proposal writer should try to find out if project staff under consideration are known to the funding agency. Funding agency staff may be more willing to fund projects when they know and recognize the capabilities of persons who will be directly involved in project implementation. Also, the funding agency staff may insist upon approval of the categories of persons to be hired, such as researchers, technicians, media practitioners, or clerical staff. Finally, many funding agencies are reluctant to approve the hiring of new persons to serve as staff for a project if there is no indication of how this staff will be continued after the project has been completed. School district administrators may find themselves obligated to pay unemployment benefits for furloughed staff unless they can be placed in other positions in the school district.

Building the Budget

The budget is the final part of the project planning. Budgets include the actual anticipated costs of the project, item by item. Governmental agencies provide a form to be completed. If no form is provided, the sample budget from the National Endowment for the Humanities included in appendix I might be helpful. This could be used to verify that the information usually required is included in the project budget.

Two budget items that may cause unexpected problems are fringe benefits and overhead. The first, fringe benefits, is a part of salary statistics. Fringe benefits are a fixed amount which must be added to all persons placed in a salary category for the project. The percentage figure used to calculate fringe benefits for proposed project personnel will be the same used for all school district salaried staff. Fringe benefits for a district employee are determined by the monthly salary, the percentage of time on the project, and the length of time of the project. That is, if a school library media specialist with a $2,000 monthly salary is to be employed half-time for six months, the project would show $1,000 x 6 or $6,000 for the project. If the school district has a fringe benefit package of 27 percent, $1,620 must be added to the project costs.

Overhead percentages may be set by school districts, universities, and private agencies. Overhead is an assessment of the use of staff, equipment, and facilities that will not be specifically included in the proposal budget. Examples would be the preparation of purchase orders, checks for payment, bookkeeping, use of office furniture and equipment, heat and lighting, and computer use. Some agencies such as state departments of education may prohibit assessment of overhead percentages.

If space or equipment is to be rented, those costs must be calculated. Also, consultants or contracted services must be listed. Consultants may be paid a per diem amount rather than a salary, in which case fringe benefits need not be calculated. School library media specialists should keep in mind that telephone charges, mailing costs, duplicating fees, online database searches, and office supplies should be added to the budget amount if the school budget cannot absorb these additional charges. Finally, if the staff or consultants require travel funds, these must be included in the budget.

Additional Considerations

When planning the project, proposal writers should check to see if evaluation points have been assigned to each part of the proposal. The number of points assigned is the highest score that proposal readers can give each part of the proposal. Very careful attention must be placed on all parts of a proposal, but special attention should be given to the sections that have been assigned the most points.

Throughout project planning and proposal preparation, school district administrators must indicate their support. It is heartbreaking to complete a project proposal and have the principal or superintendent refuse to send it to the funding agency. It is even more difficult to understand when a project is awarded funding by an agency only to have the school board refuse to permit the school district to accept the funds. Not all administrators or school boards welcome funding from an outside source, especially if they perceive that this funding comes with strings attached. This is especially true when additional personnel must be added because, as stated earlier, these persons may expect to become permanent employees at the close of the project. A successful project may encourage other administrators to demand similar materials, staff, or services from already overextended district funds. Convincing administrators of the value of the project and the potential benefit to the school building and the school district is important. This is better accomplished when the school library media specialist provides an honest, realistic assessment of the regulations and requirements for the school district at the close of the funding, the probable level of enthusiasm for similar projects in other schools, and the funds that will be required to continue even a small portion of the project.

After writing a proposal, it should be reread to see if it is written without jargon, to be sure the plan of action is logical and will achieve the objectives, to eliminate extraneous words or unnecessary materials, and to correct any spelling or grammatical errors. Finally, the proposal should be neatly typed in an easy-to-read format, or in conformity with the format outlined in the request for proposal. Format instructions might include spacing requirements, number of pages for each section of the proposal, length of abstract, and other details.

While materials not requested should not be sent, care must be taken to see that all necessary documents are included. It would be unfortunate to lose evaluation points because an item, such as a copy of the district's selection policy, was not sent when it was required.

Most funding agencies are very interested in what will happen to the project at the close of the outside funding. If parts of the project will be continued with school district funding, the project may have a better chance for funding. If administrators are involved in the planning all along the way, they should be able to help determine which parts and how much may be available to continue a project at the close of the initial funding period.

These persons who are required to sign the proposal must be available to place their signatures on the appropriate lines. If the proposal requires school board approval, copies must be distributed to members prior to the board meeting, and someone from the proposal preparation team must be ready to answer questions at the board meeting. It may not be possible to call a special meeting of the board, so the school library media specialist must pay particular attention to the closing dates of all requests for proposal so there will be time to secure board approval and all appropriate signatures.

Proposals must be submitted on time. If a deadline exists, this date must be met. Proposals that arrive after the deadline are usually returned unopened.

Writing proposals is a way of life in many situations. In others, it may be a way to get additional funds, expand a program to meet a specific need, add equipment, add materials, or try a different way to provide materials to help teach students.

Most persons who have one proposal funded are very willing to write another. They have been given an opportunity to improve their school library media center, to test a new method, to offer a new service, to provide more materials for students and teachers.[5]

To write a proposal is to enter a competition, and the process is similar to any other competitive endeavor; sometimes you win, sometimes you lose. Sometimes it may seem to be better to lose. One gains all the applause for the effort to establishing needs, developing objectives and plans of action, writing, and submitting the proposal. It is an opportunity to establish new colleagues and re-establish communication with old acquaintances.

Sometimes you win, and then you have to work to see that the project succeeds.[6]

Exercises

1. Develop a policy statement for a school library media center.

2. Using this outline, draw a Gantt chart for closing a library within two months.

    Step 1. Weeding the collection

    Step 2. Reviewing contents for integration into other collections

    Step 3. Pulling items from shelves

    Step 4. Pulling shelflist cards

    Step 5. Pulling catalog cards

    Step 6. Packing items

    Step 7. Unpacking items at new location and shelving

    Step 8. Replacing cards in shelflist

    Step 9. Replacing cards in card catalog

3.   Related Case Studies: See

Case Study 2, "Determining the Direction of the Trent Library Media Program: Goals, Objectives, Strategies"

Case Study 23, "Opportunities for Trent Special Projects: Securing Funding from External Sources."

All of these studies are in Mary K. Biagini's *A Model for Problem Solving and Decision Making* (Englewood, Colo.: Libraries Unlimited, 1988).

Notes

[1]Peter F. Drucker. *Management Tasks, Responsibilities Practices* (New York: Harper and Row, 1973), 141.

[2]Educational Products Information Exchange Institute. Educational Product Report 28, *Writing Equipment Specifications: A How-To Handbook*, rev. ed. of EPIE Report 18, 5.

[3]Ibid.

[4]Ibid., 7.

[5]Blanche Woolls. *Grant Proposal Writing: A Handbook for School Library Media Specialists* (Westport, Conn.: Greenwood Press, 1986), 96.

[6]Ibid., x.

8 On the Job
Managing Services

Four components of school library media programs—personnel, materials, equipment, and facility—are very visible. School personnel can readily observe the library media center staff at work. Because the media center is often used by teachers, students, and administrators not only for reading and research but also for meetings, it is considered an essential room in the building. It is also more comfortable and more attractive than the regular classrooms. The collection, since it is heavily used by students and teachers, is a recognizable part of the school's assets. Management and coordination of these individual components culminates in the program of services offered and, services, while less immediately visible, are the *raison d'être* of the media center.

Teachers and students may take the components of the media center for granted or they may not expect many services. After all, there should be a media specialist because the state mandates the position or the regional accrediting agency dictates it. A manager is available, therefore there is a room and a collection. Users may take for granted the services offered from this center and be very surprised when a service no longer exists. When equipment wears out and is not replaced, or reduced budgets do not permit the extension of magazine subscriptions or the renewal of the database, they will be appalled, but they will not recognize the need for their support to continue the service.

Teachers and students may expect few services because they have not been introduced to the wide variety of experiences they may choose in this room. On the other hand, they may expect a great many services, again because of their previous experiences. Deciding which services to offer and in what depth are management decisions of the media specialist, and these decisions are based upon the staff and facilities available. Services that can be offered are limited only by the creativity of the media specialist who must work with a given number of staff, within a given space, with a given collection of both materials and equipment, within a given budget available to add to these collections, and within the limit of materials available from other locations. These are the factors which form the base of possible activities. However, once these factors have been analyzed, the most important consideration is delivering the services needed to integrate media services with the curriculum.

Services are planned with full knowledge of the curriculum, teaching methods, assignments given by teachers, planned activities in classrooms that require media center support, and activities within the media center itself. To plan services for teachers, one must understand how they teach and what assignments they will make; to plan services for students, one must understand how students learn. The major task of the school library media manager is to turn units of curriculum into opportunities to blend classroom activities with use of the media center and its collections.

Understanding Curriculum

The media specialist who has elementary teaching certification or a subject speciality at the secondary level, in addition to their media certification, already knows a good deal about curriculum. These persons will be very knowledgeable about the relation of the curriculum to the classroom. Most media specialist preparation programs provide some experience in the development of curriculum units in course work and in the practicum setting, so that each media specialist will have had some practical knowledge of the planning for and execution of resource-based teaching in the school. To build on this experience, media specialists should gather both materials and information about the curriculum in the local school.

One beginning in this process of understanding the curriculum is to create a professional reference collection of all textbooks used in the building. This will be of use to teachers who need to know what has been covered in previous courses and what will be covered in the future. So, the task of maintaining the textbook reference collection is not just one to help the media staff. Media staff scan textbooks used by teachers (as discussed in chapter 3) to help plan for the semester's probable units of work. Throughout the year, the media specialist expands on the projects reviewed the first week in the building, determining what each teacher teaches and integrating the method of teaching, the materials needed beyond those provided in the classroom, and the probable use to be made of media center materials and materials secured from other libraries.

A second professional reference collection will be the copies of curriculum guides developed at the building and district levels, and at the state department of public instruction. If at all possible curriculum guides from *all* grade levels should be made available to help teachers understand experiences of their students before they arrive and learn what they should be prepared for when they move to the next level. The media specialist can continue developing this professional service by participating in both textbook selection and curriculum planning.

Media specialists volunteer to serve on textbook committees. By helping choose textbooks for the school, they can anticipate the new topics that will be covered and assess the ability of the media center collection to meet the new needs. When a new topic is added, new materials must be located, purchased, and added to the media center holdings.

Media specialists also serve on curriculum committees. By serving on these grade level or subject area committees, media specialists are better able to integrate the media center into the unit plans of all teachers. Managing time to allow for the participation in these meetings may appear to be an almost impossible task. However, this is the primary role of the media specialist in the education of students, and it must be given a very high priority. The need for backup assistance in the media center so the media specialist can attend meetings and still keep the media center open can be used to justify additional help in the media center. The media specialist asks for the services of a substitute teacher when curriculum planning meetings are scheduled for more than one period in the day.

Once curriculum units have been defined, media specialists work to provide materials to assist the teacher in teaching these units. The advent of the word processor greatly facilitates the creation and maintaining of bibliographies. Recorded unit activities on a database management program can also be updated as changes are made. The unit evaluation form can be integrated into this single database, helping teachers and media specialists assess and understand outcomes of one unit's presentation.

The process of understanding the curriculum is ongoing. No teacher or media specialist can believe that all one must know about any curriculum has been learned. Curriculum changes, teachers change, and teaching methods change.

Learning Teaching Methods

Despite efforts of educational leaders who suggest the need for changes or modification in teacher behavior, many teachers still use textbook and lecture as their primary if not only teaching method. One colleague of the author insists that this is a product of the faculty in schools of education who themselves teach almost exclusively by textbook and lecture. This model is not one that demonstrates to the student who then becomes a teacher how or why to use other methods such as independent study, the integration of library media materials into lesson plans, and instructional design. It is the responsibility of the media specialist to help teachers use more individualized methods such as independent study.

Teachers who anticipate student learning through independent study must make heavy use of materials beyond the textbook. Planning projects with teachers to ensure that their students will be able to learn about a topic of interest and be able to report this learning in a meaningful way requires much more time than preparing a lecture and then developing a test over the content. Independent study projects must be coordinated with the media staff to confirm the availability of materials. If a topic is too narrow, expanding it to a wider area, yet permitting the student to conduct the research originally suggested, takes a great deal of planning between teacher, media specialist, and student. Many teachers are better able to manage assignments that are similar from one student to the next than to manage independent study projects. Media specialists whose efforts to assist and whose collections reflect topics of interest can do much to encourage this alternative form of teaching.

The use of media beyond the textbook can be a positive experience for student and teacher. The author of this book well remembers one first grade teacher who was very textbook/ditto-sheet oriented. This teacher taught in an elementary school that was designated as a model school where each teacher had a wide variety of media available in the media center. To minimize the efforts to locate needed equipment, each classroom was issued audiovisual equipment, with the exception of a VCR and a 16-mm projector. One early afternoon, this teacher decided to try a set of cards with pictures and an accompanying audiotape designed to help students practice alphabet skills. As she said, "the children perked up, and I perked up, and I realized that media can provide a change of pace that is beneficial for all."

Research studies are ambivalent about the degree of success in the use of certain media to accomplish certain tasks. Certainly when media is used incorrectly, it is no surprise if there is little improvement in learning. However, media provides a different approach to the learning task, and the media specialist must be aware of the collection in order to offer this change of pace. For some students, media is the best way to learn because it does not require the same dependence upon reading skills. If teachers are to use media, it must be accessible. Accessibility is a management role that goes hand-in-hand with the personnel role of helping teachers change. Teachers can be encouraged to change their teaching method only if the alternative is perceived to be no more, and preferably less, work than their previous method.

Instructional design projects are very time-consuming, but the rewards are well worth the time it takes to plan. Working closely with teachers, media specialists help plan units of work, decide on appropriate teaching methods, activities related to the unit, and methods of testing, and, finally, help score the products and assign the grades. This is levels nine and ten of Loertscher's taxonomy, and media specialists should not be discouraged if very few instructional design projects are accomplished in a single semester. However, it is better to have accomplished one a semester than to have had no such experience.

The willingness of the media specialist to participate in the teaching of a lesson and in the review of final products may encourage teachers to plan units of work with media specialists. To have someone help make teaching both easier and more effective and assist with the assessment of student progress should be irresistible. Attempts at instructional design must be done on a one-to-one basis with carefully selected teachers at the beginning so that the attempt is successful. However, all teachers have very basic expectations of assistance with student classroom assignments.

Assistance with Classroom Assignments

A common use of the media center for classroom assignments is the arrival of a group of students with a book report due. At the elementary level, the assignment may be as unexciting as, "Read a book with at least 100 pages." From the management standpoint, this is a simple function. It does not take too long for the media specialist to spot books with more than 100 pages. The assignment itself is lacking in creativity, and the futile nature of this assignment is not lost on students. Only the most self-motivated will be able to place any excitement in this approach. Helping change such assignments into more positive uses is discussed briefly in chapter 5, in the section on managing with teachers, but the larger task fits within the present chapter. Offering teachers the opportunity to make creative assignments using media materials is a major task of all media specialists. For example, encouraging teachers to assign the production of a filmstrip as an alternative to a book report will be encouraging to students and may also help teachers move out of their rut.

A second response to classroom assignments is to encourage the use of media as appropriate references for a research paper. This means that the media specialist must teach students, and encourage teachers to accept another form of bibliographic reference that may not be found in every style manual.

Helping a teacher with a different and more creative assignment may seem like keeping a bag of tricks or relying too heavily on gimmicks. But suggesting new ways to do old things can change attitudes of teachers and students and can further encourage other more exciting projects, such as instructional design.

The Media Specialist in the Classroom

The role of the media specialist in the classroom is one of teacher rather than manager, but the management aspects of this role must be considered. When the media specialist is in the classroom, another individual must be placed in charge of the media center. Also, materials used by the students in the classroom during this visit with the media specialist will have been removed from the media center. That is, when the media specialist takes a set of reference books to the classroom to teach, these volumes will be missing from the media center. If the media specialist is demonstrating online database searching for a classroom, this equipment will not be available in the media center.

The placement of the media specialist, media, and equipment in a location away from the media center must be planned in advance. Students who wish to use the media center throughout the day will expect to find it open and all reference materials readily available to them. Scheduling materials and equipment away from the media center may be a great deal more difficult than scheduling the media center for class use.

The Media Center as Classroom

Many media centers have as one of their spaces an adjoining classroom. This part of the facility is scheduled by the media specialist but priorities for its use are established by the media center's advisory committee. While the media specialist is given first preference, teachers with their classes who wish to begin the lesson in the media center rather than the classroom or move to the media center in the middle of the period are considered second priority. Other non-media related activities, such as testing students by guidance counselors, would be a lower priority.

When a media center classroom is available, media materials may be easily moved into this room for teaching and practice away from the other activities in the media center. Immediate access to reference books, media, and the other materials in the media center makes lesson planning much less difficult than if the lesson and its examples must be moved into a classroom in another location in the building.

When no separate room is available, a space within the media center should be set aside for this type of instruction and use, and attempts should be made to close off the area so that activities there do not disturb other media center users. At the elementary level, storytelling should be conducted in an area away from other students so that neither group disrupts the other.

Another management dilemma occurs when media is to be shown in the media center and it is not possible to turn off the lights or cut off sound in one area of the media center. This becomes a scheduling and even a room-arrangement problem if more than one group of students wishes to use the media center while a film, filmstrip, or slides are scheduled to be shown.

Once the curriculum, teaching methods, assignments, and classroom activities have been determined, the units to be taught in the media center are reviewed. Media specialists as teachers have a library skills curriculum to cover, including teaching how to use reference books, how to view films or filmstrips, how to locate and select reference materials for a research paper, how to search databases, how not to plagiarize, and, perhaps, how to discover "truth." These are all a part of the activities to be provided in the media center.

Media Center Activities

Some activities to be provided by a school library media specialist may be determined at the state level. That is, specific curriculum components may be required by State Department of Education regulation. In other instances, programs may be directed by the district library media coordinator to include a districtwide library skills curriculum or other similar requirements. At all times the media specialist should try to integrate the library skills with a student's classroom assignments so that the lessons are not taught in isolation.

The remaining services to be offered should reflect not only the requirements of a good library media program, but also the needs and desires of school personnel, teachers, students, and administrators. School library media specialists must constantly and consistently try to discover these needs and desires.

One method to determine needs is to expand or modify the listing of services suggested in chapter 3 that the media specialist sends to teachers and students during the early weeks of the school year. The list could contain services presently offered and proposed services they might like to have. Their expectations of additional services to be offered in the library media center could be solicited under "other." Asking for such a list will give the library media specialist an indication of the reference and research sophistication of the potential users of the library. If their lists are short and most request rather traditional services, it may be that these teachers and students have little or no idea of what should be available to them. Their expectations may also be based upon their experiences with traditional, limited services offered them in other school library media centers. If they request services that are currently being offered, the media specialist must plan an awareness campaign.

A second method is to ask respondents to give a ranking of 1 (low preference) to 5 (high preference) to a list of services. This system, with no limits, allows teachers and students to assign a high priority to all items, since no penalty is attached to recognizing the importance of all. For example:

Please indicate your priority from 1 low, to 5 high for the services listed below:

low high

0 1 2 3 4 5 Provides weekly storyhour for primary children

0 1 2 3 4 5 Selects collections of books for individual classroom use for reading classes

The numbers assigned to each service could then be summed and those with the highest scores could be given high priority. However, if no penalty is attached, it is possible that each service would be rated 5, which would not help with setting priorities. The possibility of receiving all services may raise false expectations.

A third way is to offer a list of services which have been, are being, or could be offered. In doing this, the library media specialist might like to ask teachers and students which services they perceive they are receiving to confirm if they understand exactly which services are available in the library media center. Since the list contains some potential as well as actual services, it would provide a shopping list for awareness purposes as well. Media specialists may be dismayed to find that teachers are unaware of services available to them in the media center. Teachers may truly be unaware of the possibilities, or they may not understand what is being described in the list of services and misinterpret what is being asked. If a wide discrepancy exists, the media specialist should meet with faculty and try to sort out the confusion. One great value in asking library media center users to select new or expanded services is that it will provide new directions for planning activities.

It is not necessary to create a list of services, because several lists exist to help the media specialist choose wording or even add new suggested services. This shopping list can become a very subtle communication device to increase interest in expanding services into new areas. The method described below is adapted from Liesener.[1] Respondents are given 1,000 points and asked to use them to select or buy from among the choices. This method allows the distribution of weights to the most important services because those services would score the highest number of points. A final list will show teacher perception of needed services in priority order. That list will help the library media specialist decide which services to offer first and which might be postponed until more staff, materials, equipment, or space is available.

The list of services shown in figure 8.1 has been gathered from Gaver and Loertscher and expanded by the author. It may be used as a starting point for developing a list, and other services can easily be added to meet needs in individual situations.

However the original list of services is selected, responses should be studied to determine the feasibility of the requests. A second list should then be compiled and resubmitted for further priority ranking. This can be accomplished in a variety of ways. Perhaps the simplest is to ask teachers and students to indicate "yes" if they would like the service and "no" if they would not.

Some teachers and administrators do not use the services of the media center because they do not know how to use materials or equipment. They may not have been educated users of media services when they were in school, or they may have had unpleasant experiences in trying to find information. One very important service school library media specialists may offer their teachers is a good inservice program to acquaint them with all the resources of the media center and the potential use of these resources.

Good inservice programs grow out of problems perceived as vital and significant to teachers or administrators. A needs assessment is necessary to determine these problem areas, although needs assessment may be an informal query rather than a formal one. Few teachers and even fewer administrators are eager to admit they lack information-seeking skills; they are reluctant to ask for assistance in finding or using resources or equipment.

Certainly, if the library media specialist hopes to have an effective inservice program for teachers, teachers should be involved in planning inservice activities. Their input will ensure that the media specialist starts where the group is and takes it as far as possible in the allocated time period.

The library media specialist sets goals and objectives for any training session, and then keeps these in focus. Some teachers may try to turn the group into another direction. Keeping an audience on task, particularly a group of peers with whom one works on a daily basis, is accomplished more easily when objectives are shared and accepted by the participants.

_____ Individual reading guidance is given through individualized reading lists, assistance in the location of reading materials, etc.

_____ The staff assists students to develop competency in listening, visual literacy, reading, and computing.

_____ Guidance in listening/viewing is given through lists of recommended media, posting of information about mass media programs, etc.

_____ Reserved collections are provided for books and other materials in demand for _class_ needs.

_____ Photoduplication service is provided.

_____ Online database searching is available for students, teachers, administrators.

_____ Online database searches are made by library media specialists for students, teachers, administrators.

_____ _____ online databases are available in the library media center.

_____ An interlibrary loan service is provided for students, teachers, administrators.

_____ Telefacsimile service is available to _____ locations allowing access to _____.

_____ Paperback books are a part of the media center collection.

_____ Information is provided about services and materials available to students at regional and special libraries in the area.

_____ Materials in heavy demand are reserved for individual students and teachers.

_____ Facilities are provided for individual study in the media center.

_____ Facilities are provided for classroom visits to the media center.

_____ Instruction in the use of the media center and its resources is provided to small groups of students, class groups, individuals, etc.

_____ Instruction in the use of the media center and its resources is tied directly to the curriculum unit being taught.

_____ Level I of the Loertscher taxonomy is reached _____% of the time.

_____ Level II of the taxonomy is reached _____% of the time.

_____ Level III of the taxonomy is reached _____% of the time.

_____ Level IV of the taxonomy is reached _____% of the time.

_____ Level V of the taxonomy is reached _____% of the time.

_____ Level VI (VII, VIII, etc.) of the taxonomy is reached _____ times per semester.

_____ Level VI (VII, VIII, etc.) of the taxonomy is reached with _____ teachers per semester.

Fig. 8.1. Sample list of library media center services. Based on Mary Virginia Gaver, _Services of Secondary School Media Centers: Evaluation and Development_ (Chicago: American Library Association, 1971), and on David V. Loertscher, "Media Center Services to Teachers in Indiana Senior High Schools 1972-1973," Ph.D. diss., Indiana University, 1973.

The media specialist who is trying to teach the use of any resource or technology will allow for ample practice by all participants. Nothing is as futile as explaining the use of a camera to a large audience, many of whom cannot even see the camera. If the purpose is to teach simple photography, each participant should have an opportunity to load the film into the camera, take several shots, and then develop the film during the inservice sessions. Hands-on experience is essential.

In order to conduct effective inservice sessions, necessary resources and materials must be available. Enough cameras, reference books, dry mount presses, microcomputers, and online terminals must be available for *each* participant. The size of the audience should be limited to provide sufficient resources to conduct the training session.

Expertise is essential for the trainer. If the library media specialist is uncertain as to how the training should be presented, an outside consultant should be brought into the school. In some situations, an outside consultant may be better able to teach the teachers even though the library media specialist is competent to conduct the training. This is especially true if the library media specialist is trying to sell the faculty on a new technology or a new media center service. An outside presenter may help make a point that teachers would consider self-serving if made by the library media specialist.

The successful inservice trainer takes the group as far as possible in the time alloted. To do this, each participant in the session must be made to feel a vital part of the experience. Careful attention should be paid to individuals in the audience to confirm that they are following the process and understanding the instructions, keeping up with the pace of the presentation, and succeeding at the assigned tasks.

Evaluation of the inservice session will help confirm the audience's approval of the information received, the success of the experience, and the need for the next level of this training or a change to another topic. As with any evaluation process, the changes that are needed before presenting another session will be apparent. The skills of the outside consultant are assessed to determine if this person should be asked to present again.

Whatever is planned, the program must be considered as it impacts on the instructional program and the further effective use of the library media center. Through an effective inservice training program the library media specialist has an opportunity to reach reluctant teachers and to expand the services of the media center into all classrooms.

Certainly no library media specialist should promise to provide a service which is beyond the present staff, facility, collection, or budget. However, no change can be made in the condition of the media center if no new services are suggested. Also, some small pilot program may be implemented to see if it results in better service to teachers and students. Successful pilot programs can be proposed for continued funding in the next year's budget. Costing out the pilot, using methods discussed in chapter 7, will help the media specialist assign a real dollar cost to a service rather than an estimate.

This author is concerned about some less-crucial services offered to students and teachers to the neglect of others that are essential. It is far more important to work with teachers and curriculum than to catalog and process books. It is far more important to work with students on their research projects than to send them fine notices, and the time expended in both cases may be equal. Helping to complete projects at the end of the school year and doing some preliminary planning for the next year is far more important than taking inventory. Weighing "services to meet needs" against management tasks should show services in the winning column.

The most creative media specialist can plan the most helpful services. Sufficient staff, quantities of materials, and a pleasant facility exist. Yet, enticing users into the media center is a major management task; it is discussed in the next chapter.

Exercises

1. Create a list of three or more services you would hope to be able to offer your teachers and students. For each service determine the actual cost in personnel, resources, and equipment.

2. Related Case Studies: See

    Case Study 1, "What is the Value of the Trent Library Media Program? Planning a Needs Assessment"

    Case Study 16, "Trent Reads! Promoting Independent Student Reading."

All of these studies are in Mary K. Biagini's *A Model for Problem Solving and Decision Making* (Englewood, Colo.: Libraries Unlimited, 1988).

Notes

[1]James W. Liesener. *A Systematic Process for Planning Media Programs* (Chicago: American Library Association, 1976).

9 Marketing the Media Center

Introduction

The importance of the school library media program has seemed apparent to media specialists. However, this is not an automatic reaction for all teachers, administrators, and parents. For school library media programs to be given the appropriate high priority in funding and staffing plans, a marketing program must be developed. If no efforts are made, it is possible that the media program will be one of the first to be reduced or cut entirely.

Many media specialists lament inappropriate use of materials and facility by their colleagues, who sometimes send students from the study hall to the media center with no purpose, and who do not give students assignments that encourage them to use the media center. Moreover, support of colleagues is often lacking when funding is reduced. Marketing the media center can build a proper image and encourage appropriate use of the media center. When library media specialists understand, plan, and implement successful marketing projects, they draw affirmative attention to the media center program.

According to Philip Kotler, marketing is the "purposeful coalescence of people, materials and facilities seeking to accomplish some purpose."[1] If this definition is translated into the coalescence of teachers and media specialists seeking to prepare students for adult society, marketing the media center should involve the selling of services and use of the collection. The media center staff plans how to sell these services to teachers. Teachers, in turn, join with the staff to sell available resources and information to students to increase their ability to learn. The media center staff learns to market their image to gain budget support for increasing services, and the circle continues.

Before discussing the process of a successful marketing plan, it is necessary to present some aspects of the media program that cause bad impressions. It may be that the teacher and administrators, not understanding the administrative processes in the media center, misinterpret an activity. The school library media specialist must exercise care to ensure that activities in the media center that are observed by persons other than media staff are acceptable to most. Activities that are subject to negative reaction should take place elsewhere or not at all.

Among the ill-favored actions of media specialists are levying fines, taking inventory, returning misbehaving students to the teacher, and reacting negatively to student and teacher requests for service. On the other hand, positive image-builders include changing bulletin boards frequently and making special efforts for teachers and students.

The school library media specialist needs to understand marketing techniques. It may seem that too few hours are available in the school day even to consider such an uncertain return on the investment of time; in fact, marketing is an essential investment for the media center manager.

From a management standpoint, marketing is the "managerial process involving analysis, planning, implementation, and control."[2] In the broadest sense, it is the bringing together of producer and consumer. In order to carry on the marketing function, the individual must attract sufficient resources; convert resources into products, services and ideas; and distribute outputs to various consuming publics.

The marketer, by giving something, acquires something in return. The successful marketer researches the anticipated needs of the persons to whom this exchange is directed, designs a product they can't ignore, generates an absolute need for the product in the potential recipient, and communicates at an appropriate time and in an appropriate place.

School library media specialists are in the unique position of being able to provide large numbers of materials for clientele at no immediate or apparent cost to them. The media center is full of products which can easily become "gifts" the teacher or student can't refuse if those gifts are marketed at the appropriate time and place.

Marketing has three facets the library media specialist must consider: public awareness, dissemination of information (which may be a part of public awareness), and development of services to meet needs based upon marketing research. The first, a public awareness program for the media center, is centered around the person in charge.

One of the basic problems that occurs with marketing is with personnel, a problem not unique to education or to media centers. Media center staff, both personally and through the programs and information services they offer, must project a strong, helpful image to all the children and adults in the building, from kindergarten through high school, and including custodians, clerical staff, cafeteria workers, bus drivers, teachers, and administrators. Media specialists represent ALL persons in the library and media world to the clients they serve, particularly if those clients make little or no use of any other information agency.

Dissemination of information as a part of public awareness to draw attention to the media center and its services includes providing information which may not be perceived to be essential but which will be useful. Producing a list of new, recently purchased materials might not appear to be eagerly awaited. Only the more aggressive media center clients ask, "What's new?" Nevertheless, sending a list of new materials to classrooms will draw students and teachers into the center to pursue the topics that interest them.

The process of developing services based upon marketing research is another facet of the marketing process and was discussed in chapter 8. Obviously, the services offered by the media center should be a combination of services users perceive to be necessary (determined through market research) and services the library media specialist identifies as necessary and appropriate for curriculum integration and support.

A wide margin exists between offering services and having clientele use those services. Getting users to the media center to use the services is another component of the marketing process. In the media center, if teachers are given a warm welcome when they appear to collect media, produce a sign, or look up the price of some materials they wish to purchase, they will carry away with them a positive image of media personnel as well as the services offered in the center. If students are treated as serious scholars rather than nuisances, they will come. If selection and distribution of materials from the media center are simple processes efficiently managed, if information is provided willingly, correctly, and quickly, the recipient will be willing to enter the center. The next question is what offerings will keep the client returning.

What to Market

"Marketing in the firm begins and ends with the customers."[3] To the library media specialist, the customers are the media center clientele. Determining what to market is based upon an organization's choice of which of its desirable assets it wishes to place for "trade." The primary commodity of any media program is its services. The secondary commodity is the collection itself. Plans should be developed to market the following:

1. Those services determined as priorities by the majority of the users. These are the services which must be provided since they are the most often requested.

2. Other services which are offered because the need exists. Some of these may be the same as those listed above. Once services are selected to be offered, it is important that all teachers and students be made aware of their existence.

3. Those services which should be provided, but which may not be requested because teachers or students are not aware of them. Advertising these services will provide a pool of potential users.

4. New services which should be provided and will be used if an area of interest is developed in teachers and students.

5. New materials added to the equipment.

6. Special collections available for teachers and students.

Once the services have been chosen to market, media personnel must decide what methods will be most effective to carry out the marketing process.

How to Market

Rosenberg has defined marketing as "a matching process, based on goals and capabilities, by which a producer provides a marketing mix (product, services, advertising, distribution, pricing, etc.) that meets consumer needs within the limits of society."[4] His model of the marketing process, modified to fit the media center more closely, is shown in figure 9.1.

This chart shows that the marketing environment is made up of consumers and producers and is a part of the societal environment. The marketing environment for school library media centers varies from state to state, and between regions and local districts within states. A part of the marketing environment is made up of competition from other information agencies, such as the public libraries and home libraries. Also included in this environment are the suppliers and producers of products and services which are secured by media professionals to place in centers. Producers of materials for media centers include commercial vendors as well as staff and services of the production center within the media center itself. Finally, it is hoped that happy media center users will become consumer advocates.

Media specialists become *producers* who must anticipate the consumer marketplace and then offer something of value to the media center clientele as *consumers*. A planned market offering of products, services, promotion, distribution, and, in some cases, pricing (e.g., copying costs) is developed. Certainly, school library media specialists want to anticipate the market. Just as commercial vendors send sales representatives out to do just that, the media specialist must leave the media center and meet the clientele in the classroom and the school corridors. If media specialists are to anticipate markets for their products and services using the business model, they must leave the library media center to learn about needs of clientele.

In the marketing world, the consumers return something of value to the producers. If the product is offered for a cash value, the return is a dollar amount. For media specialists as producers, the value received is a much less tangible reward, such as the response of a satisfied customer's smile and "thank you," or, "Boy, was this a good book!"

Societal Environment
(Social, Political, and Econonmic System)

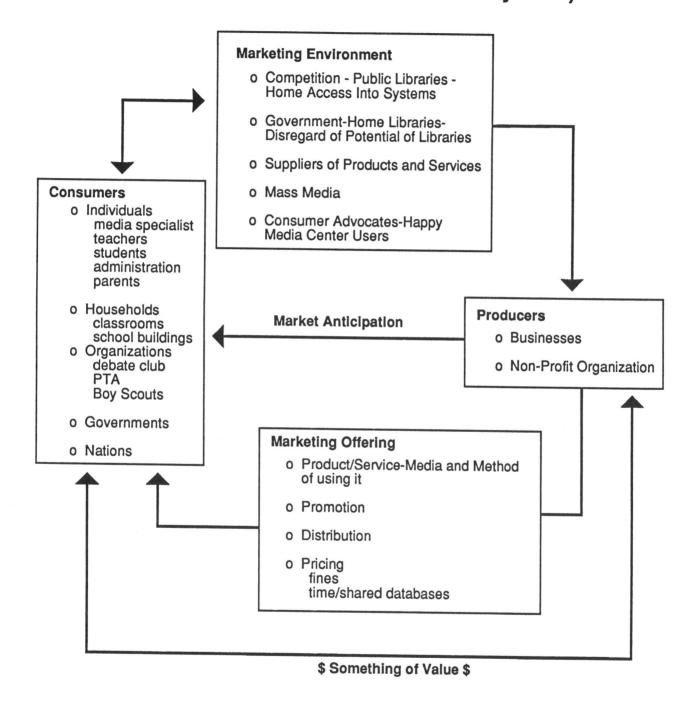

Fig. 9.1. Model of the marketing process. Modified from Larry J. Rosenberg, *Marketing* (Englewood Cliffs, N.J.: Prentice-Hall, 1977).

The *market offering* of product or service for the media program is the media (product) and the method of using it (service). *Promotion* becomes a marketing plan (which will be discussed in depth later). *Distribution* becomes the system which provides the information requested by the consumer. Distribution in the media center is translated into access to and ease of use of information from the media center. In most areas of the media program, *pricing* is not a consideration since services are and should be free. All types of librarians have been debating fee vs. free services, usually connected to a need to reimburse the high-cost services such as database searching. However, pricing may be a part of a database search or a photocopying system. Charges are made to the library media specialist for the database search, and a ceiling may be placed on free searching. When the ceiling is reached, a student might be asked to help support the system. Certainly, few schools offer free photocopying services.

Market planning is "the act of specifying in detail what will be done, by whom, to whom, with what and when, to achieve the organization's objectives."[5] Market planning resembles the process described in the section on proposal writing. It begins with setting goals and objectives for the planning process for the district or school media program, developing a proposal for funding, or writing educational objectives for a new facility. The four steps in this process and some additional suggestions follow.

The first step is to analyze the situation, that is, conduct a *market analysis.* A market analysis may resemble a needs assessment conducted for program planning. Media specialists do not have time to spend convincing clientele to use services of little value. The old saying, "That person could sell ice to Eskimos," gives credit to someone who can sell an unnecessary product. Library media specialists have products to sell that are needed if teachers are to have the best teaching materials and students are to be given the best opportunities to learn. At some times, these products may be perceived to be less helpful because of the difficulty of securing them, the lack of quality of the product, or simply the audience's unawareness of their existence. For example, the need determined by the library media specialist is for better management of the periodical literature. Students have been unable to find current events literature for class reports and are concerned about the length of time between requesting a periodical from the stacks and receiving it in the limited time they are in the media center.

The second step is to develop a strategy of what to do and how to do it. This also resembles a step in responding to a request for proposal, that of planning activities. What can be done to meet the need within the constraints of the present media center and its services? For our example, the media specialist has recorded the provision of research information in periodical literature for two weeks. A "test" was completed using two measures. The first was to ask students preparing a research paper for one class to record their success or failure in finding information in the media center in the periodical collection and also to note the amount of time between requesting and receiving a magazine from the stacks. The second measure was for the library media specialist to record use of periodicals by tabulating requests for them. Also, the library clerk was asked to turn through three years of *Time* magazine and note the number of articles that had been cut from the issues. It was thereby determined that providing back issues of periodicals for research was a problem and that the solution might be to change from providing hardcopy periodicals to making back issues available on microforms.

Microforms are often not popular with an audience, so the market strategy will be to convince the audience that a wider choice will be available, that a reader/printer will permit taking away hard copy, and that the number of missing articles within a periodical or missing volumes hampers in-depth research. A list of missing journals could be posted in several locations to point out numbers of missing volumes and the need for better storage of this information. Media specialists then offer inservice sessions with teachers and students to demonstrate the new equipment and alert all clerical staff and volunteer helpers to suggest microforms before seeking hard copy.

Step three is to evaluate the effectiveness of the activities. A good evaluation technique is to keep a brief record of any comments made about the posting of the holdings. From the preproject record of the number of uses of hardcopy periodicals it will be easy to determine if this number goes down and microform use goes up that amount or more. If students begin using microforms as much or more than hard copy, it may be that the marketing has been successful.

The fourth step is final evaluation. A brief questionnaire could be developed for distribution to teachers and students asking them their opinions about microform copies of periodicals, with some question included about if, how, or why they were accepting or rejecting the transfer of back issues to hard copy.

In the above example, a marketing strategy was planned. The library media specialist wished to sell the use of microforms to the user. The objective was to achieve acceptance of a new format for materials in the media center. When a strategy is less successful and the product is still very important, the library media specialist should analyze the marketing process and try a new strategy.

A marketing program is ongoing, and statistics should be available to respond instantly to inquiries from interested parents, community members, teachers, or administrators. Major corporations and university athletic departments publish fact books for media reporters. General information on the media program would include statistics about the media center—its size, amount of seating, numbers of volumes and media available, budget, amount of library use by class and individuals, and type of use (e.g., storytelling, viewing, research). Output measures such as circulation figures should be included, as well as interesting input measures such as the number of new books or periodicals purchased each year and the average cost of each. The fact book might also contain a description and photos of the facility. Finally, a statement concerning curriculum integration based upon the Loertscher taxonomy will highlight the heavy use of the media center for instructional purposes.

Marketing experts also suggest that an image be selected for the media center, an image that can change from time to time. Students might be asked to help choose a theme for the year and to suggest ways to follow through with an ongoing plan to keep the media center in the center of attention at the school. In order to maintain a full marketing program, the media specialist should ask the following questions.

The first question is, "What is the timeframe for market planning? Weekly, monthly, or annually?" If survival is an issue, more frequent market planning should be done. Otherwise, a regularized system can be maintained during monthly staff planning sessions. If this does not happen, then some discussion of the market plan should be conducted during the first staff meeting of the school year with a follow-up at the beginning of the second semester.

Who should do this planning? In the single-person media center, the planning is done with the advisory committee. Additional assistance is needed for marketing, especially in the single-person center. If the media center has more than one on the staff, they must all be involved in the planning for they will all be involved in the implementation.

As stated earlier, a marketing plan follows the format of proposal writing. Objectives are developed, the current situation is described, and the expected progress is outlined. Alternative strategies are written for achieving the objectives with reasons given for each strategy. Specific actions are then listed and any needed budget proposed. Staff are assigned to specific implementation tasks. Finally, evaluation of each step is indicated with a timeline showing how often to review.

Promotion

One of the more important points made under market planning is that of promotion as a form of communication. Kotler lists several promotional tools, which have been modified for the school library media program setting.[6] The first, "space and time advertising," could be accomplished by providing an article for the student newspaper. If the school publishes a literary newsletter or magazine with articles by students, a well-written book review or other media review could be sponsored by the media center. A media column with critiques of films shown in local theaters could be patterned after the entertainment column in the local newspaper.

Loudspeaker advertising of the media center could be offered through school intercoms. Sometimes the only public relations message school library media specialists provide is a notice concerning the necessity for students to return books at the close of the semester (penalty noted: grade cards withheld); this is clearly not a very positive marketing mechanism. A better plan would be to announce the winner of the latest reference question quiz. The message system should publicize happenings in the media center that will attract students and teachers to the center.

The equivalent of *mailings*, another method of marketing, could be achieved by putting information in teachers' boxes or distributing notices during students' homeroom period. All such messages must be carefully planned with thought given to the type of ads used to sell products. Examples which come to mind are the enclosures that often accompany billing from department stores or oil companies to highlight new products or special sale items. If the message is clever, brief, and attractive, it will be read. If not, it will be discarded immediately.

The *sales presentation* could be equated to the presentation of new materials at the teachers' meeting. The presentation should be relaxed with some "reward" at the close of the meeting when teachers are given sample products described during the presentation. Demonstrations provided at these meetings may promote the possible use of a new piece of equipment. Certainly, any demonstration should provide new information for the audience and offer them something they will be eager to use. A brief demonstration should leave teachers eager to use the product.

Contests are another very successful ploy when they pique the interest of the intended audience. Contests should be planned with specific goals and objectives to expand the market, not just to bring attention to an existing service. One does not need to offer a prize to the teacher who used the most films in a year when film use is high. However, providing a prize for the best research paper using media center materials should expand students' use of the center.

Free samples are another marketing tool. Students love bookmarks. Bringing posters from professional meetings to share with teachers or students can also be very acceptable free samples. A production workshop in the media center from which teachers or students can take away the products they have created is an excellent strategy.

Displays of posters, signs, and show cards produced in the media center can bring teachers and students there to create them for classroom and club. Posters, signs, and show cards are an excellent promotional tool to advertise the media center. If production of attractive posters is not possible in the school, the district or regional production center should be used to produce them. Library media specialists should try to locate sources for developing in-house posters, because the local aspect of this type of advertising adds a positive dimension. Microcomputer software such as *Print Shop* also provides excellent poster and sign graphics which will be sought after by teachers and students.

Another marketing device is the *point-of-sale display*. Used in grocery stores to get rid of tall stacks of boxes, bags, or bottles of a given product, a poster and a stack of books near the charge-out desk encourages students to borrow something to read.

Sales literature could take the form of bibliographies generated to help users understand what is available on a single topic. Other forms of sales literature may be the flyer to describe a special workshop opportunity or a guest speaker who would be available to talk to students or teachers, or an exhibition book about a special exhibit that a student or teacher might place in the media center.

In developing another marketing device, the *brochure*, one should consider the development of the copy. Most advertising personnel choose a particular theme for copy. If several themes are possible, an in-house contest with the participation of library media center staff or students might help select the best. The possibilities of the product to be sold should always be kept in mind as the sales literature is being developed.

Another marketing tool is the *formal presentation* made by the library media specialist to groups both inside and outside the school. An enthusiastic, carefully orchestrated talk, with interesting visuals can draw far greater positive attention to the media center than can many of the methods discussed earlier. Such a presentation, followed by a lively question-and-answer period, can do much to change any negative images of media professionals and media programs.

Preparing Presentations

Many books have been written to help the novice prepare and deliver a speech. Persons who have managed to make as few formal presentations as possible in their high school and college years are probably not as comfortable in front of a group as they perceive their colleagues to be. Yet, it is essential that the media program be articulated to a wide variety of audiences if the program is to be understood and given the high priority that it deserves. A few simple suggestions may help the reluctant speaker accept this responsibility.

First, the length the presentation should be predetermined and observed. No audience wants to sit longer than they expect to sit, as witnessed by participants who begin to yawn or wriggle in their seats. Nor does a host wish to have the program come to a close too quickly and have the audience "demand their money back."

An outline of the presentation, to confirm the sequence of points to be made, should be prepared and followed. A presentation that moves back and forth from a point will confuse the audience and the point will be lost.

The shy speaker should plan visuals to help illustrate points and to cut down the actual speaking time required. The author has always found it useful to make copies of important visuals to distribute so the audience listens rather than starts making hasty notes of what they are seeing.

Successful speakers tell their audience what they are going to say, say it, and, finally, summarize what they have said. If the speaker is enthusiastic about the topic, that enthusiasm will be transmitted to the audience. Bringing along written testimonies, or having children present their projects in person, will add substantially to the audience's enjoyment of the presentation.

Marketing the media center is a continuous activity. Perhaps one of the media specialist's easiest marketing techniques is to greet everyone who comes into the door of the media center with a smile and an eagerness to help.

Exercises

1. See if you can match a media center activity or service with each of the promotional tools listed below:

Space and time advertising

Loudspeaker advertising

Mailings

Sales presentations

Contests

Free samples

Displays

Point-of-sale display

Sales literature

2. Design a brochure to advertise the addition of new materials or equipment to the media center.

3. Outline a presentation for teachers or parents describing a needed addition to the media center. "Sell" this to the group to get their support for encouraging administrative approval of additional funds for the media program.

4. Case Studies: See

Case Study 5, "Is the Library Media Program Central to the Mission of the Trent Schools? Creating a Rationale"

Case Study 8, "Opportunities for Partnership: Planning In-Service Programs for Trent Teachers"

Case Study 22, "Celebrate Libraries! Planning a Public Relations Campaign for Trent Libraries"

Case Study 24, "A Visible Community Presence: Gaining Community Support for the Trent Library Media Program."

All of these studies are in Mary K. Biagini's *A Model for Problem Solving and Decision Making* (Englewood, Colo.: Libraries Unlimited, 1988).

Notes

[1]Philip Kotler. *Marketing for Nonprofit Organizations* (Englewood Cliffs, N.J.: Prentice-Hall, 1975), 5.

[2]Ibid., 6.

[3]William J. Stanton. *Fundamentals of Marketing* (New York: McGraw-Hill, 1978), 35.

[4]Larry J. Rosenberg. *Marketing* (Englewood Cliffs, N.J.: Prentice-Hall, 1977), 6.

[5]Kotler, 238.

[6]Ibid.

10 Managing the Media Program
Evaluation

Introduction

A library educator, David Loertscher, once queried his audience, "If you had ten cents for each time you had helped a teacher with a curricular need, what could you buy—a new suede jacket or an ice cream cone? If you were arrested for contributing to the education of a student, would there be enough evidence to convict you?" Both are very thoughtful questions, and progress toward the dual goals of helping teachers and contributing to the education of students must be documented if these successes are to benefit the media program.

Evaluation has many definitions. According to one dictionary, to evaluate means "to ascertain or fix the value or worth of; to examine and judge, appraise."[1] Determining the worth of a project, product, service, person, or program in order to fix a value to it is threatening. The judging process is frightening, for it may point out what was thought to be helpful is, in fact, not helpful at all. From early years, children are tested and retested for scholastic achievement, experiences that are often anxiety-provoking. This tension is not something that is outgrown, and adults are seldom secure in what they perceive to be a test atmosphere. The same is true when the outcome of the evaluation is to fix a value to a program.

A less threatening approach is to analyze program progress through *measurement* rather than *evaluation*, particularly when evaluation is viewed as assigning a rank order score from high to low, good to bad, or "A" to "F." Top programs receive "A" while a less effective program is only a "B." Just as in assigning grades to scores in the classroom, cutoff levels on the scale of scores appear to be very arbitrary. Students regret missing an "A" by one point or enjoy the experience of having their grade raised from a "C" to a "B" when the teacher lowers the scale by one or two points. For example, a media program with only 19,999 books "fails" while 20,000 books is considered "successful."

Program evaluation of the school library media program and its components occurs for one or more of the following reasons. The school library media specialist may choose to test a single program facet. School district administrators may wish to compare all programs or any part of their media program at the local level, or they may wish to be given approval by a regional accrediting agency. In other instances, the school library media program may be a part of a network, and the network requires an analysis of a media service. In each of these cases, a different approach may be necessary to provide the proper responses to evaluation.

Two perspectives of evaluation exist: (1) to find out what is right; (2) to find out what is wrong. Both perspectives are useful. Certainly, school library media specialists need to learn what is wrong so that repairs, changes, or alternatives can be put into place. Finding out what is right is satisfying, for this confirms that proper decisions have been made, adequate procedures are in place, and the program is running smoothly in those areas. Evaluation is not a threat when it confirms accomplishment or provides constructive plans for improvement.

One major problem with any evaluation is that most elements of the school library media program are not easily quantified. Many quantity measures are not real measures of a program. For instance, circulation statistics tell you only what materials have moved out of the media center. They do not tell the amount of use, or, for that matter, if there was any use at all.

A second major problem is that few yardsticks exist against which to measure. One yardstick is national standards, and these are developed by school library media specialists. They are sometimes questioned by school administrators and other members of the education community when they are based upon intuition rather than research results.

Standards exist in many states, but these often outline only minimum requirements for the media program. Most are within easy reach of school library media programs because they are mandated by the state, and the quantities cited are meager. State standards which would require large numbers of materials, a substantial amount of special equipment, many professional and clerical workers on staff, and large facilities are often challenged by school board members who say they cannot raise adequate funds for implementation. The local officials might demand that state funding be supplied to meet state-imposed standards, and this might not be politically popular.

Local standards may be established by administrators to ensure that all programs have minimum materials, staff, and services. If local standards are to be developed, they should be designed to judge the progress of the school library media program to meet districtwide objectives. This type of evaluation helps with planning all programs, policy making, and with the revision, continuance, substitution, or cancellation of program components or media center services. Evaluation can also serve as an awareness device for teachers and administrators. It is particularly useful for those who have misunderstood the purpose of the media program.

Most school personnel base their expectations upon models they observed when they, themselves, were students in elementary and high school, in their teacher training programs, and in their student teaching or practicum experience. School library media specialists who served as role models in previous teaching and learning situations may have been mediocre to excellent. After graduation, teachers and administrators added to their perceptions when they accepted positions in schools and observed the media program and its relationship to their classes. While some of these experiences may have provided excellent models, many did not. An effective evaluation designed with teacher and administrator input can raise their awareness and expectations.

Simply saying that the school library media program is essential to the learning environment of the school is not enough. Media programs can be scrutinized by program appraisal methods that test the value of the program. Media center program appraisal helps analyze which services are meeting the needs of the school. Are services being offered which meet objectives established by the media center advisory committee? Measuring progress toward these objectives is the first step in evaluating the media center. For example, if a program objective was to provide online database searching for research papers, the evaluation could be a simple, "yes, online database searching has been added to the library media center services." A better value statement tells how many searches were made for how many students, the number of students trained to do their own searching, the average length of time for each search, and the number of relevant citations found. If the response is "no, we have not been able to provide this," analysis should be made to show if the problem was lack of funding, equipment, staff time, or staff training.

The importance placed upon the role of the media specialist and the concept of the media program must be assessed in relation to those persons who make up the school district and the community at large. If students and teachers have access to a wide variety of information sources such as public and academic libraries, they may need a totally different type of collection and service program in the school. If the library media center is the only source for the student, a different concept may prevail. Relationships between nearby information agencies and the use of these outside sources should be a part of the evaluation process.

When school staff and students are involved, they must understand the evaluation process so that an accurate study can be conducted. All persons must view the process as a self-evaluation which requires responding with accurate and well-considered answers. Again, it is impossible to improve a program if the flaws are not recognized by the media staff. The counterpoint is that successes should be confirmed rather than assumed.

Designing methods for testing must be done with care to determine exactly who will be queried, which items are necessary to measure, and what procedures should be used to acquire the needed information. Careful consideration must be given to the choice of statistical methods with which to tabulate and analyze the responses to any evaluation documents. Furthermore, individual components of any media program should not be measured in isolation.

The curriculum of the school is the essential element in the planning and evaluation of the media program, because the major test is the degree to which the media program complements, supplements, supports, and is an integral part of curriculum offerings. Collections are tailored to meet needs of teachers and students, and these needs change as the curriculum changes, as grade levels are shifted between buildings, and as teachers are replaced. Students and teachers may need more audiovisual materials or high-interest/low-vocabulary materials rather than a larger collection of higher level materials. The type of learner in the school affects the collection just as the teaching method dictates some aspects of collection development.

Four components of the media program can be measured without too much difficulty: staff, collections, facilities, and services. They can be measured by quantitative or qualitative methods patterned after existing models or planned for by the total media staff with assistance from other building-level or central administrative staff. Documents are available that show measuring techniques. A search of recent literature will point to these.

Quantitative Measures

As mentioned earlier, school library media standards often provide quantitative measures, but these may appear to be either too high, as in the case of the 1975 national standards, or too low, as in the case of most state standards.[2] A major flaw with quantitative measures is that administrators place too much emphasis upon counting *things* with little regard to their quality. In an effort to meet a required size of the media center, areas of the school such as equipment storage closets or even a storage area in the basement may be designated a part of the media center with little regard to the proximity to the media center or to the convenience of access. The necessity of providing a certain number of books or filmstrips per pupil may result in neglect of the weeding process. Collections, while meeting an arbitrary numerical count, may be out-of-date, in poor condition, or of no value to the current school curriculum. Equipment may be left in storage closets gathering dust because, by discarding obsolete machines or items needing major repairs, the library media center totals fall below the required numerical "score." Administrators may also buy inferior products to achieve a standard number of holdings rather than purchase high-quality merchandise.

Increasing the size of the library media center may not increase its use if teachers do not make assignments that require use of materials in the library media center. If new spaces are not thoughtfully created or attractively arranged, they may not encourage use. library media staff can, through the use of rigid rules or a grudging behavior, discourage media center use regardless of the size or ambiance of the facility. Arbitrary assignment of classes to the media center or overloading it with escapees from study hall will also discourage proper use of the facility.

Quantitative measure of services can be done, but this may give a one-dimensional perspective. School library media specialists may distribute a checklist asking teachers to indicate which services they are receiving. A wide variety of services may be offered, but the list resulting from such a survey will give a very inaccurate picture if a majority of students and teachers are unaware that these services exist, or if many services are offered that are not requested by teachers or students. It will not matter if a service is available if no one makes use of that service for any reason. While quantitative measures are often less helpful, some output measures are useful in describing the media program. Counting output will certainly confirm media center use. Output is the number of teachers and students who come into the media center each day, an estimate of the number of materials that circulate, the percentage of the student body using the media center at least once a month, and other similar statistics. The better measure is the relationship of quantity to quality.

Qualitative Measures

The fact that quantity measures are very specific and have little cause-and-effect value mean that they do not test a program adequately. Quality measures are much more significant but are much more difficult to determine. Quality can be measured from the basis of "What is" to "What should be."

What Is	**What Should Be**
A place to send students for teacher's fifty-minute break.	A place with open access for research and reading based upon planned programming.
One hundred periodical titles with no duplication. Files maintained on thirty titles for five years.	A collection of seventy subscriptions with multiple copies of ten titles which have been determined to have heavy use. Files maintained for five years of thirty titles. Fifteen titles purchased on microfilm for ten years or more.

Administrators, teachers, students, and media staff can measure *what is* against *what should be* and calculate the discrepancy as an actual dollar amount. While this sounds as if it is a quantity count, it actually is not. The *what is* becomes a qualitative count of persons, equipment, materials, or the facility and the services. That is, a service or other component must reach a certain qualitative standard before it can be counted. *What should be* outlines what is needed to provide quality. These qualitative factors are applied to facilities, staff, collection, and services. That is, an obsolete projector would not be eligible for the tabulation of holdings in audiovisual equipment.

Appraising the Facility

Analyzing the facility has been discussed in chapter 4 under planning and remodeling the media center. Students and teachers can be asked to make suggestions for improving the ambiance of the media center. In so doing, they may take responsibility for helping raise the funds to make simple adjustments.

Staff or Performance Appraisal

Performance appraisal is easy in the world of sports where the height of the basketball player and the weight of the football player are easily determined facts. Success is calculated by baskets scored, rebounds made, yards gained, or number of tackles or passes completed. The ultimate test for the team is not the score for the individual players but the season's number of wins and losses.

Such statistics are not as readily available for media center staff, and the calculation of wins and losses is arbitrary most of the time. Asking teachers or students to determine wins and losses is difficult because the qualities which appeal to one student or teacher may not appeal to another. Frances Henne's basic rule for media staff quoted in chapter 5 bears repeating here:

> For some students, and in certain schools this may be many students, the only library skills that they should have to acquire is an awareness, imprinted indelibly and happily upon them, that the library is a friendly place where the librarians are eager to help.[3]

The score for "friendly place" and "librarians eager to help" may be determined in part by the numbers of students who seek the advice and counsel of the media specialist not only for curriculum needs, but also for matters which go beyond the scope of the classroom. Compatibility of personalities is very difficult to score. Interpersonal relationships, though identified, are not easy to describe in terms of quantity or quality. Communication patterns between media center staff and the users of the media center can best be determined if someone spends periods of time observing such patterns, and this method is seldom possible to implement. Another measurement is to ask students and teachers to describe what they like best about the media center. If a student likes the media specialist "best," this would indicate rapport between that student and the media specialist. On the other hand, if the response to "What do you like least about the media center?" was also "the media specialist," one would evaluate this as lack of rapport. In-between measures on the scale would be much more difficult to determine.

In some states evaluation of all teaching staff is mandated, and a state-approved form is provided. Most school library media specialists lament the fact that the items do not seem to apply to their unique assignments, and their evaluation using this mechanism, while not inaccurate, is incomplete. A better method is to match performance to previously determined job expectations. George B. Redfern has listed the following as basic components of performance evaluation:

1. Clarification of performance criteria or definition of the scope of the job;

2. Establishment of performance objectives or job targets;

3. Formulation of performance activities or a plan of action for implementing objectives;

4. Agreement on monitoring techniques for measuring the effectiveness of activities;

5. Development of a means for assessing the monitored data; and

6. Arrangement for one or more conferences with follow-up to utilize the feedback gained from the process.[4]

The actual application of these components was discussed in chapter 5 in the section on evaluating personnel. However, the activities expected of the media specialist should be the baseline for appraisal of that person's success or failure. Expectations should be written as job descriptions and discussed with each individual.

Clerical staff should also be measured on preestablished performance criteria. These criteria are related to their job descriptions and evaluation may be based upon a districtwide process. If not, documentation of work falling below the established standard must be maintained if changes in behavior are to be expected.

Another measure of performance is the ability of the media center personnel to provide the necessary information for their clientele. If materials are well organized, if patrons are given correct and pertinent information in an efficient manner and with a minimum of difficulty, the staff are performing well. If patrons are reluctant to ask for assistance, or if they are consistently provided with misinformation, performance of the staff is considerably below adequate achievement levels.

Staff may be evaluated on how many services they offer as well as on how well they deliver those services. Mary Virginia Gaver verified the assumption that size of staff can affect the number and quality of services offered.[5] If the size of staff is large enough to permit a media center to offer a wide variety of services and it does not, one would investigate why not. On the other hand, it is not practical to attempt to offer a wide variety of services with limited staff. Media specialists would not be exercising good judgment to offer many services and offer no service well.

The principal may define quality as the ability of the media center staff to get along with teachers, to control the behavior of students in the media center, and to limit the number of books lost during the school year. While these items may be of assistance in the evaluation of the media specialist, it is unfortunate if these are the *only* criteria used for performance appraisal.

Collection Measurement

While analysis of the media collection should be done yearly, this is impractical in most situations. Rather, a *part* of the collection may be analyzed each year. Certainly each item in the total collection should be reviewed at least once every five years. Materials that have become obsolete, have worn out, or, because of curriculum changes, are not pertinent, should be removed from the shelves. Materials that will probably be used later can be stored, but no quality collection contains large blocks of unused materials.

Several measures are useful for the collection. Some are simple, and others are more time-consuming. As discussed in chapter 6, an excellent measure known as *collection mapping* has been developed by David V. Loertscher. Collection mapping is a review of the collection matched to particular curriculum areas. The collection is analyzed, and areas with large numbers of materials above this base number are reviewed for probable emphasis areas which can support the curriculum in an exemplary way. This process is thoroughly explained in *Drexel Library Quarterly*[6] and in the book, *Computerized Collection Development for School Library Media Centers.*[7]

Records should also be maintained of materials borrowed from outside the school district. Items used more than once a year should be purchased, if available, for the media center, except in the case of very expensive items which may be borrowed from a regional or state center or rented from a rental library. Collecting statistics on materials borrowed will help in budget requests for future years.

The relevance and timeliness of the collection can be easily measured. Different areas of the Dewey Decimal Classification System have different copyright date requirements. The books and other materials given 310, almanacs and yearbooks, should be superseded by each new edition as they have very little value after five years. On the other hand, a history of the Civil War that is accurate and well written, relevant to the curriculum, and suitable to the reading ability of most students might be of use for many years. A simple chart which tabulates shelflist holdings could help one determine the quantity and the timeliness of the collection with specific areas outlined (see table 10.1).

As shown in table 10.1, more than 50 percent of the reference books in this collection are more than twenty years old, and 75 percent are more than ten years old. If the five counted as copyright after 1980 are sets of encyclopedias, students would have general up-to-date information. However, one would be very skeptical about the quality of reference information in this school and its relevance to the curriculum.

Relevance can be measured only by asking teachers and students if materials they used were relevant to their needs. This does not mean that an item should be discarded because it did not meet a specific need for one assignment. However, an item lacking relevance for the topic it covered under all circumstances should be discarded. This was particularly pointed out to the author when she counted materials in school districts and found twenty-year-old books in 629.9 Aeronautics.

Table 10.1. Collection Age Inventory

Dewey Number	Copyright Date									
	Before 1970		1971-1978		1978-1984		After 1980		Total	
	#	%	#	%	#	%	#	%	#	%
000	40	50	10	25	5	12.5	5	12.5	60	100
100										
200										
300										
310										
320										
340-350										
360										
etc.										

Many school media specialists with computerized circulation systems can program the system to tabulate the circulation by each Dewey class number. An analysis can be made of the use or the lack of use of material in each area. Individual books can be tracked to see how often the book has circulated. While neither of these procedures can determine how the materials were actually used, knowing the topics being researched may be helpful.

Actual use can be identified in several ways. Teachers and students can be interviewed concerning their use of the materials when they return them to the media center. Students can also be asked to keep a log of the materials they select and to note how they use them. They might also be willing to record those materials secured from another sources. The usefulness of all materials should be assessed.

At the completion of a unit of work, a citation count (long a favorite in academic research) can be applied to students' research papers. Citations can then be checked against the media center's holdings to see if materials are available in the collection or if students chose items from other libraries. Jacqueline Mancall and Carl Drott provide an excellent example of this process.[8]

If a bibliography is generated for the unit, or if a classroom collection is pulled for use in one classroom, both teachers and students can be asked to indicate use and to evaluate the quality of items on the bibliography or in the classroom collection. A simple evaluation checklist, as shown in figure 10.1 can be used.

Collections can be checked to see how many materials have not been circulated within the past three years. If these materials are relevant and useful, why haven't they been located and used by students or teachers? If they do not appear to be relevant or useful, they should be reviewed to determine if they would be more appropriate at a different grade level or in a different building. Some materials cease being relevant when curriculum changes, in which case they could be stored until a later time. If they are not being used, do not appear to be likely candidates for use in the near future, or are unused because they are out-of-date or in poor condition, they should be discarded and all records removed. No collection, no matter how large, can be judged to have high quality when the collection is cluttered with out-of-date, worn, unused, or irrelevant materials.

Author	Title	Type of Material	Material Was	Did you Use?	If Used, What?	Other Comments
			Very Good Adequate Out-of-date Useless	___Yes ___No	All Most Very Little	
			Very Good Adequate Out-of-date Useless	___Yes ___No	All Most Very Little	

Fig. 10.1. Material use analysis.

After the First Year

Evaluation is a process of deciding what to tell, who to tell, and why to tell. Sometimes one statistic can be used for two purposes. When large numbers of students use the media center for assignments, these numbers can be used in a positive report showing media center success. If those students cannot find materials because the collection is out-of-date, the same statistics become part of a failure report. Both are equally "good" because failure statistics can be used to support a request for additional funding.

By the middle of the media specialist's second semester in the school, the year's goals and objectives should be under scrutiny for their success to date. The degree of accomplishment may be high, and this appears in the annual report to the principal. If it has been much lower than expected, a careful analysis of the reasons should be made so that needs for the next year may be stated.

Exercises

1. Design an evaluation project to test one component of the library media program. If possible, implement this project and prepare a written report of the data analysis.

2. Related Case Study: See

   Case Study 1, "What Is the Value of the Trent Library Media Program? Planning a Needs Assessment"

   Case Study 3, "Measuring Up: Comparing the Trent Library Media Program with State, Regional, and Professional Standards."

Both these studies are in Mary K. Biagini's *A Model for Problem Solving and Decision Making* (Englewood, Colo.: Libraries Unlimited, 1988).

Notes

[1]*American Heritage Dictionary of the English Language* (Boston: American Heritge Publishing Co., Inc. and Houghton Mifflin Co., 1969), 453.

[2]At the time of preparation of the present volume, the new AASL/AECT *Information Power: Guidelines for School Library Media Programs*, containing school library media standards, was also in preparation. Therefore, actual quotations from that document were not available.

[3]Frances Henne. "Learning to Learn in School Libraries," *School Libraries* 15 (May 1966): 17.

[4]George B. Redfern. *How to Evaluate Teaching* (Worthington, Ohio: School Management Institute, 1972).

[5]Mary Virginia Gaver. *Services of Secondary School Media Centers* (Chicago: American Library Association, 1971), 39.

[6]David V. Loertscher. "Collection Mapping: An Evaluation Strategy for Collection Development," *Drexel Library Quarterly* 20 (Spring 1985): 10-11.

[7]David V. Loertscher and May Lein Ho. *Computerized Collection Development for School Library Media Centers* (Englewood, Colo.: Hi Willow Research and Publishing Co., 1986).

[8]Jacqueline C. Mancall and M. Carl Drott. "Materials Used by High School Students in Preparing Independent Study Projects: A Bibliometric Approach," *Library Research* 1 (1979): 223-36.

11 Cooperation and Networking

Introduction

Cooperation between schools and public libraries began as early as there were both schools and public libraries. This cooperation was "institutionalized" in 1896 when the National Education Association made libraries eligible for membership.[1] Relationships flourished, and the Certain Standards, the first school library standards, stated

> To relate the work in the high school library to that of the public library and to make clear the uses to pupils, after school days are over, of an institution which should be a factor in their future mental development, classes should be taken to the public library, where its book resources, rules, methods, departments, catalog and support can be briefly explained by one of the staff.... Where visits to the library are an impossibility in school hours because of distance, competent members of the library staff may be invited to talk on the subject.[2]

By the early 1960s, increased attention to research in schools, particularly scientific research, and the lack of good school libraries created a problem for public libraries. Student use of public libraries appeared to be halting efforts to serve all other clients. Efforts to meet students' needs within the schools were assisted by the passage of the Elementary and Secondary Education Act, but even those funds did not provide all the materials needed.

The need to share resources resulted in a variety of efforts at cooperation and networking. Consortia and networks were created linking academic and large public libraries. However, school library media centers were not really a part of the basic planning; therefore, input concerning the appropriate configurations, shared funds, and other necessary elements in the sharing process created problems for the library media specialist who wished to join a network. Thus a vital avenue for providing materials for teachers and students is still missing. With the steady growth of information in an ever-increasing variety of formats, the need for agencies to cooperate is even more acute now than it was twenty years ago. In a few locations, however, some efforts have been made to include school library media centers in consortia and networks.

In 1978, the National Commission on Libraries and Information Science (NCLIS) published a report of its Task Force on the Role of the School Library Media Program in the National Program. In the final report, the role of the school library media program was described with the following introduction:

Just under fifty million young people are enrolled in public and private elementary and secondary schools in the United States — 23 percent of the country's total population. The Task Force believes that the information needs of these young citizens are important. The quality of the information services to which students and their teachers have access affects directly what they learn and how well they learn it — a factor of no little consequence for this Nation's future.[3]

The NCLIS idea was cited:

Providing every individual in the United States with equal opportunity of access to that part of the total information resource which will satisfy the individual's educational, working, cultural and leisure-time needs and interests.[4]

The Task Force then stated that, to meet the NCLIS ideal, not only students, but parents, teachers and others

should find their school library media centers to be effective points of access to the appropriate parts of that total information resource. This will happen only when schools are involved as full participating members in a library network.[5]

Almost as many definitions exist for the term, *network*, as there are networks. The reality of this concept may exist under another name such as *cooperative, consortium,* or *services authority.* NCLIS defines network as "a formal arrangement whereby materials, information, and services provided by a variety of types of libraries and/or other organizations are made available to all potential users."[6] For school library media centers to be full participating members, library media specialists must understand their role and what's in it for them, and for their teachers, students, administrators, and parents.

This author participated in two recent studies that provide an answer to, "What's in it for me and my library media users?" Information was gathered about the possible value of networking for school library media specialists. Study A was a national view of elementary, middle, and high schools in several states compared with rural school library media centers in one county in Pennsylvania.[7] Study B offered a more detailed look at a sample of high schools in Pennsylvania.[8] Both projects were designed to study the feasibility of sharing resources with libraries of all kinds within a single district, a county, or a specific geographic or governmental area.

Study A determined the costs for joining a national bibliographic utility; Study B analyzed the costs for producing machine-readable records from high school card catalogs or shelflists. A common element in the two studies was discovering the quantities of materials available within the schools and the degree of overlap in titles in the various collections.

In order to assess overlap, a methodology designed by Ellen Altman for her dissertation at Rutgers was adopted.[9] Three master checklists were developed, one for each type of school: elementary, junior high, and senior high.

Ten Dewey Decimal Classification numbers and fiction, author's last name beginning with "E," were chosen. The high school topics matched those selected by Altman and included *math* and *Civil War*, subjects that could be less current but still relevant, as well as *drugs* which requires current information. Middle school included *automobiles* and *football*, while elementary topics were *dogs, ghosts, fairy tales,* and *seasons.* The one Dewey Decimal Classification number consistent on all three lists was 629.2, *aeronautics.*

Specific titles were listed from three H. W. Wilson publications, *High School Catalog, Junior High Catalog,* and *Children's Catalog.* Additional titles were added from the library media center collections in high schools in the Pittsburgh, Pennsylvania Public Schools, and from a middle school and an elementary school in one school district in the rural county chosen for the study.

As shelflists were checked for titles in the master checklist, all titles under that number, but not appearing on the master checklist, were added. A final compilation matched all the added titles from each school in both studies.

For Study A, the national study, shelflists were checked for a small, suburban district in California, a large urban district in Florida, selected schools within a large intermediate district which included urban, suburban, and rural schools in Iowa, and two small urban districts, one in Ohio and the other in Texas. Included also was the rural county in Pennsylvania with thirty-five elementary schools (of which twenty-two were respondents), twenty-three middle schools (of which eighteen were respondents), and twenty high schools (of which nineteen were respondents).

For Study B, the state study, thirty-one high schools were visited throughout Pennsylvania, including one of the high schools in the rural county chosen for Study A. These high schools represented a variety of sizes in both urban and rural sections of the state and ranged from a large school serving 4,000 students to a small school with 270 students.

The commonality and uniqueness of the collections were measured in order to point out the potential for shared cataloging and interlibrary loan and to anticipate the costs for retrospective conversion (entering all card catalog and shelflist records), if collections were to be made machine-readable. The resulting statistics demonstrate one major value of networking for library media specialists, that of resource sharing.

From Study A, a total of 177 titles were chosen from *Children's Catalog.* These titles were checked against the holdings in the rural Pennsylvania county. Of these, fourteen titles were not found in any of the twenty-two elementary schools, and only nine titles were found in more than fourteen of the twenty-two schools. A total of 238 titles were listed from *Junior High Catalog* with fifty-seven found in none of the eighteen schools. Only two titles were found in more than nine schools. Of the 170 titles listed from *High School Catalog,* sixteen were found in none of the nineteen high schools, and only five were found in more than twelve high schools.

A total of 145 titles were added to the master checklist from one elementary school. Of these, twelve titles were unique to that school and only four were found in more than fourteen. A total of 484 titles were added to the master checklist from the junior high. Of these, ninety-seven were unique to that school while only two were found in more than fourteen. A total of 538 titles were added from the shelflist of the high schools in Pittsburgh. Of these, 125 were found only on that list. Only two of these additional titles were found in more than twelve schools.

The titles most often found in schools are as follows. Three books were found in eighteen of the twenty-two elementary schools: Edmonds, *The Matchlock Gun*; Estes, *The Middle Moffat*; and Estes, *The Moffats.* Seventeen schools had purchased many of the holiday books by Barth, including *Hearts, Cupids, and Red Roses; Holly, Reindeer and Colored Lights; Turkeys, Pilgrims, and Indian Corn;* and *Witches, Pumpkins, and Grinning Ghosts.* Sixteen schools owned Estes' *Pinky Pye* and Miller's *Story of the Liberty Bell,* while fifteen had Kettlekamp's *Haunted Houses* and Wyndham's *Thanksgiving.*

Of the eighteen junior high/middle schools reporting, seventeen had Adamson's *Born Free* and Frank's *Diary of a Young Girl.* Sixteen schools had Pratt's *Monitor and the Merrimac* and fifteen had Tregaskis' *Guadalcanal Diary.* Another Landmark Book was in fourteen schools, Jackson's *Witchcraft of Salem Village.* Taylor's *Battle in the Arctic Seas* was also in fourteen schools. Adamson's *Living Free,* Kantor's *Gettysburg,* and Reynold's *Battle of Britain* were found in thirteen schools.

In checking overlap of the balance of titles added, that is, those titles which were added to the original lists, there were 978 titles added to the elementary list of which 630 were unique to one school, and only four were found in more than nine schools. A total of 1,473 were added to the middle school list of which 1,035 were unique to one school, and only four were found in more than nine schools. An additional 1,098 titles were added to the original checklist from the nineteen high schools. Of these titles added beyond the basic list, 829 were found in only one school. Only fifteen titles were found in more than nine schools.

From Study B of thirty-one high schools in Pennsylvania, no titles were found in more than twenty-two schools. The book found most often was George Eliot's *Mill on the Floss.* Another ten titles were found in twenty or twenty-one schools. These were Bergamini's *Mathematics* and *Book of Ancient Rome,* Alden's *The American Revolution,* Catton's *This Hallowed Ground* and his *Mr. Lincoln's Army,* and several of Churchill's histories of World War II.

A final compilation of data from Study A is shown in table 11.1.

Table 11.1. Overlap and Unique Titles in School Library Media Centers

Place	Overlap	Unique Titles
Pennsylvania county	45%	55%
Iowa intermediate unit	45%	55%
Suburban California	17%	83%
Urban county, Florida	20%	80%

This means that 55 percent or more titles found in school library media centers will be unique to the single school, and will not be duplicated in any other school in the immediate area. Communication about the contents and the capability of sharing would expand information to students at little additional cost compared to purchasing those materials for limited use. Possibilities of sharing are further increased when school media center collections are compared with those in public libraries.

Carol A. Doll studied eight school library media centers and four public libraries in four Illinois communities in 1980.[10] She selected 200 book titles at random from each shelflist and then checked for duplication in each of the participating libraries. Her findings showed that the average overlap was 50 percent when comparing the school's collection with the public library collection. This means that half the titles were the same and half different. Doll also found that there was less overlap between two school library media centers than between a school and a public library.

In all of the cases reported above, libraries, both school and public, have a great many book titles which would be of interest to library users if made available to all. This underscores the value of resource sharing among schools and is an interesting prelude to the New York study.

A study completed in New York in 1983-84 showed that the twelve school library system pilot projects (serving over 446,000 students in 117 public school districts and fifty-six nonpublic schools) provided interlibrary loan for more than 50,300 items borrowed, four times the pilots' first year level in 1979-80.[11] The most compelling statistic of all was that, of the 50,300 items borrowed, 43,034 were from other school library media centers, confirming that media specialists borrow most of their materials from another school library media center rather than another type of library. However, access was available to all types of libraries, and students and teachers were able to secure 7,700 items where were not available in their own school library or another school library.

This report shows that sharing provides an expanded variety of materials for students to use in preparing research reports or for extending their interest in a subject beyond what is in the local school. Whether or not any savings in acquisition or cataloging accrued from sharing, the expanded access and service was significant.

Cost of Network Membership

The cost of network participation varies by type of network (some are only consortia of libraries sharing a union list of serials and communicating over local telephones and through established delivery systems). However, there are differences in costs between networks offering similar services. The costs of participating in a consortium with a union list might be the purchase cost of the union list and the time it takes to provide materials to other members. When one becomes a member of an automated network, costs are often much higher.

When joining a network, first-time members may have to pay an initiation fee. This fee may or may not cover the annual membership cost, purchase of necessary equipment, training of staff, and any other fees for service such as costs for cataloging or database searching. After the first year, an annual membership fee may be assessed; charges for specific services are continued based upon use of those services. As additional services are chosen, additional fees may be charged for equipment, database searching, acquisition, serials control and other items; these fees vary from network to network.

Joining a Network

Since most networks serve specific regions of the United States, media specialists must join the network serving their area, state, or region. Networks differ in services offered and the cost of those services. Requirements for membership also vary, and those requirements must be measured against the services offered.

Upon becoming interested in joining an automated network, the school library media specialist should first review the positive and the negative aspects of belonging to any network, particularly a national bibliographic utility. Testimony and recommendations are available in the literature for successful networking. In national and state journals, research reports, personal experiences, published activities, and the costs and benefits of networking may be detailed. Many conference programs offer information about selecting services within a network configuration.

A second step in learning how to join a network would be to seek out another librarian who is participating in that network. Network members can answer questions about the cost of services and benefits, and they will be able to make specific recommendations. Network officials are the final source of information; they help establish the level of service based upon an analysis of the needs of the prospective member.

When potential network members can join in clusters or groups of libraries, such as all school and public libraries in a city or county, some charges may be reduced. The initiation fee and the annual membership fees are divided among group members. School library media specialists are then charged only for the costs of the services they use. A major savings for a cluster member of an automated bibliographic network is in use of a single record. For instance, if one library in the group purchases cataloging for *St. George and the Dragon*, the first-time use (FTU) of the bibliographic record will be assessed. All others purchasing a copy of that book will be charged a lesser fee. A careful check of the costs of services, using anticipated usage levels, will help determine which services should be chosen and how much use can be made of any service purchased.

The third step is for library media specialists to sell the administration of the school district on the merits of belonging to a network. Start-up as well as continuing membership costs will be difficult to explain to administrators who do not understand the underlying rationale for purchase of the services being proposed. Media specialists must provide carefully thought-out examples of the benefits of each service, written in lay-person terminology, so that administrators are sold on the project before they review any costs. If possible, costs should be presented with options such as single membership and cluster membership. This may help administrators select a less expensive initial experience rather than turning down full membership.

The fourth step is to make presentations to the school board and to organizations in the community in an effort to secure the necessary funds. An attractive feature might be to make the project a community project with long-term positive benefits accruing through the use of high technology. Parents and school board members will often be ready to help if they understand why networking is important.

School library media specialists proposing membership in a cluster should be aware that comingling funds is not always easy. In a cluster arrangement, one unit must assume fiscal responsibility for all members. School boards may be reluctant to agree to what they perceive as paying another school district, the public library, or an academic library for services. This arrangement is sometimes difficult to understand.

After joining a network, active participation provides opportunities for the school library media specialist to keep up-to-date. Network meetings and training sessions provide information concerning state-of-the-art equipment and services for members and permit interaction with librarians in other types of libraries.

Certainly school librarians will continue to provide such traditional materials as books, films, microcomputer word-processing programs, periodicals, online database access and even telefacsimile transmission. However, the quanity and quality of the information which can be provided to students and teachers is greatly increased when the school library media center is a member of a network and school patrons have ready access to a wide variety of sources outside the building.

It is up to school library media specialists to meet this challenge *today*. Horizons must be widened for *all* children. Students and teachers must have access to services through networks. School library media specialists will continue to provide all types of information in their centers, from picture books, films, word-processing programs, to online databases and telefacsimile transmission. But they must expand their resources. Third graders must learn to use magazine indexes and then to request missing articles online. This is networking. Sharing allows all children to have equal access to the world's knowledge, and it is the responsibility of each individual school library media specialist to help this happen.

When parents and teachers recognize that even the youngest child needs access to materials which may be beyond the ability of the local school or public library to provide, school library media specialists will remain a necessary component in all schools, small or large, elementary or high school, to help locate resources from other locations, be they in hard copy or online. When this happens, school library media specialists, opening the world of information to their users, will be present in all schools and will be actively contributing to "providing every individual in the United States with equal opportunity of access to that part of the total information resource."[12]

Exercises

1. Determine the network in your region, e.g., NELINET, SOLINET, PALINET, PRLC, OHIONET, etc. Ask for their information available to librarians wishing to join that network. If you were managing a school library media center with 25,000 items, what would it cost your school district to

   a. Join the network as a first year member
   b. Secure the hardware needed for use of the bibliographic utility
   c. Retrospectively convert the collection
   d. Add 600 titles to your collection for one year

2. Determine the costs for remaining a member of your network for subsequent years by determining the following:

   a. Annual membership of $____
   b. Cost of adding 600 titles to your collection
   c. Cost of interlibrary loan component anticipating 200 loans
   d. Cost of training
   e. Cost of attendance at annual meeting

Notes

[1] Melvil Dewey. "New Library Development of the National Education Association," *Public Libraries* 1 (September 1986): 185.

[2] C. C. Certain. *Standard Library Organization and Equipment for Secondary Schools: New York State Library: Library School Bulletin 45* (Albany, N.Y.: The University of the State of New York, 1920), 22.

[3] Task Force on the Role of the School Library Media Program in the National Program. *The Role of the School Library Media Program in Networking* (Washington, D.C.: National Commission on Libraries and Information Science, September 1978), 5.

[4] National Commission on Libraries and Information Science. *Toward a National Program for Library and Information Services: Goals for Action* (Washington, D.C.: U.S. Government Printing Office 1975), xi.

[5] See note 3 above.

[6] National Commission on Libraries and Information Science, 82-83.

[7] Blanche Woolls. "Optimum Configurations and a Proposed Package for Schools and School Districts to Join OCLC: Final Report" (Unpublished report to OCLC, July 15, 1987).

[8] "High School Libraries: Expanding Information Through Automation: The Final Report" (Unpublished report to the State Library of Pennsylvania, April 1985).

[9] Ellen Altman, "The Resource Capacity of Public Secondary School Libraries to Support Interlibrary Loan: A Systems Approach to Title Diversity," Ph.D. diss., Rutgers University, 1971.

[10]Carol A. Doll. "A Study of Overlap and Duplication Among Children's Collections in Selected Public and Elementary School Libraries," *Library Quarterly* 54 (July 1984): 277-89.

[11]"Lasting Benefits for Libraries: The Final Report of the Commissioner of Education Gordon M. Ambach to the New York State Legislature on the Library Pilot Projects" (Albany, N.Y.: The University of the State of New York, The State Education Department, The New York State Library, 1985), 48.

[12]National Commission on Libraries and Information Science, p. xi.

12 Leadership and Professional Associations

> "The time has come," the Woollsrus said,
> "To talk of many things:
> Of shoes—and ships—and sealing-wax—
> Of cabbages—and kings."

With apologies to Lewis Carroll, the time has come for all school library media specialists to step back from behind the looking glass and assume a leadership role in both their professions; educator and librarian. In the almost one-hundred-year history of professionals in school library media centers, it has seemed difficult at times for many media specialists to become leaders in either role. Difficulty occurs in the role of educator because

1. The first school librarians were more often part-time than full-time. That is, they were teachers in academic classrooms as well as librarians or responsible for two or more schools, and it was difficult to establish a power base.

2. School library media specialists were considered "specialists" rather than "regular" teachers.

3. The perception of the school library media specialist was one of a quiet, retiring person rather than a dynamic, aggressive program advocate.

Difficulty occurs in the role of library professional because

4. Media specialists have nine- or ten-month contracts and may be unavailable to meet with other professionals for two or three months each year.

5. Some media specialists, because of their undergraduate preparation in schools of education, are identified as educators rather than professional librarians.

6. Many professions, librarians included, consider members who work with youth rather than adults as somehow less likely to lead.

For these reasons, school library media specialists are working to change perceptions of their fellow educators and library professionals. They are accomplishing this by joining professional associations in both education and librarianship and working within them as capable, creative, confident members and leaders.

Education Associations

An exciting array of opportunities exist for the media specialist in a variety of education associations. At the national level, educators choose to belong to either the National Education Association (NEA) or the American Federation of Teachers (AFT). Both of these associations have state and local affiliates, and school media specialists may teach under contract to a local affiliate of NEA or AFT that acts as the bargaining unit. While local school districts may not be "closed shops," it is usually an uncomfortable situation for a media specialist to refuse to join with fellow teachers in the contract unit. Anger directed at the media specialist may extend into anger toward the media program.

When the school district has a local bargaining unit, membership in both the state and national association is required and automatic. Also, the teacher and media specialist cannot join only the national association, but must join their local and state associations as well. These teachers' associations offer media specialists the opportunity to attend local and state meetings and may give them the opportunity to become a delegate to the national association.

Media specialists who belong to their education association should work within that association to improve perceptions of the media program. Teachers, especially at the elementary level, often feel that the media center is their "free" period. The author is aware of one situation where a grievance was filed against the media specialist because this person was not assigned lunchroom duty. Helping teachers understand the importance of having the media center open for students throughout the day is part of the role of the media specialist.

It is also very important that at least one library media specialist be a member of the contract unit's negotiating team. In this way, library media specialists, representing the needs of the media center, can be kept a part of the bargaining team. When library media specialists neglect this important opportunity, it is possible that they may be moved into a special category, apart from the teaching staff. When this happens, additional time may be assigned to the media specialist role. For example, in one state, it was ruled that, since library media specialists did not have student work to take home to grade, they were expected to report to school thirty minutes earlier and stay thirty minutes later than classroom teachers.

School library media specialists with interests in specific subject areas may join the relevant associations to help keep the library media center visible to other educators. Special subject associations include the National Council of Teachers of English, the International Reading Association, and others. Choosing to become active in the Association for Supervision and Curriculum Development will bring library media specialists in direct contact with principals and curriculum directors in school districts.

Library and Media Associations

Library media specialists who wish to join with other librarians may be able to participate in a local association, which is usually a very informal group of librarians. In the Pittsburgh area, the Council of Suburban School Librarians has two meetings each year. These meal functions feature a children's book author and are sometimes preceded or followed by workshop sessions. They provide an opportunity for school librarians to meet and discuss their local situations with others in the immediate area. Membership is quite inexpensive, and the time required to participate is minimal, except perhaps for the officers.

Some states have two media-related associations while others have only one. Annual conferences provide workshops, speakers, exhibits, and communiction with other library media specialists. The success of a state association is in direct relation to the willingness of members to volunteer their services, because few state associations have sufficient income to maintain paid office staff. Participation in the state association provides an excellent opportunity to build leadership skills. At this level it is often very easy to become active in committee work and to offer presentations at the annual meeting.

One national body, the Association for Educational Communications and Technology (AECT), provides members with a journal, a newsletter, and the opportunity to attend a yearly conference. AECT is governed by a president, who is elected yearly by mailed national ballot, an executive board, and a council. Presidents of divisions and affiliate representatives from state associations serve on the AECT Council.

AECT offers many opportunities for members to write articles for publication in *Tech Trends* and to make presentations at the annual meeting. Exhibits for this association specialize in audiovisual media and equipment. Many state library/media associations are affiliates of AECT.

A second national association for school library media specialists is the American Association of School Librarians (AASL). AASL is a division of the parent association, the American Library Association (ALA), and members of AASL receive the benefits of ALA, including a lobbying effort in Washington, D.C. Two meetings are held each year, a midwinter conference and an annual conference. The midwinter session is for members of the boards of directors of divisions and both ALA and division committees. Many exhibitors provide new items for participants to consider for purchase.

The Annual Conference is a much larger experience. It offers not only meetings of boards and committees, but also speakers, preconference workshops, the Newbery/Caldecott dinner, and a vast array of exhibits. A number of meetings of library-related groups are held at the same time, such as the membership meeting for Beta Phi Mu, International Library Science Honor Society.

The American Association of School Librarians is governed by an Executive Board made up of the past president, the president, the recording secretary, the president-elect, and the executive director, ex officio. In addition to the executive board, a board of directors is elected by the membership and by other sections within the association.

A wide variety of committees exist for AASL members. These include the Standards Committee, whose members work to develop standards for library media centers, and the Evaluation of School Library Media Centers Committee, whose members study methods for the effective evaluation of media center staff, facilities, and services. The AASL Editorial Advisory Committee reviews the publication of the association journal, *School Library Media Quarterly*. The AASL also provides national conferences at three-year intervals and maintains relations with state associations through its Affiliate Assembly. The Affiliate Assembly is made up of officers from state associations. These state associations may affiliate with AASL only if its president is a member of AASL.

Certainly, more opportunities for association membership exist than school library media specialists can hope to take advantage of. Nevertheless, choosing as many as possible and participating actively is essential to the effectiveness of the school library media specialist and the profession. Membership in an association provides library media specialists with an opportunity to join forces with peers and to lobby for the continuation and expansion of school library media programs at the local, state, and national levels.

School Library Media Specialists and the Political Process

School library media specialists are becoming aware of and effective in the political process. That school library media specialists are a public good is a fact that has not been universally acknowledged in the past or present. It will happen only when effective methods are used to bring the status of media centers into the public view. One method of doing this is for media specialists to learn how to sell a program, to lobby.

For some school library media specialists, the word *lobby* may seem threatening, or beneath or above the abilities of a building-level person. Lobbying is the process of making opinions heard and getting ideas to decision makers. It is collecting appropriate information and using it for advocacy. Finally, it can result in influencing legislation. Library media specialists need not begin trying to change federal laws. There are many persons who should be made aware of the media center programs, and it is much easier and more obviously effective to begin at home.

Lobbying can begin at the local school building as the library media specialist presents the needs of the media program to teachers and the principal. Efforts can be expanded when the library media program is brought to the attention of the school board. Suggestions for beginning this process are covered in chapter 9 on marketing. A wider audience is needed to secure the consideration of state-level funding agencies and legislators. Finally, attention can be drawn to school library media centers at the national level. When library media specialists begin to meet "players" in the state and national arena, they are meeting legislators and legislative aides.

Articles, books, and pamphlets are available from a variety of sources to help understand the lobbying process. A pamphlet distributed by the ALA Washington office, "Who Me? A Lobbyist?," suggests getting to know your legislators. These men and women are interested in hearing from their constituents; they often do not understand the issues involved in particular pieces of legislation and welcome information. Another source of help in communicating with a legislator is a single sheet distributed by the ALA Washington office, "How to Write a Letter to Your Legislator" (see appendix J).

State and national associations often support Legislation Days where members of the association go to the capitol to call on legislators; this can be very effective. However, school library media specialists often cannot be away from their schools on these days. That does not mean that they cannot be effective as lobbyists. Indeed, it may be even more effective to meet legislators at their local office. The addresses of local offices of both state and national legislators is readily available in local telephone directories.

The ALA Washington office has also published "Five Basic Rules for Effective Communication." These include:

1. Be Brief. A legislator's time is limited. So is yours.

2. Be Appreciative. Acknowledge past support, and convey thanks for current action.

3. Be Specific. Refer to local library and district needs.

4. Be Informative. Give reasons why a measure should be supported.

5. Be Courteous. Ask; do not demand or threaten. Be positive but polite.

Legislators most often hear from their constituents when they want something. It is well to establish communication with legislators and their office staff before a crisis arises. Then, a visit "in time of need" may seem less harassing for all parties. Again, remember that legislators need information from their constituents to better understand issues. Becoming a reliable information provider should convince your legislator that library media specialists are friends of lawmakers, there to help them understand the educational needs of students.

Sometimes the library media specialist must move to block proposed legislation. Professional associations usually have a legislative network in place to notify members when it is necessary to visit legislators, write letters, or make telephone calls against, as well as for, a bill.

For the library media specialist who becomes totally immersed in local, state, and national politics, some golden rules exist.

1. Give legislators carefully researched and correct information. To tell a state legislator that the average per-pupil expenditure for media materials in a state is a very low figure only to have incorrect information contradicted will be embarrassing to everyone, perhaps critically so to the legislator.

2. Follow legislation of interest to school library media specialists from introduction through signature. Carefully choose legislators to support the issue. Learn to gather support from news media, local newspapers and television, as well as lawmakers.

3. Follow up with legislators after the legislation has been passed, and thank supporters. Also thank legislators who vote against an unwelcome bill.

4. Learn to write letters to lawmakers, and then write them. The image of library media programs must be a positive one, and lobbying will help create a positive image of library media specialists and their programs.

Exercises

1. Review the charges to AASL committees found in the *ALA Handbook of Organization*. Compose a letter to the president-elect of AASL (who will make new appointments) volunteering to serve on the committee of your choice. Be sure to state your qualifications for this committee as well as your desire to serve.

2. Compose a letter to a state legislator requesting support for an increase in the per-pupil allocation for school library media materials. You may wish to use statistics concerning the rising costs of media materials from the *Bowker Annual* to support your position.

13 Managing School Library Media Centers in the Twenty-first Century

Focus on Curriculum: Responsibilities to Students

In the nearly 100-year spectrum of school librarianship in the United States, the relationship of the library media specialist to the curriculum and to students has been greatly affected by the way teachers teach. In the last sixty years, many changes have taken place, and these changes have affected the barometer of the relationship of the school library (now library media center) to teachers, students, and curriculum. One measure of the focus on curriculum and responsibility of the library media specialist to students might be reflected in the number of students who can be seated in the media center. This is calculated as the proportion of the media center used for seating students as compared with the proportion of the center used for other purposes.

The school library began as a stack of books, often on the corner of the teacher's desk, placed in the classroom to encourage reading. The practice of reading took precedence over the use of the books for any learning. Reading was an end unto itself, and books were not used even for the teaching of reading. Reading texts, beginning with the Murray readers in the nineteenth century, did contain some passages from literary works, but by the 1930s, reading texts were created by reading specialists and their contents reflected "run, Dick, run" rather than stories from leisure reading tales written by children's book authors.

In the 1930s, few elementary school administrators or teachers conceived of the possibility of a library in an elementary school. At the secondary level, which usually housed grades seven through twelve, many school libraries were located at the back of the study hall, and the proportion of seating to materials was probably 90 percent seating and 10 percent materials. The limited shelving adequately housed the limited number of leisure reading books placed in the library for use by students in their spare time. The major teaching method was lecture by an all-knowing instructor, with assignments and tests reflecting the chosen textbook. The school librarian taught (most often English) when she (and it was mostly shes) was not on study hall duty. Little if any time could be allocated to encourage the use of supplementary materials, except during the unit the eleventh grade students were writing their term papers. Certainly little effort could be placed on developing lifelong library habits among students.

That school librarian dreaming of the library of the future would have longed for a private room, many more books, and a library teaching and management role without the distraction of study hall and classroom teaching responsibilities. The librarian actually had little responsibility to help students learn how to use a library.

Thirty years later, in the middle 1960s, federal funds poured into school districts. Administrators hired coordinators to renovate classrooms into elementary school libraries. Librarians in junior high schools, which were fast becoming middle schools, enlarged their facilities; and high schools added media to the existing book collections. The proportion of seating to the materials dropped to 50 percent seating capacity, 50 percent other use of available spaces. Librarians, and they were still school librarians in the 1960s, became responsible providers of materials to supplement the curriculum. They could now offer a wide variety of materials, both print and nonprint. Instructional design was introduced to teachers and librarians; but, the librarian was consultant TO rather than instructor WITH the teachers.

One idea for a media center of the future was described by Doris Young Kuhn in the late 1960s. She proposed an

underground school, air conditioned, well-lighted, with building units for 2,000 children ages four to twelve. A moving sidewalk took students to the central instructional materials center where he stepped off at a desk, gave a card to a librarian, and moved on to a comfortable reading area. In a few minutes he received the book created for him. He might choose to read in one of the carrels or return to his class living room. While he waited, a group of children entered a small viewing room. On the walls are projected pictures of a desert, the domed ceiling presented the vivid sky so realistically one can almost feel the desert heat as he heard the snort of a camel and moved toward the opening in the pyramid. As the pictures changed, the children descended into the tomb. Later, they examined pots, jewelry, papyrus scrolls— facsimiles to be sure, but they faced the question, How can we learn about the people who made these materials? Their study created the need for other films, recordings and books.[1]

She also suggested that a curator of a small museum, an audiovisual media librarian, and a more book-oriented librarian would staff this model center. The activities described were beginning to be perceived more as teaching activities, and the librarian as a teacher creating an environment of learning, facilitating discovery, and sharing in the excitement of learning. The librarian was becoming one who listened and encouraged, one who worked with the teacher rather than for the teacher.

Shortly before this author read the Kuhn article in 1967, she had moved to Roswell, New Mexico, a city with an underground school built as a bomb shelter. Roswell was the city with missile silos to protect the White Sands Missile Range and the Los Alamos laboratories. To get to and from Roswell travelers used Love Field in Dallas and rode along the moving sidewalks there.

Roswell used some ESEA Title III funds for an innovative project in which a planetarium was built onto the local museum, somewhat like the planetarium the author had visited in Chicago. The domed ceiling was not that unusual for students in Roswell or in the environs of Chicago. However, elementary schools in Roswell did not have professional librarians, and the possibility of combining the museum program with elementary teaching units seemed very exciting. In 1967 it appeared that, by 1990, these things should be available in most school districts where personnel were enjoying the euphoria of free-flowing funds from the federal government. It did not seem possible that these funds would dwindle in the 1970s. No one was predicting the pill and the resulting fallout; no one expected that the school that had grown to 2,000 elementary children would close because there were fewer than 200 children in the neighborhood.

In 1969 the American Association of School Librarians prepared new standards and renamed the person in charge of the school library. The library media specialist now maintained a media center. Media centers included television studios purchased with federal funds as well as expanded production centers for teachers and students to develop their own learning materials. Library media specialists continued to offer technical assistance by beginning to help plan curriculum, to work with teachers, and to help teach students.

It is now nearing the third decade of this 30-year cycle which began in 1960, and the reduction in support for schools and the consequent reduction in support for school library media programs seems to be halting. School enrollments are increasing from the public school enrollment which dropped between 1971 and 1981 by 5.9 million students or 5.9 percent. In the District of Columbia this decrease was 33 percent. The economy seems to be improving, and it is hoped that funds for education will increase. This may mean that, in less than ten years, school library media centers will reach to an expected 25 percent seating and 75 percent for other uses.

Laser-disk and CD-ROM technology will revolutionize all information services. Encyclopedias are available on CD-ROM, and the accompanying hardware is not as expensive as a complete set of book-format encyclopedias.

Picture a school library media center serving any number of students. The enrollment will make little, if any, difference. The 25 percent seating provided will be comfortable chairs for recreational reading and relaxing. Students will unlikely need library tables or carrels and chairs at which to work. They will bring no notebooks or pencils with them. Rather, they will want a larger surface equipped with new technologies. More about that in a moment.

Another 25 percent of this center will store materials in "concrete" form. This will be the housing for books, filmstrips, films, tapes, periodicals, pamphlets, and microforms. The third 25 percent of the space will be used for the production of learning materials, the television studio, the darkroom, the tape-duplicating equipment, the off-air recording devices, and the laser-disk production department.

The final 25 percent will be the surfaces for fluid information transfer. Fluid information is information that is ever-changing, the information that flows over communictions lines from a digital location fifty feet to 5,000 miles away. This part of the media center will have the communication and computer devices, the laser-disk readers, the capability to retrieve from tape storage. Students entering the media center will select an online database to locate the information needed. If the periodicals are available in the media center, they will be carried to the work area. If not, a telefacsimile will be requested from the nearest library with the periodical in its holdings. A lap-held microcomputer will be used to record notes from films and filmstrips while they are being viewed.

Appropriate printed material and the recently transmitted telefacsimile will be taken to the work area where the student will place a disk into a microcomputer and begin to create the report with a word-processing program. Some material may already be on the disk because the student spent the previous evening in the nearby public or academic library getting a head start on the project. If, during the time in the media center, students need additional information, they will go to the laser-disk reader and locate the material wherever it is in the United States. Back to the work area, the material can be requested through electronic mail to the holding libraries. If material is needed but cannot be found in existing records, an electronic mail request can be placed to locate information from all persons with electronic mail addresses.

What has this to do with curriculum and students at this time? It has everything to do with the way they perceive their information-seeking role and how they anticipate preparing for 2001. Present and potential school library media specialists must encourage their professional associations to work with state departments of education to implement a library curriculum that includes online training for students. Pennsylvania has published an online curriculum for students, and both state and federal funds have been used to develop online training sites in elementary, middle, and high schools. Many state departments have published curriculum sequences for integrating library media skills into the curriculum. The need to revise such skills sequences regularly makes it imperative that any publication be in a format for easy addition and deletion as methods and skills change.

School library media specialists should plan to attend workshops and learn new technologies. They should then share what they have learned with their colleagues. Planning and presenting inservice for teachers and students in these technologies will be necessary if they are to be accepted, learned, and used.

Costs for new technologies present a challenge for the school library media specialist. However, in preparing budgets, many complain about the per-pupil allocation which does not cover the cost of one new book per child per year. Rather, budgets should be developed to include the needed technologies. Too many are trying to sell administrators on "ho-hum" changes or additions when they should be developing a request for the $100,000 funding that may be necessary to move students and teachers into the new information sources.

The role of the library media specialist in the immediate future becomes even more interwoven with that of the other teachers as they learn to depend upon the technical expertise of the library media specialist. The media specialist will understand the use of the more traditional holdings as well as the realm of electronic media to teach units of instruction. Teachers will continue to send students to the media center to be taught how to retrieve information which may be found in that familiar area, the 25 percent devoted to concrete information. They will also want their students to be competent users of fluid information. Library media specialists are teaching students to conduct searches, to choose descriptors, to analyze the documents retrieved, and to decide what information to place in their research reports. Library media specialists will help everyone adjust to the world full of electronically published information.

Electronic publishing may generate a little less enthusiasm because the real reader likes to read books in bed and in the bathtub. However, the speed with which information can be transmitted is exciting, and the storage capacity of information on optical disk is mind-boggling. There will be other, dynamic, exciting innovations to learn about, share with teachers, and transmit to students. This will help the school library media specialist be prepared, in 2020, to manage a library media center which may be, at best, 10 percent seating and 90 percent other items.

Present Problems Overcome

School library media specialists in the late 1980s may have perception problems, and these problems may not be theirs, but others. An example used earlier was one in which the library media specialist had a grievance filed against her because she did not have lunch duty. Teachers, in this instance, considered the role of the library media specialist one of teaching; teachers had lunch duty, so should the library media specialist. No consideration was given to the educational use of the media center over the lunch period. Another example given was of a state in which teacher certification was not required for the library media specialist, only library courses. This state lengthened the hours in the school day for library media specialists.

One remedy to the perception of the school library media specialist has to do with power. The assumption is that knowledge is power, and that the library media specialist has knowledge therefore power. Some suggestions for assuming a power role and overcoming present problems are:

1. The deluge of information is unmanageable for school library media specialists. Imagine how this avalanche of knowledge must appear to teachers and students. Take an aggressive stance on finding information outside the media center. Be their expert.

2. Do not give "library lessons!" Build research skills into the nooks and crannies of the classroom. Help students learn that all libraries provide information. If the information is not available in the school library media center, a telephone call or an online request can have it sent from another location. The library media specialist will *find it for them!* A power move.

3. Show the school users online retrieval. It is magic they will enjoy watching someone else accomplish. Then, when the media specialist is too busy to do a search, students and teachers will have their curiosity piqued and demand to know how to search.

4. Spend time with teachers planning and deciding what students must learn and the best methods to employ in this process. Assume some of the responsibility for the actual teacher. Be delighted when a mandated curriculum thrusts the media specialist back into a lost teaching role. When too little time is available to teach all students research skills, *link* with teachers encouraging them to help with skills instruction. In exchange, agree to help analyze the quality of research used by students in preparing their papers.

5. Treat new rules and regulations as a challenge to be met, a life preserver rather than a burden, a concept to be tried rather than something to fight. Mandated activities assigned to the media specialist as teacher can save positions, because teaching is not a task for a volunteer or a clerk. Help the teacher teach research "library" skills.

6. Help students by providing a viable program, with new materials purchased *for* the curriculum, not *for* the collection.

7. Continue in the curriculum support role while striving for the development of resource-based teaching units. Obviously one- or two-person library media centers cannot work with *all* teachers on *every* unit. Pick a percentage of the teachers with whom to develop resource-based units each year. Not all units spring newborn every year. Choose to plan three new units and to review and expand three repeat units each semester while continuing your support for the other teachers. It will become apparent to those teachers who are left out that they and their students are being deprived. They will become more interested in having help from the media center in preparing their own integrated resource-based units.

8. It will be difficult to have time for lunch duty if an online search is underway for the principal or for another teacher or for students in the media center.

9. Constantly reevaluate the tasks and services of the media center. Burnout is really burning up energy with the nonessential. Nonessential tasks are seldom understood and rarely rewarded by others. They are often tasks such as inventory, the importance of which teachers do not understand. Remove all activities that do not actively support the curriculum, those tasks that are not essential to the functioning of the school or media center.

10. The library media center is that place in the school where no child need fail. The library media specialist is the magician who provides the best information for every teacher and every child in the school. It is *the* place in the school that touches all children. When someone asks, "What have you done to affect the life of a child today," what will you answer?

Notes

¹Doris Young Kuhn. "The School Librarian—Catalyst for Learning," *School Libraries* 17 (Winter 1968): 9.

Appendix A
Pennsylvania and Ohio
Required Programs

Expected Competencies
Library Science
Section B

The candidate shall demonstrate the competency to:

- Integrate library media curriculum that develops information management skills and processes.

- Demonstrate in the skills that comprise the library media curriculum.

- Utilize current pedagogical techniques (methodology).

- Apply a variety of classroom management techniques (discipline).

- Recognize individual differences in students and accommodate varying learning styles.

- Develop lesson plans.

- Develop, jointly with classroom teachers, a comprehensive plan of school library media instruction to include identification of goals, specification of objectives, design of activities, identification of resources, and development of assessment techniques.

- Develop a comprehensive plan of school library media instruction to include, but not be limited to the following general categories:

  - media production
  - literacy appreciation
  - technological access to information
  - reading/listening/viewing guidance
  - location of resources
  - selection of resources
  - evaluation of resources
  - synthesis of resources

- Apply collection development principles to achieve and maintain a collection of resources and equipment to respond to the curricular objectives of the educational programs to reflect readability levels and selection principles.

- Recognize and apply the principles of intellectual freedom to address censorship challenges.

- Develop search strategies and conduct on-line searches to meet specific information needs.

- Identify appropriate reference sources of information and the processes necessary to access them, including but not limited to electronic data bases, networking systems and community resources.

- Assist teachers and administrators in research procedures.

- Plan and utilize time effectively to administer a total school library program.

- Apply group and interpersonal skills in working with the total school community.

- Demonstrate the ability to cope with change.

- Market services and resources to school and community.

- Conduct ongoing evaluation of the school library program.

- Perform technical processing, operations, including acquisition, classifying, cataloging, processing, filing and circulation.

- Formulate procedures and policies to ensure the effective operation of a school library program.

- Develop and expend a budget reflecting sources of funding and program needs.

- Implement a schedule to meet program needs.

- Plan a new or existing facility which permits achievements of program goals.

- Use technology as a library management tool.

- Assign appropriate duties and manage library staff to ensure the implementation of the school library program.

- Develop a working knowledge of all laws and regulations which affect school library media programs.

- Develop program goals which reflect community values and the school program.

- Conduct appropriate staff development sessions for teachers and administrators.

- Apply general principles of educational supervision.

- Participate in local, regional, state and national professional organizations.

- Engage in self-evaluation to identify the areas of need for continuing education and professional growth.

Academic and Professional Preparation
Library Science
Section C

I. The candidate shall successfully complete:

A. Indepth academic preparation in the following areas:

Teaching Methodology
Administration of School Library Programs
Reference Sources and Processes
Classification and Cataloging Principles
Technological Applications for School Library Programs
Materials and Equipment Selection, Evaluation and Utilization

K-12

Materials Production
Practicum (Student Teaching—Elementary and Secondary Programs)

B. Academic preparation beyond the introductory/survey levels in the following areas:

Communication Skills
Child Development
Interpersonal and Group Relationships
Tests and Measurements
Classroom Management (Discipline)
Curriculum Design (K-12)
Storytelling
Learning Styles
(Field Experiences should be included in appropriate courses)

C. Academic preparation at the introductory/survey levels in the following areas:

School Finances (grants, funding, proposal writing)
School Law
Reading
Problem Solving and Decision Making
Field Experiences shall be included in appropriate courses

II. The candidate shall successfully complete:

A. Indepth professional preparation in the following areas:

- How to manage classroom instruction
- How to plan a lesson
- How to organize a course and a curriculum
- How to give an explanation
- How to arouse student interest
- How to give helpful correction and feedback
- How to avoid unfair biases in interacting with students
- How to increase the proportion of academic engaged learning time during a school day
- Human development and learning and its implications for classroom instruction
- How to teach developmental reading and reading in the content area
- Student teaching that is based on the preceding items

B. Professional preparation beyond the introductory/survey levels in the following areas:

- Psychology and learning theories
- Methods and materials for specific area of certification
- Curriculum analyses
- Curriculum development
- Assessment and measurement of student achievement
- Standardized tests—how to interpret and use data for instructional planning
- Grading and reporting student achievement
- How to use district, IU and state special services for students with personal, social, academic problems.
- How to use technological advances as a teaching tool
- State and federal laws that affect teachers, students and schools
- Field experiences in classrooms

C. Professional preparation at the introductory/survey levels in the following areas:

- School organization
- Philosophy and foundations of education
- Social and cultural aspects of the public school
- Sociology with emphasis on community and the school

Minimum Standards Leadership Series 1985
Ohio Department of Education
Quality Library Services K-12

Personnel

School Librarian — responsible for administering the school library and providing leadership in curriculum support to students and teachers. The librarian's teaching skills should be complemented with skills in technical production. In buildings where more than one librarian is employed, it is recommended that a head librarian be designated to ensure coordinated management.

    Educational Qualifications
        Bachelor's degree
        Appropriate Ohio certification

Responsibilities might include the following:

— Administrative

- Demonstrate effective interpersonal relations with students, teachers, administrators, other school library specialists, and the community

- Apply principles of effective communications which reinforce positive behaviors in children and young adults

- Evaluate the library program for compliance with the Minimum Standards for Elementary and Secondary Schools

- Establish regular evaluations of the library program based on the district library plan

- Establish and administer a building library plan

- Establish policies and procedures for effective utilization of materials, resources, and staff

- Develop, justify, administer, and evaluate a budget for the school library program

- Maintain records of expenditures

- Make recommendations in hiring personnel and recruiting volunteers

- Supervise and schedule staff and volunteers

- Conduct staff development programs demonstrating an understanding of the adult learner for volunteers, staff, and administrators

- Arrange the library to support a variety of learning activities

- Create an atmosphere conducive to learning

- Maintain positive public relations through announcements, brochures, and newspaper publicity

- Supply current statistical data and reports to the library supervisor and other administrators

- Cooperate with other school and local library personnel and organizations

- Participate in professional association

- Plan for personal and professional growth and career development

—Instructional/Curricular

- Exhibit an understanding of curriculum developments through active participation on curriculum committees

- Become familiar with courses of study

- Provide students and staff with services, media, and equipment needed to support courses of study

- Converse with students to determine interests

- Survey faculty and students to determine needed resources

- Evaluate and select media in cooperation with students and staff

- Plan, instruct, and evaluate a comprehensive library skills program to help students develop basic information gathering and research skills

- Prepare individual or group instruction in library skills, media production, and the use of audiovisual equipment

- Teach students responsibility in the care of materials, equipment, and environment

- Develop programs to motivate the acquisition of reading, listening, viewing, communication, and inquiry skills

- Provide reading guidance and assist in referrals

- Provide reference services for students and staff

- Plan with individual teachers to integrate media into instructional experiences

- Attend faculty and department meetings

- Serve on committees

- Collaborate with teachers on special projects

- Introduce and publicize media of special interest

- Apply principles of research to improve the library program

—Informational

- Promote professional reading for staff

- Read and scan professional journals

- Route materials of interest to staff members

- Select and organize materials for the professional collection

- Keep current with educational trends

- Identify existing information patterns and determine information needs in the school

- Demonstrate a strong commitment to the right of students and teachers to access information within the legal framework

- Demonstrate knowledge of and understanding of up-to-date print and online databases to meet the needs of students and teachers

- Develop special procedures which provide access to information not readily available, such as community resource files and special collections

- Identify and cooperate with other information agencies in networking arrangements to expand access to information for students and teachers

- Evaluate available and emerging information technologies and their application to school libraries

— Technical

- Acquire and organize materials

- Order, catalog, and classify media

- Supervise the physical preparation of materials

- Supervise check in, stamping, labeling, and filing

- Supervise the withdrawal of obsolete and damaged items including the adjustment of inventory records

- Direct assistants in charging and discharging materials, writing notices, counting, filing, and keeping circulation records

- Plan circulation policies and procedures

- Maintain records of materials ordered

- Keep circulation statistics

- Inventory materials regularly

- Compile records of library holdings for annual reports

— Other

- Perform other related library duties as assigned or needed

Appendix B
Pittsburgh and Kent State Programs

Courses Required in Competency-Based Program for
Pennsylvania School Library Teacher Certification

COURSE		CREDITS
LS 200	Organization of Information	3
LS 201	Librarianship and the Structure of Libraries	3
LS 202	Resources: Information Collection, Evaluation and Use	3
LS 203	Behavioral Perspectives for the Information Professions	3
LS 222	Materials for Children	3
LS 223	Materials for Young Adults	3
LS 225	School Media Center in the Educational Process	3
LS 258	Online Bibliographic Retrieval	3
LS 261	Applications of Microcomputer Software	3
LS 274	Introduction to Media Center Management	3
LS 278	Practicum in School Media Programs	3
ADM PS 258 or	Seminar on Inner City Education LS 215 Library Services to the Underserved	3
SP ED 200	Foundations of Special Education	3
TOTAL CREDITS		
		39

Notes concerning this program:

1. This program fulfills the requirements for the MLS degree, as well as for Pennsylvania School Library Teacher Certification.

2. Students who have demonstrated competency in areas covered by specific courses may have those courses waived as requirements.

3. In selecting courses in specific terms, students should keep in mind that LS 278 should be taken toward the end of the program. It may be spread over more than one term or session; but, except in unusual cases, should not be taken in the Summer Session. Students must spend full days at the practicum site.

February 1987

Kent State Program of Studies

School Libraries Concentration

General Rationale

The School Libraries Concentration is offered as a Joint Certification Program with the Educational Technology program of the Department of Educational Psychology Administration, Technology and Foundations of the College of Education.

Requirements of this concentration significantly exceed the minimum credit hour requirements for Educational Media set by the Ohio Department of Education.

The purpose of this concentration is to provide students with the competencies and knowledge base needed to serve as librarians in school settings — elementary through high school.

Requirements

Requirements for each of the three options vary slightly based upon the type of certification students desire: (1) Elementary (K-8); (2) Secondary (7-12); or (3) Comprehensive (K-12).

A. Elementary (K-8) Option Requirements

1. Selection of Educational Media, Effective Utilization, & Production

LSCI	60614	Sel. & Acq. of Lib. Mats.	3 sem. hrs.
C&I	57400	Sel. & Utiliz. of Ed. Media	2 sem. hrs.
C&I	57401	Design & Prod. of Ed. Media	3 sem. hrs.
C&I	57403	Instructional Design	3 sem. hrs.
C&I	64795	Intro. to Microcomputers in Ed.	3 sem. hrs.

Total Requirements in Sel./Utilization/Production: 14 sem. hrs.

2. Bibliography, Including Children's Literature

Choose *one* of the following:

LSCI	60629	Lib. Mats. & Services for Children	3 sem. hrs.
C&I	67315/	Survey of Children's Literature	3 sem. hrs.
ENG	61051		
C&I	67316/	Criticism of Children's Literature	3 sem. hrs.
ENG	61052		

Total Requirements in Bibliography: 3 sem. hrs.

3. Reference Tools

LSCI	60601	Information Sources & Services	3 sem. hrs.

Total Requirements in Reference Tools: 3 sem. hrs.

4. Cataloging & Classification

LCI	60602	Organization of Lib. Materials	3 sem. hrs.

Total Requirements in Cataloging & Classification: 3 sem. hrs.

5. Organization, Administration & Utilization of the Educational Media Center

C&I	67491	Seminar: Adoption & Diffusion of Innovation	3 sem. hrs.

Choose *one* of the following:

LSCI	60607	The School Library	3 sem. hrs.
C&I	57402	Organization & Administration of Educational Media Programs	3 sem. hrs.

Total Requirements in Organization & Administration: 6 sem. hrs.

6. Other Library Science Requirements

LSCI	60600	Foundations of Librarianship	3 sem. hrs.
LSCI	60604	Intro. to Lib. Sc. Research Methods	3 sem. hrs.

Total Requirements of Other Lib. Sci. Courses: 6 sem. hrs.

Total Hours Required in Elementary Option: 35 sem. hrs.

Total Hours Required for MLS Degree: 36 sem. hrs.

B. Secondary (7-12) Option Requirements

1. Selection of Educational Media, Effective Utilization, & Production

LSCI	60614	Sel. & Acq. of Lib. Mats	3 sem. hrs.
C&I	57400	Sel. & Utiliz. of Ed. Media	2 sem. hrs.
C&I	57401	Design & Prod. of Ed. Media	3 sem. hrs.
C&I	57403	Instructional Design	3 sem. hrs.
C&I	67495	Intro. to Microcomputers in Ed.	3 sem. hrs.

Total Requirements in Sel./Utilization/Production: 14 sem. hrs.

2. Bibliography, Including Children's Literature & Adult Literature Suitable to the Middle & High School

LSCI	60625	Lib. Materials & Services for Adolescents	3 sem. hrs.

Total Requirements in Bibliography: 3 sem. hrs.

3. Reference Tools

LSCI	60601	Information Sources & Services	3 sem. hrs.

Total Requirements in Reference Tools: 3 sem. hrs.

4. Cataloging and Classification

LSCI	60602	Organization of Lib. Materials	3 sem. hrs.

Total Requirements in Cataloging & Classification: 3 sem. hrs.

5. Organization, Administration & Utilization of the Educational Media Center

C&I	67491	Seminar: Adoption & Diffusion of Innovation	3 sem. hrs.

Choose *one* of the following:

LSCI	60607	The School Library	3 sem. hrs.
C&I	57402	Organization & Administration of Educational Media Programs	3 sem. hrs.

Total Requirements in Organization & Administration: 6 sem. hrs.

6. Other Library Science Requirements

LSCI	60600	Foundations of Librarianship	3 sem. hrs.
LSCI	60604	Intro. to Lib. Sci. Research Methods	3 sem. hrs.

Total Requirements of Other Lib. Sci. Courses: 6 sem. hrs.

Total Hours Required in Secondary Option: 36 sem. hrs.

Total Hours Required for MLS Degree: 36 sem. hrs.

C. Comprehensive (K-12) Option Requirements

1. Selection of Educational Media, Effective Utilization, & Production

LSCI	60614	Sel. & Acq. of Lib. Mats.	3 sem. hrs.
C&I	57400	Sel. & Utiliz. of Ed. Media	2 sem. hrs.
C&I	57401	Design & Prod. of Ed. Media	3 sem. hrs.
C&I	57403	Instructional Design	3 sem. hrs.
C&I	67495	Intro. to Microcomputers in Ed.	3 sem. hrs.

Total Requirements in Sel./Utilization/Production: 14 sem. hrs.

2. Bibliography, Including Children's Literature & Adult Literature Suitable to the Elementary, Middle & High School

LSCI	60626	Lib. Mats. & Services for Adolescents	3 sem. hrs.

Choose *one* of the following:

LSCI	60629	Lib. Mats. & Services for Children	3 sem. hrs.
C&I ENG	67315/ 61051	Survey of Children's Literature	3 sem. hrs.
C&I ENG	67316/ 61052	Criticism of Children's Literature	3 sem. hrs.

Total Requirements in Bibliography: 6 sem. hrs.

3. Reference Tools

LSCI   60601   Information Sources & Services   3 sem. hrs.

Total Requirements in Reference Tools: 3 sem. hrs.

4. Cataloging & Classification

LSCI   60602   Organization of Lib. Materials   3 sem. hrs.

Total Requirements in Cataloging & Classification: 3 sem. hrs.

5. Organization, Administration & Utilization of the Educational Media Center

C&I   67491   Seminar: Adoption & Diffusion of Innovation   3 sem. hrs.

Choose *one* of the following:

LSCI   60607   The School Library   3 sem. hrs.
C&I   57402   Organization & Administration of Educational Media Programs   3 sem. hrs.

Total Requirements in Organization & Administration: 6 sem. hrs.

6. Practical Experience in an Educational Media Center as Part of the Student Teaching Experiences

Choose *one* of the following:

LSCI   60692   Practicum   2-3 sem. hrs.
C&I   67492   Advanced Practicum & Internship in Ed. Media   2-3 sem. hrs.

Total Requirements in Practical Experience: 2-3 sem. hrs.

7. Other Library Science Requirements

LSCI   60600   Foundations of Librarianship   3 sem. hrs.
LSCI   60604   Intro. to Lib. Sci. Research Methods   3 sem. hrs.

Total Requirements of Other Lib. Sci. Courses: 6 sem. hrs.

Total Hours Required in K-12 Option: 40-41 sem. hrs.

Total Hours Required for MLS Degree: 36 sem. hrs.

Appendix C
NASSP Checklist*

Circle correct response to each question	-1	0	1	2	3	4	5
1. How does the media center compare to others in the district?	do not have one	don't know	not as good as	almost as good as	as good as	better than	much better than
2. How many books per student are available in media center?	don't know	1 per student	3 per student	5 per student	10 per student	15 per student	more than 15
3. In general, the collection of books is	out of date	peripheral value	few recent titles, fair cond.	some recent titles, some relevant	mostly relevant, most in acceptable condition	mostly recent titles	recent titles relevant, in good condition
4. How many filmstrips per student are available in media center?	don't know	1 per student	2 per student	3 per student	4 per student	5 per student	more than 5
5. In general, the filmstrip collection is			(use same scale as for books)				
6. How many records/tapes per student are available in the media center?			(use same numbers as filmstrips)				
7. In general, the records/tape collection is		(use same scale as for books, filmstrips)					
8. The media collection is weeded (evaluated to discard out of date, etc.)	don't know	we never discard anything	rarely discard anything	occasionally	yearly	semi-yearly	constantly evaluate and discard
9. The media center is used for	discipline	study hall	entertainment	supplementary use	support of curriculum	extension of learning	integral part of learning
10. The media center is used by ___% of potential users	don't know	0-9	10-20	21-40	41-60	61-80	over 80
11. The media center collection is used by at least 50% of students	don't know	never	once a year	each semester	once a month	every two weeks	once a week
12. Students enjoy going to the media center	don't know	never	occasionally	some of the time	often	most of the time	always
13. The media center collection is used by at least 50% of the teachers	don't know	never	once a year	each semester	once a month	every two weeks	once a week
14. Teachers choose time for use of the media center based on instructional needs	never; rigid schedule	occasionally	when reminded	some of the time	often	most of the time	always
15. The media center is open before and after school	never	only for faculty	by special plans	either, or, not both	open both for some	heavy use at one time	heavy use both times
16. Students and teachers may produce learning materials in the media center	teachers	only 1 format	2 formats, quick & dirty	fair quality 3-4 formats	average 3-4 formats	above 5-6 formats	high quality 7-8 formats

*From Blanche Woolls, "Where Will Your Library Media Center Be in 1985?" *NASSP Bulletin* (April 1982): 76-77. Used by permission.

17.	The media center specialist may leave the media center	no, has study halls	don't know	only for lunch	sends classroom collections	visits classrooms occasionally	often visits classrooms	visits most classes each semester
18.	The media center specialist serves on curriculum committees	don't know	no such committee exists	sends suggestions	attempts to assist if asked	serves on one committee	serves on two committees	is an integral part of planning
19.	The media specialist and the principal have a 5-yr. plan for media center facilities, staff, collection, and services	don't know	no plan	principal speaks to specialist when passing	principal meets with specialist once/year to discuss program	specialist submits annual report during annual meeting	specialist keeps principal informed of needs	plan is provided by specialist and approved by principal
20.	The principal supports the media center	never	occasionally	whenever reminded	some of the time	often	most of the time	always
21.	The teachers support the media center program			(use	same scale	as 20)		
22.	The students support the media center			(use	same scale	as 20)		
23.	The media center has an impact on the school	never thought about it	don't know	perhaps	occasionally	often	most of the time	always

Appendix D
International Association of School Librarianship, "Joint Policy Statement on School Libraries"*

At the World Confederation of the Teaching Profession Assemblies in the late Sixties, delegates interested in school libraries met to discuss their common concerns. These meetings led, first to the creation of an ad hoc Committee of WCOTP, and then, in Jamaica in 1971, to the founding of the International Association of School Librarianship as an International Associate Member of WCOTP.

During 1980 and 1981 at the suggestion of John Thompson, the Association worked on the creation of a position paper on school libraries and resource centers. The draft paper was circulated to WCOTP member organizations for comment in August 1981. A revised draft was examined by the WCOTP Executive Committee in March 1982, and further comments were then offered to the IASL. In turn, IASL made additional changes.

The draft presented was, therefore, the result of a long process of discussion and exchange of viewpoints. The Executive Committee of WCOTP recommended its adoption as a statement of WCOTP policy at the 1984 Assembly of Delegates.

A Policy Statement on School Libraries

Principle 7 of the UN Declaration of the Rights of the Child states: "the child is entitled to receive education which shall be free and compulsory at least in the elementary stages. He shall be given an education which will promote his general culture, and enable him on a basis of equal opportunity to develop his abilities, his individual judgement, and his sense of moral and social responsibility, and to become a useful member of society."[1]

The existence and utilization of the school library media center is a vital part of this free and compulsory education to which the child is entitled. The school library media center is essential to "the development of the human personality as well as the spiritual, moral, social, cultural and economic progress of the community."[2]

The purpose of the school library media center is to aid in the fulfillment of the instructional goals and objectives of the school and to promote this through a planned program of acquisition and organization of information technology; and dissemination of materials to expand the learning environment of all students.

---

*Accepted by IASL Board of Directors, August 1983. Adopted by WCOTP XXX Assembly of Delegates Lome, Togo, August 1984.

The school library media center provides a wide range of resources, both print and audiovisual, and access to data which promotes an awareness of the child's own cultural heritage, enhances his knowledge of people different from his own and provides the basis for an understanding of the diversity of other cultures.

Functions

The school library media center functions as a vital instrument in the educational process, not as a separate entity isolated from the total school program but totally involved in the teaching and learning process. Its goals could be expressed through the following functions:

1. Informational

   a center for reliable information, rapid access, retrieval and transfer of information.

2. Educational

   promotion of continuous lifelong education through provision of the facilities and atmosphere for learning; guidance in selection and use of materials, training in information skills and promotion of intellectual freedom.

3. Cultural

   to improve the quality of life through the presentation and support of the aesthetic experience, guidance in appreciation of arts, encouragement of creativity and development, of positive human relations.

4. Recreational

   to support and enhance a balanced and enriched life and encourage meaningful use of leisure time through provision of recreational information, materials and programs of recreational value, and guidance in the use of leisure time.

Materials

"Appropriateness" implies:

(a) an awareness of the total range of information and communication technology;

(b) variety concerning many fields of knowledge and recreational activities;

(c) materials devised to serve children within the range of their cognitive, affective and psychomotor skills;

(d) appeal to children's interests;

(e) utilization of the student's primary language;

(f) reflection of the cultural interests valued by the children's families

(g) application to the economic environment.

Facilities

All school media centers from basic preschool through secondary level, need adequate space in which to exploit the technology available for preparation, processing and storage of all library materials, as well as space to enable students and teachers to utilize fully these materials through reading, viewing and listening skills. The plans should fit functionally into the general architectural design of the school, located near natural centers of traffic with easy accessibility to all users including the disabled and handicapped. Consideration might also be given to the use of the media center outside normal school hours. There is a need for flexibility and scope for future expansion and rearrangement of space and use with adequate provision of electrical outlets to allow this. Attention must be given to lighting, acoustical treatment of floors and ceilings, control of temperature and humidity and furniture and shelving suitable to the age of the users.

Personnel

Establishment of the school library media center requires that all persons who are affected by the use of it learn how it should be used effectively and efficiently. Administrators provide the leadership for such use. Preparation for these administrators, as for all teachers, should include information about the role of the school library media center in the learning process and in the planning and implementation of the teaching activities. The administrator should be aware of the specialist librarianship skills which the school librarian needs in addition to his/her professional training as a teacher, so that he/she can more effectively coordinate the role of the librarian in the school, including the preparation of the budget and arranging the school schedule so that students can make greater use of library materials and facilities.

This greater understanding of the librarian's role will enable the administrator to encourage teachers to work more closely with him [or her] in planning learning activities for the students; assisting the school librarian with the evaluation of the effectiveness of library media services and with plans for continually improving the materials, equipment and services offered by the school library media center so that it keeps pace with developments in information and communication technology.

The International Association of School Librarianship advocates that professional school library media specialists be qualified teachers who have, in addition, completed professional studies in librarianship. This type of preparation ensures that teachers receive assistance from professional personnel who have an understanding of the educational program and practices of the child's school. This assistance to teachers may concern: development of the curriculum, the educational activities offered by the school to the child, as well as daily and intermittant planning concerning the uses of materials, information technology and equipment for the child's education.

Lifelong Education, Skills, Literacy Development

The skills learned by the student through the school library media center provides the child with the means of adapting himself/herself to a wide variety of situations, enabling education to be continued throughout his/her life even in adverse conditions. The school library media center promotes literacy through development and encouragement of the reading habit. The reading habit is encouraged by the school library media center through the selection of appropriate and appealing reading materials, promotion of activities to attract students to use reading materials, encouragement of activities to help the child express recreational interests as well as to fulfill instructional assignments. Reading, viewing and listening activities all stimulate and reinforce the child's interest in the development of reading skills.

In addition, the student is provided with an insight into the full range of information and communication technology, as it is available to him or her; he/she is provided with instruction into the utilization of this technology so that he/she can locate and evaluate information to answer educational and recreational needs and interests, thus being able to construct visual, recorded and audio-visual messages as appropriate for purposes of communication. These skills promote lifelong learning. Acquiring these skills enables the child to continue independent learning even where his or her education is interrupted by natural disasters and social unrest.

In lesser developed countries, education systems should be encouraged to extend the learning environment beyond textbook and teacher into the school media center, rudimentary as it may be. This could well reduce the incidence of lapsed literates who swell the number of genuine illiterates, making government programs to eradicate illiteracy expensive and prolonged.

Government and Public Support

The establishment of good school library media services can demonstrate that public authorities are fulfilling their responsibilities to implement education which will enable children to become useful members of society.

The school library media center provides materials as sources of information for parents and social agencies to use in serving the needs of children in the home, pre-school, school, and after-school environments. The informational and recreational needs of girls as well as boys in both rural and urban areas are served.

For societies and public authorities endeavoring to promote the education of the child, one of the measurable achievements which can be observed is the provision of the tools for education where there were none or the improvement in the quality of the tools provided where formerly these were inadequate. Where education shall be free and compulsory, the need of the child for educational tools is greatest. The society that invests in tools for the child invests in its own future.

Notes

[1]Adopted unanimously by the General Assembly of the United Nations, November 20, 1959.

[2]Guiding Principle of the UNESCO/ILO Recommendation re the Status of Teachers.

Appendix E
Presentation of a Five-Year
Long-Range Plan for
Library Development to
Meet ALA Standards*

The following material is a demonstration of a method for preparing a plan to present to a principal or superintendent.

* * *

Introduction

This plan has been developed to meet the standards as described in *Media Programs: District and School* published by the American Library Association in 1975, and will be updated when the new standards are published in 1988.

Throughout the planning process it is assumed that the existing media program will be maintained and kept current. The current ongoing media center costs are approximately $30,000. As we come into compliance the ongoing costs will increase.

Funding for all improvements and maintenance have been assured by Dr. W_____, head of the program.

Comparison of AASL Standards
and Current Program

The following pages outlines the AASL standards and compares them to our current program, showing the items needed to comply with standards and the estimated costs.

*Developed by Marjorie Lovell at University of Pittsburgh, January-April 1986. Courtesy of Marjorie Lovell.

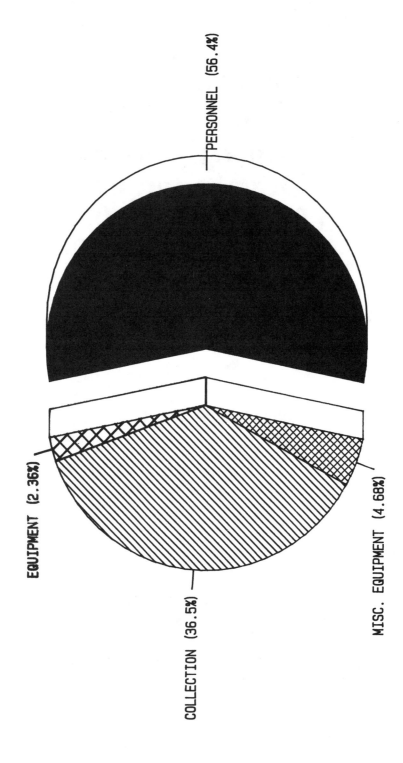

COMPLIANCE COST

PERSONNEL (56.4%)

EQUIPMENT (2.36%)

COLLECTION (36.5%)

MISC. EQUIPMENT (4.68%)

COMPARISON TO STANDARDS AND COMPLIANCE COST

	AASL STANDARDS	CURRENT PROGRAM	NEEDED TO MEET STANDARDS	ESTIMATED FIVE YEAR COMPLIANCE COST
PERSONNEL				
Head of Media	1	1 Librarian	1	$1,000
Media Professional	1	0	1	$72,000
Technician	1-2	0	1	$45,000
Media Aide	2-3	0	2	$60,000
Total Personnel Compliance Cost				$178,000

COMPARISON TO STANDARDS AND COMPLIANCE COST

COLLECTION	AASL STANDARDS	CURRENT PROGRAM	NEEDED TO MEET STANDARDS	ESTIMATED FIVE YEAR COMPLIANCE COST
Books	20000	11000	9000	$90,990
Periodicals	50-175	33	17	$207
Pamphlets	To meet local needs	2 File Drawers	0	$0
Microforms	Varies with program	0	0	$0
Filmstrips	500	375	125	$11,250
Slides and Transparencies	2000	1000	1000	$750
Graphics	800	1200	0	$0
16-mm Films	Access to 3000 titles	Access to over 3000	0	$0
Audio	1500	600	900	$9,000
Games and Toys	400	500	0	$0
Models and Sculpture	200	197	3	$600
Specimens	200	150	50	$2,500
Software	0	150	0	$0
Total Collection Compliance Cost				$115,297

COMPARISON TO STANDARDS AND COMPLIANCE COST

EQUIPMENT	AASL STANDARDS	CURRENT PROGRAM	NEEDED TO MEET STANDARDS	ESTIMATED FIVE YEAR COMPLIANCE COST
Microform	0	0	0	$0
Filmstrip				
Projectors	10	5	5	$1,500
Viewers	30	3	27	$1,350
Slide				
Projectors	5	3	2	$1,000
Viewers	10	2	8	$40
Overhead	1	1	0	$0
16-mm Sound Projection				
Projectors	6	4	2	$1,000
Video Playback	5	2	3	$1,200
Audio Recorders	15	15		
Reproduction Units	30	10	20	$800
Listening Units	21	3	18	$360
Radio	5	1	4	$200
Computers	0	16	0	$0
Total Equipment Compliance Cost				$7,450

COMPARISON TO STANDARDS AND COMPLIANCE COST

	AASL STANDARDS	CURRENT PROGRAM	NEEDED TO MEET STANDARDS	ESTIMATED FIVE YEAR COMPLIANCE COST
MISCELLANEOUS EQUIPMENT				
Opaque Projector	1	1	0	$0
Microprojector	1	0	1	$2,000
Auditorium Equipment				
Auditorium Overhead	1	0	1	$800
Auditorium Screen	1	1	0	$0
Auditorium 16-mm Projector	1	1	0	$0
Auditorium Slide Projector	1	1	0	$0
Projection Carts				
Motion Picture	6	4	2	$60
Overhead	10	3	7	$210
Opaque	1	1	0	$0
Video Tape	2	2	0	$0
Audio Recorder	30	0	30	$3,000
Projection Screens	30	20	10	$400
Television	0	2	0	$0
Copy Machines	2	1	1	$2,000
Duplication Machines	2	2	0	$0
Paper Cutters	1	1	0	$0
Transparency Makers				
Thermal Unit	1	0	1	$500
Photocopier	1	0	1	$800

COMPARISON TO STANDARDS AND COMPLIANCE COST

	AASL STANDARDS	CURRENT PROGRAM	NEEDED TO MEET STANDARDS	ESTIMATED FIVE YEAR COMPLIANCE COST
:MISCELLANEOUS EQUIPMENT CONT.				
:Typewriters for Graphic Production:	1	0	1	$5,000
:Cameras				
: Slide	1	1	0	$0
: Videotape Recorder	1	1	0	$0
: Videotape Camera	1	1	0	$0
:Film and Video Production	1			
: Film Splicers	1	1	0	$0
:Telephones				
: Inhouse	0	1	0	$0
: Outside Line	0	1	0	$0
:Bulletin Boards	0	1	0	$0
:Chalkboards	0	1	0	$0
: Total Misc. Compliance Cost				$14,770
:Total Compliance Cost				$315,517

Specific Five-Year Plan

In order to have the library come into compliance, as well as maintain its existing activity level, we have established a five-year plan.

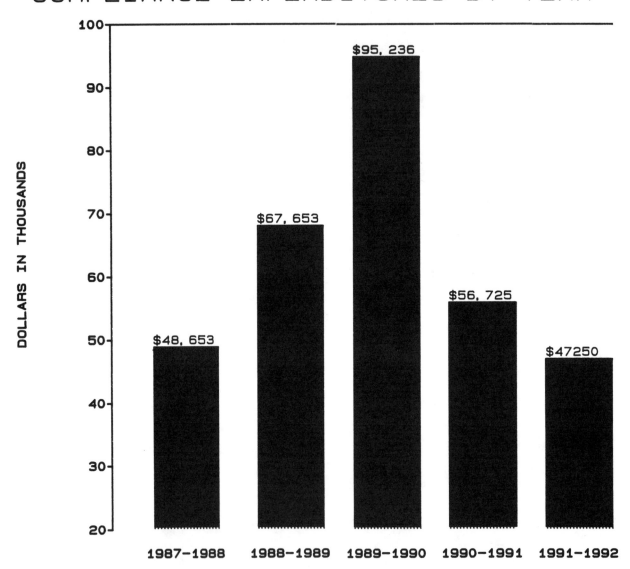

PROJECTED FIVE YEAR PLAN

	ESTIMATED FIVE YEAR COMPLIANCE COST	YEAR EXPENDITURE WILL BE MADE				
		1987-1988	1988-1989	1989-1990	1990-1991	1991-1992
PERSONNEL						
Head of Media	$1,000	$1,000				
Media Professional	$72,000		$18,000	$18,000	$18,000	$18,000
Technician	$45,000			$15,000	$15,000	$15,000
Media Aide	$60,000	$12,000	$12,000	$12,000	$12,000	$12,000
Total Personnel Compliance Cost	$178,000	$13,000	$30,000	$45,000	$45,000	$45,000

PROJECTED FIVE YEAR PLAN

COLLECTION	ESTIMATED FIVE YEAR COMPLIANCE COST	YEAR EXPENDITURE WILL BE MADE				
		1987-1988	1988-1989	1989-1990	1990-1991	1991-1992
Books	$90,990	$30,330	$30,330	$30,330		
Periodicals	$207	$73	$73	$61		
Pamphlets	$0					
Microforms	$0					
Filmstrips	$11,250	$2,250	$2,250	$2,250	$2,250	$2,250
Slides and Transparencies	$750			$375	$375	
Graphics	$0					
16-mm Films	$0					
Audio	$9,000	$3,000	$3,000	$3,000		
Games and Toys	$0					
Models and Sculpture	$600			$600		
Specimens	$2,500			$2,500		
Software	$0					
Total Collection Compliance Cost	$115,297	$35,653	$35,653	$39,116	$2,625	$2,250

PROJECTED FIVE YEAR PLAN

EQUIPMENT	ESTIMATED FIVE YEAR COMPLIANCE COST	YEAR EXPENDITURE WILL BE MADE				
		1987-1988	1988-1989	1989-1990	1990-1991	1991-1992
Microform	$0					
Filmstrip						
Projectors	$1,500			$1,500		
Viewers	$1,350			$1,350		
Slide						
Projectors	$1,000			$1,000		
Viewers	$40			$40		
Overhead	$0					
16-mm Sound Projection						
Projectors	$1,000			$1,000		
Video Playback	$1,200			$1,200		
Audio Recorders						
Reproduction Units	$800			$800		
Listening Units	$360			$360		
Radio	$200			$200		
Computers	$0					
Total Equipment Compliance Cost	$7,450	$0	$0	$7,450	$0	$0

PROJECTED FIVE YEAR PLAN

MISCELLANEOUS EQUIPMENT	ESTIMATED FIVE YEAR COMPLIANCE COST	YEAR EXPENDITURE WILL BE MADE				
		1987-1988	1988-1989	1989-1990	1990-1991	1991-1992
Opaque Projector	$0					
Microprojector	$2,000				$2,000	
Auditorium Equipment						
Auditorium Overhead	$800				$800	
Auditorium Screen	$0					
Auditorium 16-mm Projector	$0					
Auditorium Slide Projector	$0					
Projection Carts	$0					
Motion Picture	$60			$60		
Overhead	$210			$210		
Opaque	$0					
Video Tape	$0					
Audio Recorder	$3,000			$3,000		
Projection Screens	$400			$400		
Television	$0					
Copy Machines	$2,000		$2,000			
Duplication Machines	$0					
Paper Cutters	$0					
Transparency Makers						
Thermal Unit	$500				$500	
Photocopier	$800				$800	

PROJECTED FIVE YEAR PLAN

	ESTIMATED FIVE YEAR COMPLIANCE COST	YEAR EXPENDITURE WILL BE MADE				
		1987-1988	1988-1989	1989-1990	1990-1991	1991-1992
:MISCELLANEOUS EQUIPMENT CONT.						
:Typewriters for Graphic Production:	$5,000				$5,000	
:Cameras						
: Slide	$0					
: Videotape Recorder	$0					
: Videotape Camera	$0					
:Film and Video Production						
: Film Splicers	$0					
:Telephones						
: Inhouse	$0					
: Outside Line	$0					
:Bulletin Boards	$0					
:Chalkboards	$0					
Total Misc. Compliance Cost	$14,770	$0	$2,000	$3,670	$9,100	$0
:Total Compliance Cost	$315,517	$48,653	$67,653	$95,236	$56,725	$47,250

1987-1988

Personnel

The media skills of the librarian will be updated to comply with the head of media description for a total cost of $1,000.

Two media aides will be hired to aid the head of media in various administrative functions. Their salary is estimated to be $12,000.

Collection

Additional books, periodicals, filmstrips and audio material will be purchased over the five-year period to bring the media center into compliance. The first year cost is estimated to be $35,653.

1988-1989

Personnel

The personnel staff will be increased to include a media professional at an estimated annual cost of $18,000. This person will be in charge of all media.

Collection

The second-year purchase of additional books, periodicals, filmstrips and audio materials will be purchased at an estimated cost of $35,653.

Miscellaneous Equipment

The purchase of an additional copy machine will be made to assist with various reproduction tasks, at an estimated cost of $2,000.

1989-1990

Personnel

The personnel staff will be increased to include a media technician at an estimated annual cost of $15,000. This person will maintain and repair media equipment.

Collection

The final installment of additional books, periodicals and audio materials will be purchased at an estimated cost of $35,653. Also slides and transparency materials, models and sculptures, and specimens will be purchased for an estimated cost of $3,463.

Equipment

Filmstrips, slides, 16-mm sound projection, audio recorders, and radios will be purchased for $7,450.

Miscellaneous Equipment

Projection carts and screens will be purchased for $3,670.

1990-1991

Collection

Filmstrips, slides, and transparencies will be purchased at an estimated cost of $2,625.

Miscellaneous Equipment

Microprojector, auditorium overhead, transparency makers and a typewriter for graphic production will be purchased at an estimated cost of $9,100.

1991-1992

Collection

The remainder of the filmstrips will be purchased at an estimated cost of $2,250.

Appendix F
Volunteers

Volunteers may be asked to assist in the library media program in many school districts. Care must be taken to make sure that this does not violate the teacher's contract and that the school administrators are aware that volunteers are being recruited. A districtwide policy about the use of volunteers in schools may exist. If the district provides orientation and coordination, this part of the process can be taken from the other responsibilities of the library media specialist.

If no districtwide program is in place, the library media specialist must do the following:

1. Inform the principal and other appropriate administrators of the scope of the volunteer program and the person(s) designated to take responsibility.

2. Develop "job descriptions" of the tasks expected of volunteers so that interested persons may anticipate their activities once they volunteer. These job descriptions will help the library media specialist plan the training to be given to volunteers.

3. Recruit volunteers through the parent-teacher organization in the school, through notes sent home with students, through pleas to service organizations in the area, and any other means available.

4. Recruit a manager of the volunteers. That is, get another person to assume responsibility for the attendance of volunteers. This person frees the media specialist of such time-consuming tasks as volunteer scheduling and rescheduling, accepting telephone calls for volunteers who cannot appear on their scheduled day, etc.; otherwise, the volunteer program could become more trouble than it is worth.

5. Ask volunteers to complete an information form (sample follows).

6. During orientation, inform the volunteers of your expectations. If there is no district orientation, volunteers *must* be cautioned of their expected behavior toward students and toward any information they may learn about students. All information about the school, the teachers, or the program learned at school must remain confidential and should remain at school. Volunteers must not discuss the activities in the media center with their friends and neighbors. This may be violating the rights of students. Any volunteer who is unable to come at the designated time should call the volunteer coordinator well in advance to allow opportunity to call a substitute. Volunteers should also recognize that they will serve as "media specialists" while in the media center and should dress and behave appropriately.

7. Careful records should be maintained of the attendance of volunteers, their activities, and their comments concerning possible revision and volunteer program improvement. Careful evaluation can help reinforce good work by volunteers, assist in encouraging better performance, and help remove those who can be "more trouble than they are worth."

8. Plan a reward system for the volunteers. Parties to honor the volunteers are essential, or any other acknowledgment of their efforts will be appreciated by them and will encourage them to continue another semester or another year. The true test of a volunteer's devotion comes when volunteers continue after their children leave the school.

9. Remember at all times that volunteers are directly linked to the school and to those persons who can support the library media program. Volunteers can be enthusiastic advocates of the media activities in the school.

PARENT VOLUNTEER FORM

PLEASE COMPLETE THIS FORM AND RETURN IT TO THE LIBRARY MEDIA SPECIALIST.

NAME _____

ADDRESS _____

TELEPHONE NUMBER _____

DAY(S) YOU ARE AVAILABLE TO VOLUNTEER: (Please indicate 1, 2, 3, for your preferences).

MONDAY   TUESDAY   WEDNESDAY   THURSDAY   FRIDAY

TIMES YOU ARE AVAILABLE TO COME TO THE LIBRARY MEDIA CENTER:

A.M. only   P.M. only   A.M. and P.M.

GRADES YOU PREFER TO WORK WITH:

Primary   Elementary   Middle School   High School

I would like to (check as many as apply)

_____ read stories to children   _____ type orders, booklists

_____ prepare a bulletin board   _____ assist with microcomputers

_____ duplicate learning materials   _____ help circulate books

_____ other, please specify _____

Suggestions for the use of volunteers in the school

1. Circulating materials

2. Shelving books

3. Reading the shelves

4. Preparing bulletin boards

5. Preparing other displays

6. Setting up learning centers

7. Pulling books from the shelves for classroom projects

8. Preparing materials for the vertical file

9. Processing new books

10. Preparing bibliographies, hopefully on the word processor

11. Reading stories to children

12. Listening to children read

13. Producing audiovisual materials

14. Presenting programs

15. Keeping records

Appendix G
ALA Intellectual Freedom
Policy Statements*

53.1 Library Bill of Rights

The American Library Association affirms that all libraries are forums for information and ideas, and that the following basic policies should guide their services.

1) Books and other library resources should be provided for the interest, information, and enlightenment of all people of the community the library serves. Materials should not be excluded because of the origin, background, or views of those contributing to their creation.

2) Libraries should provide materials and information presenting all points of view on current and historical issues. Materials should not be prescribed or removed because of partisan or doctrinal disapproval.

3) Libraries should challenge censorship in the fulfillment of their responsibility to provide information and enlightenment.

4) Libraries should cooperate with all persons and groups concerned with resisting abridgment of free expression and free access to ideas.

5) A person's right to use a library should not be denied or abridged because of origin, age, background, or views.

6) ... (Concerns meeting rooms and exhibit spaces)

53.1.1   Challenged materials which meet the materials selection policy of the library should not be removed under any legal or extra-legal pressure.

53.1.2   Expurgation of any parts of books or other library resources is a violation of the Library Bill of Rights because it denies access to the complete work and, therefore, to the entire spectrum of ideas that the work was intended to express.

*Source: *American Library Association Manual* (Chicago: American Library Association), annual.

53.1.3   Denying minors access to certain library materials and services available to adults is a violation of the Library Bill of Rights since it is the parents—and only the parents—who may restrict their children—and only their children—from access to library materials and services.

53.1.4   Evaluation of library materials is not to be used as a convenient means to remove materials presumed to be controversial or disapproved of by segments of the community.

53.1.5   Restricting access to certain titles and classes of library materials for protection and/or controlled use is a form of censorship.

53.1.6   Labeling certain library materials by affixing a prejudicial label to them or segregating by a prejudicial system is a practice which seeks to close paths to knowledge; such practices violate the Library Bill of Rights.

53.1.7   ... (Concerns meeting rooms and exhibit spaces)

53.1.8   A policy on library-initiated programming should reflect the library's philosophy regarding free access to information and ideas. Selection of library program topics, speakers, courses, classes and resource materials should be made by library staff on the basis of the interests and needs of library users and the community.

53.1.9   Restricted access to rare and special collections is solely for the protection of the materials, and must in no way limit access to the information or ideas contained in the materials. Library cards, reference services, use of meeting rooms and exhibit spaces should be examined for conformance to the Library Bill of Rights.

53.1.10   Diversity in Collection Development
        Librarians have a professional responsibility to be inclusive, not exclusive in collection development and in the provision of interlibrary loan. Access to all materials legally obtainable should be assured to the user and policies should not unjustly exclude materials even if offensive to the librarian or the user. Collection development should reflect the philosophy inherent in Article 2 of the Library Bill of Rights. A balanced collection reflects a diversity of materials, not equality of numbers. Collection development and the selection of materials should be done according to professional standards and established selection and review procedures.
        Librarians have an obligation to protect library collections from removal of materials based on personal bias or prejudice, and to select and support the acquisition of materials on all subjects that meet, as closely as possible, the needs and interests of all persons in the community which the library serves. This includes materials that reflect political, economic, religious, social, minority, and sexual issues.
        Intellectual freedom, the essence of equitable library services, promotes no causes, furthers no movements, and favors no viewpoints. It only provides for free access to all expressions of ideas through which any and all sides of a question, cause, or movement may be explored.

Appendix H
Pennsylvania School Librarians Association Publication List

The following list was prepared for a workshop presented at an annual conference of the Pennsylvania School Librarians Association (PSLA). The goal of the workshop was to assist building-level library media specialists to increase the sharing of information about exciting programs and activities. This list of publishers was produced to assist media specialists in choosing an audience for any article they might produce. This list contains the name of the periodical, the address, telephone number, and editor, and, when available, information concerning the editorial policy and requirements for publication.

The American School and University

North American Publishing Co.
401 N. Broad St.
Philadelphia, PA 19108
Telephone: (215) 238-5300
Editor: Dorothy Wright
   No written procedure is stated. It is suggested that anyone wishing to submit an article should send an outline of the subject area and the basics that will be covered in the article. The editor will respond from this point. Articles must be double-spaced and between 800-2,000 words.

Book Report: Journal for Junior and Senior High School Librarians

Linworth Publishing Co.
2950 N. High St., Box 14466
Columbus, OH 43214-0466
Telephone: (614) 261-6584
Editor: Carolyn Hamilton
   No information given.

Emergency Librarian

Dyad Services
P.O. Box 46258, Station G
Vancouver, BC V6R 4G6
Canada
Telephone: (604) 734-0255
Editor: Carol-Ann Haycock
   Emergency Librarian is a professional journal for teachers and librarians working with children and young adults in school and public libraries.

Instructor Magazine

545 5th Ave.
New York, NY 10017
Telephone: (212) 503-2888
Editor-in-Chief: Leanna Landsmann

Thirty percent freelance written. Emphasizes elementary education. Pays on acceptance. Buys all rights or first North American serial rights. Submit seasonal/holiday material six months in advance. Photocopied submissions OK. Computer printout submissions acceptable; prefers letter-quality to dot-matrix. SASE. Reports in six weeks. Free writer's guidelines: mention *Writer's Market* in request. Nonfiction: How-to articles on elementary classroom practice—practical suggestions as well as project reports. Query. Length: 750-2,500 words. Pays $35-$300 for articles: $150-$250 for short articles. Send all queries to Marge Schere, managing editor/editorial. No poetry.

Tips: "The most frequent mistake made by writers is that the material is better suited for a general audience than for teachers."

National Association of Secondary School Principals' Bulletin

1904 Association Dr.
Reston, VA 22091
Telephone: (703) 860-0200
Editor: Thomas F. Koerner

A pamphlet is available upon request giving guidelines for publication and required format.

Phi Delta Kappan

Phi Delta Kappan, Inc.
Box 789
Bloomington, IN 47402
Telephone: (812) 339-1156
Editor: Robert W. Cole, Jr.

A brochure is available upon request giving all publication policy guidelines and formats.

An example of a state association publication is

Learning and Media

c/o Editor
1419 Hillcrest Rd.
Lancaster, PA 17603
Telephone: (717) 397-9383

Learning and Media publishes theoretical and practical articles that are of interest and value to library media specialists and teachers in public, private, and parochial schools as well as to library educators and students in colleges and universities. Articles must be of general interest to most PSLA members and should deal with issues or with the application of principles to the library media program.

Manuscripts and letters are invited for publication and should be sent to the Editor for consideration. Two copies of a manuscript should be submitted. The manuscript should be typewritten and double-spaced. There is no prescription set for minimum or maximum length. Citations should be consistent with Kate L. Tarabian's *A Manual for Writers of Term Papers, Theses, and Dissertations* (4th ed. Chicago: University of Chicago Press, 1973) and with PSLA's *Citations for Nonprint Media Formats in Term Papers and Theses* (Lancaster, Pa.: PSLA, 1978). Standard formal usage should be observed in manuscript preparation. Terminology should be consistent with PSLA policy and practice (e.g., library media center, library media specialists, etc.). The editor has the final responsibility for all action taken on a manuscript.

All material in *Learning and Media* subject to copyright by PSLA may be photocopied for the noncommercial purpose of educational advancement.

Publication in *Learning and Media* does not imply official policy endorsement by PSLA or endorsement of the opinions expressed by individual contributors.

Deadlines for submitting manuscripts are: December 1st for the Winter issue; March 1st for the Spring issue; June 1st for the Summer issue; September 1st for the Fall issue.

Library Journal

R. R. Bowker Co., Magazine Division
205 E. 42nd St.
New York, NY 10017
Telephone: (800) 257-7894
Editor-in-Chief: John N. Berry III

Nonfiction: *"Library Journal* is a professional magazine for librarians. Freelancers are most often rejected because they submit one of the following types of articles: 'A wonderful, warm, concerned, loving librarian who started me on the road to good reading and success'; 'How I became rich, famous, and successful by using my public library'; 'Libraries are the most wonderful and important institutions in our society, because they have all of the knowledge of mankind — praise them.' We need material of greater sophistication, dealing with issues related to the transfer of information, access to it, or related phenomena. (Current hot ones are copyright, censorship, the decline in funding for public institutions, the local politics of libraries, trusteeship, etc.)" Professional articles on criticism, censorship, professional concerns, library activities, historical articles, information technology, automation and management, and spot news. Outlook should be from librarian's point of view. Buys fifty to sixty-five unsolicited manuscripts/year. Length: 1,500-2,000 words. Pays $50-$350. Photos: Payment for black and white glossy photos purchased without accompanying manuscripts is $30. Must be at least 5x7. Captions required.

School Library Journal

R. R. Bowker Co., Magazine Division
205 E. 42nd St.
New York, NY 10017
Telephone: (800) 257-7894
Editor: Lillian N. Gerhardt

Nonfiction: Articles on library services, local censorship problems, and how-to articles on programs that use books, films or microcomputer software. Informational, personal experience, interview, exposé, and successful business operations. "Interest in history articles on the establishment/development of children's and young adult services in schools and public libraries." Buys twenty-four manuscripts/year. Length: 2,500-3,000 words. Pays $100.

School Library Media Activities Monthly

LMS Associates
17 E. Henrietta St.
Baltimore, MD 21230
Telephone: (301) 685-8621
Managing Editor: H. Thomas Walker
Content Editor: Paula Montgomery

School Library Media Activities Monthly welcomes unsolicited articles and reader contributions to *all* columns and departments. All unsolicited manuscripts become the property of LMS Associates. Prompt notification of publication will be made to all contributors, and appropriate attribution of all contributions will be made. LMS Associates reserves the right to make editorial changes in unsolicited manuscripts and will copyright each issue of *School Library Media Activities Monthly* as a collective work unless prior arrangements are made by individual authors with LMS Associates.

School Library Media Quarterly

American Association of School Librarians
A Division of the American Library Association
50 E. Huron St.
Chicago, IL 60611
Telephone: (312) 944-6780
Editor: Marilyn W. Greenberg

Articles to be published should be mailed to AASL and they will be forwarded to the editor for review.

Tech Trends

Association for Educational Communications and Technology
1126 Sixteenth St.
Washington, DC 20036
Telephone: (202) 466-4780
Editor: Dan Levin

How to submit a manuscript: *Tech Trends* welcomes submissions on any aspect of new technology in education and training in schools, colleges, and private industry. Authors are not paid for their contributions. Please write in a direct, conversational style. Manuscripts should be typewritten double-spaced or submitted in ASCII on IBM PC-compatible DS/DD diskette. Manuscripts also may be sent over the TechCentral network to d.levin. All manuscripts will be scheduled for publication at the editor's discretion and will be edited to conform to the magazine's style. Unaccepted manuscripts will not be returned unless accompanied by a self-addressed envelope with correct postage. Author's guidelines are available upon request.

Top of the News

Association for Library Service to Children and Young Adults
A Division of the American Library Association
50 E. Huron St.
Chicago, IL 60611
Telephone: (312) 944-6780
Editor: Joni Bodart

Articles to be published should be mailed to ALSC to be forwarded to the editor for review.

Wilson Library Bulletin

950 University Ave.
Bronx, NY 10452
Telephone: (212) 588-8400
Editor: Milo Nelson

Eighty percent freelance written. Monthly (September-June). For professional librarians and those interested in the book and library worlds. Pays on publication. Publishes manuscript an average of two months after acceptance. Buys first North American serial righs only. Sample copies may be seen on request in most libraries. "Manuscript must be original copy, double-spaced; additional photocopy or carbon is appreciated." Computer printout submissions acceptable; prefers letter-quality to dot-matrix. Deadlines are a minimum two months before publication. Reports in three months. SASE.

Nonfiction: Uses articles "of interest to librarians throughout the nation and around the world. Style must be lively, readable and sophisticated, with appeal to modern professionals; facts must be thoroughly researched. Subjects range from the political to the comic in the world of media and libraries, with an emphasis on the human as well as the technical aspects of any story. No condescension; no library stereotypes." Buys thirty manuscripts/year. Send complete manuscript. Length: 2,500-6,000 words. Pays about $100-$400, "depending on the substance of article and its importance to readers." Sometimes pays the expenses of writers on assignment.

Tips: "The best way you can break in is with a first-rate black and white photo and caption information on a library, library service, or librarian who departs completely from all stereotypes and the commonplace. Libraries have changed. You'd better first discover what is not commonplace."

Appendix I
NEH Budget Form*

PROJECT BUDGET National Endowment for the Humanities Washington, D.C. 20506	III. Date Prepared	Page 1
	IV. Project Title	
I. Type of Budget Submission ☐ application budget ☐ budget revision grant or application number		
	V. Project Director	
II. Applicant Organization	VI. Grant Period From ____ ____ To ____ ____ month year month year	

VII. Project Costs (include all charges to NEH and cost sharing funds)

Summary Budget for Entire Grant Period

DIRECT COSTS	Amount
Salaries and wages	$_____
Fringe benefits	_____
Consultant fees	_____
Travel domestic $_____	
foreign $_____	_____
Supplies and materials	_____
Services	_____
Other	_____
Total Direct Costs	_____
INDIRECT COSTS	_____
TOTAL PROJECT COSTS	$_____

VIII. Project Funding for Entire Grant Period
  (1) Requested from Endowment:

	Outright funds	$_____
	Federal Matching	_____
	Total Requested from Endowment	$_____

  (2) Cost Sharing

a. Cash Contributions
(list applicant's anticipated cash outlay and the sources
and amounts of third-party donations, grants, etc.)

b. In-Kind Contributions
(list each item, source, and value)

_____ $_____	_____ $_____
_____ _____	_____ _____
_____ _____	_____ _____
_____ _____	_____ _____
	Total Cost Sharing $_____
	TOTAL PROJECT FUNDING $_____

IX. Estimated Outlay of Endowment Funds During Grant Period

1st twelve-month period ending ____ ____ ____	$_____
month day year	
2nd twelve-month period ending ____ ____ ____	_____
3rd twelve-month period ending ____ ____ ____	_____
4th twelve-month period ending ____ ____ ____	_____
5th twelve-month period ending ____ ____ ____	_____

X. Institutional Grant Administrator

_____   _____   _____
Name and Title (please type or print)   Signature   Date

1/1/83   Telephone: (____) _____

---

*National Endowment for the Humanities, Washington, D.C., April 1, 1978.

Page 3

5. Supplies and Materials (list each major type and indicate the cost computation)

type	basis/method of cost computation	Amount
		$

Total Cost of Supplies and Materials $

6. Services (list each major type and cost computation)

type	basis/method of cost computation	Amount
		$

Total Cost of Services $

7. Other (list each major type and cost computation)

type	basis/method of cost computation	Amount
		$

Total Cost of Other $

INDIRECT COSTS

1. Rate(s) established by negotiation with Federal agency:

Amount

_____% of $_____ $_____

_____% of $_____   _____

Name of Federal agency: _____

Date of negotiation agreement: _____

2. Rate requested in attached indirect cost proposal or estimate of indirect
cost rate if submission of indirect cost proposal will be delayed:

_____% of $_____ $_____

1/1/83   **Total Indirect Costs** $_____

Appendix J
How to Write a Letter
to Your Legislator*

The most frequently used, correct forms of address are:

To your Senator:	To your Representative:
The Honorable ___(full name)___	The Honorable ___(full name)___
United States Senate	U.S. House of Representatives
Washington, D.C. 20510	Washington, D.C. 20515

"Sincerely yours" is in good taste as a complimentary close. Remember to sign your given name and surname. If you use a title in your signature, be sure to enclose it in parentheses.

Forms similar to the above, addressed to your state capital, are appropriate for your state representatives and senators.

Where possible use your official letterhead. If this is not in order, and you write as an individual, use plain white bond paper, and give your official title following your signature as a means of identification and to indicate your competency to speak on the subject.

DO's

1. Your Legislators like to hear opinions from home and want to be kept informed of conditions in the district. Base your letter on your own pertinent experiences and observations.

2. If writing about a specific bill, describe it by number or its popular name. Your Legislators have thousands of bills before them in the course of a year, and cannot always take time to figure out to which one you are referring.

3. They appreciate intelligent, well-thought-out letters which present a definite position, even if they do not agree.

4. Even more important and valuable to them is a concrete statement of the reasons for your position—particularly if you are writing about a field in which you have specialized knowledge. Representatives have to vote on many matters with which they have had little or no first-hand experience. Some of the most valuable information they receive comes from facts presented in letters from people who have knowledge in the field.

5. Short letters are almost always best. Members of Congress receive many, many letters each day, and a long one may not get as prompt a reading as a brief statement.

6. Letters should be timed to arrive while the issue is alive. Members of the committee considering the bill will appreciate having your views while the bill is ripe for study and action.

7. Don't forget to follow through with a thank-you letter.

DON'Ts

1. Avoid letters that merely demand or insist on votes for or against a certain bill; or that say what vote you want but not why. A letter with no reasoning, good or bad, is not very influential.

2. Threats of defeat at the next election are not effective.

3. Boasts of how influential the writer is are not helpful.

4. Do not ask for a vote commitment on a particular bill before the committee in charge of the subject has had a chance to hear the evidence and make its report.

5. Form letters or letters which include excerpts from other letters on the same subject are not as influential as a simple letter drawing on your own experience.

6. Congressional courtesy requires Legislators to refer letters from non-constituents to the proper offices, so you should generally confine your letter-writing to members of your state's delegation or members of the committee specifically considering the bill.

7. Do not engage in letter-writing overkill. Quality, not quantity, is what counts.

---

*American Library Association, Washington, D.C., office.

Index